LightWave 3D® 8
Character Animation

Timothy Albee

Wordware Publishing, Inc.

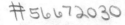

3-06

Library of Congress Cataloging-in-Publication Data

Albee, Timothy.
  LightWave 3D 8 character animation / by Timothy Albee.
     p. cm.
  Includes index.
  ISBN 1-55622-099-5 (pbk., companion cd-rom)
  1. Computer animation.   2. Computer graphics.   3. LightWave 3D.   I. Title.
  TR897.7.A425 2004
  006.6'96--dc22   2004023270

© 2005, Wordware Publishing, Inc.

All Rights Reserved

2320 Los Rios Boulevard
Plano, Texas 75074

No part of this book may be reproduced in any form or by any means
without permission in writing from Wordware Publishing, Inc.

Printed in the United States of America

ISBN 1-55622-099-5

10 9 8 7 6 5 4 3 2 1
0410

All inquiries for volume purchases of this book should be addressed to Wordware
Publishing, Inc., at the above address. Telephone inquiries may be made by calling:

(972) 423-0090

Contents

Foreword

Perhaps you're one of those people who, as a kid, sat in a darkened movie theater watching a great animated movie and said to yourself, "I want to do that."

I know I was. At the time, all I could do was draw my own "flipbooks," as there was very little written about the technique of animation. The big breakthrough for me came when I discovered something called an "Animation Kit" at Disneyland some 45 years ago. It consisted of a simple light board, some model sheets of Disney characters, a booklet on "How to Animate," and some punched paper.

With this animation kit, I could finally create my own animation! After seeing my first pencil tests, I was hooked. My fate was sealed. I knew this was what I wanted to do with my life.

Of course, my first work was quite crude; so my next task was to find a way to learn the skills it took to become a real animator.

A generation or two ago, there were no schools teaching animation. About the only way to learn "the craft" was to serve an often lengthy apprenticeship with a journeyman animator. Slowly, under this apprenticeship, the secrets of animation would be revealed at a rate designed (no doubt for job security) by those who held the few positions there were for animators.

I was lucky in that I was able to study under the great master animator Art Babbit, who animated the queen in *Snow White* and Geppetto in *Pinocchio*. Art maintained that an animator should be something of a Renaissance man. He should be well-read and be well versed in the arts, including painting, drawing, music, dance, and films. In other words, in order to *portray* life, you needed to *understand* life. In 1980, Art disliked intensely the idea that computers might someday "take over" the animation business. He said if they did, the operator would have to be an animator. He was certainly right about that.

The art of animation was brought to one of its high points during the 1940s at the Disney studios by a group of animators known as "the nine old men." They were revered by their underlings as almost "god-like" and have since been accorded the greatest of respect by everyone in the industry. The performances they leave us today are among our greatest cultural treasures. Their work has served as an inspiration to countless young students of the craft. Any serious study of animation must include the works of these masters.

Animation has changed much in recent years. A great deal of this change is due to a resurgence of interest in it as a medium, and the introduction of the computer as an animator's tool. Although the work of the early computer animation pioneers was revolutionary and impressive, I believe it was not until experienced traditional and stop-motion animators learned to use computers that the CG industry as we know it today was born. The responsibilities of the animator did not change when animators exchanged their pencils for mice and keyboards. Now they simply had a very powerful assistant that relieved them of the burden of drawing and could quickly generate perfect inbetweens. But it will always require someone with the skills of an animator to bring a character to life, no matter what the medium.

With all this activity, there is now a great demand for the knowledge that created the big CG hits of today. There are a few good schools that teach animation, but of course, the quality of instruction is only as good as the instructors themselves. And not all of them have hands-on experience in the field. There is nothing like learning from someone who has been in the trenches as the author of this book has been for many years. Until recently, there has been relatively little written about the actual hands-on, nuts-and-bolts process of creating an animated performance. The problem I find with most animation books today is they give you only part of the picture. Some books on animation have emphasized only the technical side. Other books talk only about acting. Still others concentrate on action analysis. This book represents one-stop shopping for the aspiring computer animator. Not only does it deal with all the technical mysteries of such things as Inverse Kinematics, but it also reveals all of the time-honored principles of classical character animation.

In my career, I have met only a very small handful of individuals whose knowledge encompasses both the technical and the artistic aspects of animation. Such a person is a rare bird indeed, and Timothy Albee is one of these. Tim takes you step by step through all the stages you will need to bring your characters to life. You have here, distilled into one book, all the skills and knowledge you need to begin to create your own performances.

Now the rest is up to you.

Tom Roth
Animator, *Hercules* (Hades), *Dinosaur* (Yar), *Stuart Little*, *Shrek*, *All Dogs Go to Heaven*, *Scooby Doo*

Chapter 1

About This Book

1.1 Who Is This Book For?

This book is for anyone who has ever had a character in their heart that they've wanted to bring to life with as much fluidity, power, and grace as can be seen in the best animated feature films. This is a book for anyone who has wanted to become an animator but hasn't gone to Sheridan College in Toronto or CalArts in Valencia. This is a book for animators who have progressed as far as they can on their own and want to hone their skills to the level of feature-quality animation. This is a book for feature-quality animators skilled on other software platforms who have a project that requires them to use LightWave.

This is the book I wish had been available when I was starting out as a LightWave animator.

This is not just a book on how to set up and point weight characters. It is not yet another book that covers the same basics that nearly every other book on animation presents as "all-there-is-to-know." This book covers the complex animation mechanics that are locked inside every beautifully animated scene but that are difficult to understand until someone shows you how. It took many gifted people with careers in animation going back over 30 years to show me what I hadn't learned in school or in the books I'd read. I've taught many people who've worked for me on projects ranging from films to video games how to see, understand, and internalize these techniques and subtleties. It is my goal in this book to pass this information on to a much larger audience, and by doing so, raise the level of animators and the way others perceive animators all across the board.

Animation is an incredible art. It encompasses so much technical and artistic skill that in my experience, nothing else comes close to the impact it has on the artist or the viewer. We're moved by good animation in a way we can't explain. And there are those of us who are so touched by it that it consumes us and we have to make it a part of ourselves. We give our lives to it. And once we finally understand how to breathe life into these ideas and archetypes we have had deep within our own mind's eye, there is no better place to be than in the space that is created when you're animating.

When you're working on a piece, time drops away. And it's not like working on a painting where the characters never move. You're working on a "drawing" that lasts through time; you're drawing in four dimensions. Your characters evolve ever so slightly from the beginning to the end of your scene, and they begin to breathe life of their own. This only happens, however, when you know the simple and complex mechanics of animation so well that they become a part of you; you don't have to think about them and you can just let the scene flow out through you.

We, as computer animators, have a much bigger challenge than traditional animators. Sure, the computer takes care of perspective for us, and we don't need an army of inbetweeners and digital ink and painters to see our work in the smoothness of animating on "ones" (a new image on every frame) and the beauty of brilliant color. But we do have issues and problems that traditional artists have never had to think about. I don't think it's ever been on record that a pencil has frozen or crashed and erased a stack of drawings — a day's work — because the animator forgot to save. Traditional animators don't also have to be "technical directors" and understand how to build setups that let them be creative, rather than fighting the computer every step of the way. They don't have to figure out why even though their character's hand is still flat on the table, his arm is now sticking straight out behind him. More often than not, we as computer animators have had to learn how to cope with all of this on our own, even if we did go to school for it.

This book is here to give you the tools you need to stop fighting the computer. It is here to let you learn and internalize the things that make animation come to life so your evolution as an animator can really begin. This is only the first step, but it is a first step from the point of view of feature-quality animation, and that is what will make all the difference in the world.

Yes, this book focuses on LightWave, and the sections on character setup show step by step how to use LightWave's Inverse Kinematics (IK) to build strong, dependable setups you can use for any character you envision. But even if you are using another package, if it supports a strong, dependable IK engine, the information will help you all the same. The buttons may be different between packages, but IK is still IK. What separates 3D packages in terms of those that are good for character animation and those that aren't is the solidity of the package's IK engine. LightWave has one of the best — quietly and without hype. (If you are using another software package, I'd suggest trying LightWave; you might just be pleasantly surprised. I've used all the major packages on projects from feature films to video games, and I keep coming back to LightWave. I've amazed motion technical directors with how much more powerful the setups on LightWave can be than on packages costing many times more.)

Everything else in this book will be directly useful to you regardless of what 3D software you're using (even if you're animating on paper)! Whether you are a traditional animator or computer animator, you must first and foremost be a good animator. Understanding the mechanics of animation, both the simple and complex, should be your primary goal. The computer provides the tools; you provide the force that drives them.

1.2 How to Use This Book

This book is broken down into sections. Each section deals with a different aspect of the character setup and animation process. If you're like most folks out there, you want to learn as much as you can about all parts of this gig. That's great! This book will cover everything you need to know to take your model, set him up for animation, learn the controls that make him move, and get him moving like a character that should be on the big screen.

If you're only interested in one aspect of this process, that's okay too! In today's high-end studios people are highly specialized and oftentimes an animator won't know anything about modeling and is happy to keep it that way. If your focus is on learning to become a better animator, and that's it, the latter sections will give you all you need to know. There are scenes you can load that have all your setups and props made for you so you can jump right into bettering your skills as an animator.

If you want to be a better technical director and you don't really see yourself as having to ever animate a scene, the sections you'll be most interested in are the ones close to the front of the book. Pre-bending, boning, IK, and point weighting are all covered there.

Then there are those who are already masters at one aspect but want to get a handle on the others. This is a really good idea because then you'll understand the issues those on the "other side" have to deal with, and if you're a hot-shot animator, you're much more likely to treat a TD with understanding if you know what it takes to get that character set up the way it is, and vice versa. For you folks (and the people new to LightWave from another package), there are two things you'll want to keep your eyes open for: Newbie Notes and Newbie Blocks.

Newbie Note:

Newbie notes are short little blips that give bits of information that you might not be familiar with, things to watch out for, and the like.

Newbie Blocks

These are longer sections that will help you to get up to speed if you know Modeler but not Layout, or the other way around, or if you're new to LightWave from another package. Those of you who know how to get around inside these modules can most likely skip right over these blocks. Newbie Blocks are here so you don't have to break your flow of concentration by turning to the LightWave manuals. There's no way for me to cover everything in these blocks, just the basics. It's my attempt to eliminate a bit of the frustration I remember trying to make an origami model when the book left out some important step because "everyone" was supposed to know it already.

Note:

Notes, on the other hand, are things that everyone should watch for. Notes are things that might help you right away, or they may be things that you'll keep in the back of your mind for a time later on down the road. They're bits of information that I've picked up along the way that will probably help you too.

Advanced Note:

Advanced notes are for the hard-core group. These are for people who like to pull things apart to find out how they work. These are for the folks who aren't satisfied with just using something that works; they want to know how it works and how they can modify it to suit their needs. You know who you are and these notes are for you.

1.3 **The Models**

This book ships with a CD that has models and test scenes on it. You're welcome to use the models for your own work; that's why they're there! (Not everyone is a modeler, right?) But if you do use one or some of the models, please give credit to the guy who built them for ya. Doesn't have to be much, just a passing nod — that's all I ask.

So, there are a couple of human characters on the CD for you to start creating character interaction. There are also some cartoony characters for you to squash and stretch to your heart's content. (There's also a realistic animal, if you're feeling daring. I have to tell you, though, quadrupedal animation is enough for a book unto itself.) Use these and have fun! Create some wonderful animations that'll look fantastic on that demo reel of yours! The exercises in the book will show you how!

1.4 **The Exercises**

This book is full of exercises, from life drawing in 3D to analyzing animation. Please take the time to do every one. There may be things you've already encountered, especially in the chapter on the basics of animation, but treat each exercise as though it were a scene you've been assigned that will eventually be reviewed by a director (and his entourage). Never knowingly leave anything wrong with your scene. Even if it is something rudimentary, like having your character getting up out of a chair or swinging a baseball bat, give that scene feeling, let your character have a reason for being in that chair at that moment, and let that reason show through in the action. Like Degas, show a moment in time. Let it seem that your character existed before the scene began and will go on after the scene ends. In treating each scene like this, your animation skills will grow further and faster than you ever thought possible.

It is my greatest wish that you'll use this information to become the animator you've always wished you could be. Though I cannot promise to respond to every e-mail, if you have a movie of a scene that you're particularly proud of, pack it up as small as possible (and still have it readable) and send it my way (TimothyA@ ptiAlaska.net); I'd love to see it. If I can, I'll make comments on it and get them back to you. Hopefully, in the not-too-distant future, I'll be watching for your name in the credits of a cool animated piece!

Chapter 2

Inverse Kinematics, Forward Kinematics, and IK Booster

What the heck is a "kinematic"? Why would anyone care whether it's "forward," "backward," or somewhere in between?

Kinematics refers to the study of mechanics concerned with motion. Where 3D animation is concerned, kinematics defines the way in which you manipulate a system of hierarchical (parent/child) items.

2.1 **FK (Forward Kinematics)**

Forward Kinematics (most often referred to simply as FK) is the "old reliable" way of animating. It is labor-intensive, but there are no surprises — everything that's in an animation must be put there, on purpose, by the animator.

Figure 2.1. Forward Kinematics. Here, you see a hierarchical set of bones that could easily be a character's bicep, forearm, and hand.

With FK, if you wanted to make the tip of the character's "forearm" reach the null object (represented as the "+" in Figure

2.1), you'd have to first rotate the bicep and then the forearm, evaluate how close you got to your objective, and then refine.

As you can see in Figure 2.1, the tip of the forearm overshoots the null. I'd have to go back and tweak the rotations of the bicep and forearm again and again (and probably again).

As you can see, there are no surprises in this kind of animation — everything that's done must be done on purpose by the animator, and as such, it is a painfully slow way to work all the myriad of bones that make up a character's *rigging* (skeleton).

2.2 IK (Inverse Kinematics)

Inverse Kinematics (IK) uses an exacting set of calculations to figure precisely the rotations that need to be applied to each item within a hierarchical system in order to have the system strive to have its puller remain in constant contact with its goal.

What Is IK?

Figure 2.2. Inverse Kinematics.

With IK, you set the hand as the *puller* for the chain of bones and the null as the puller's *goal*, and the bicep and forearm automatically figure the perfect set of rotations that will keep the puller's base at the exact location as the goal's base.

IK lets an animator focus on the broad strokes of a pose or gesture while the IK solver handles many of the small but important details. Using IK, you simply pose a character's hand control, and the character's arm bones do what they need to do to remain in contact with the hand's base.

Figure 2.3. IK in action, driving the positioning for a character's arm.

> **Note:**
>
> *Not all IK is created equal!* IK requires very precise calculations in order for it to work *dependably*. In this, LightWave's precision floating-point mathematics engine, which keeps its calculations accurate to many places to the right of the decimal point, makes it one of the best packages for character animation.
>
> Other software may have great salesmen, but LightWave has it where it counts, "where the rubber meets the road." Thanks to LightWave's robust IK, which is dependable and predictable in every situation, I was able to do nearly ten times the feature-quality animation per day as is expected from feature animators using other packages.

"Standard" IK Basics

I'm saying "standard" IK basics here because LightWave's IK Booster is as much an advancement on IK as IK itself was on character animation back in the early '90s. It's important to know how standard IK works and is set up because I've found IK Booster to be put to its best use when it supplements standard IK, giving you the best of both ways of working.

Note:

You may want to change your viewport layout to allow for multiple views on your project at once (as opposed to the single viewport that is LightWave Layout's default). I find this helps me get a better handle on items' true positions and rotations in 3D space.

Figure 2.4

Under Edit|Display Options, you'll find the Viewport Layout setting. I've experimented with a lot of options and have settled on 2 Top, 1 Bottom as my current favorite.

Make sure you have one of your viewports set to right by selecting Right (ZY) from the view's View Type list. (This will let us more easily work with the bones in this simple example.)

We'll be driving our character's motion with bones eventually, so let's use them to explore a standard IK setup. Bones in Light-Wave need to belong to an object, so we'll need to first create a null object to which they'll belong.

1.   Click on **Items|Add|Null**, and a requester window opens up, asking what you'd like to name your new null object. Press **Enter** (or click **OK**) to leave the null object's name "Null." (See Figure 2.5.)

> **Note:**
>
> Null objects are one of the handiest little things in 3D CGI. They are "placeholders," treated by LightWave with all the respect of a "real" object that has geometry, without taking up any memory or hard drive space. Null objects don't show up in a render or cast shadows (and like vampires, don't show up in reflective objects either).
>
> Nulls are super-handy when you want to have a "handle" to move a bunch of different objects, lights, and/or cameras at the same time, and they're perfectly suited for the job of being a *goal object* in an Inverse Kinematic system.

Figure 2.5

2. Click on **Setup|Add|Bone**, and a requester window opens, asking for the name you'd like for your new bone. Accept the default name of "Bone."

Figure 2.6

3. You can add a second bone that is automatically set to be the child of the first, automatically positioned at the exact tip of the first bone, by clicking **Setup|Add|Child Bone** (or by pressing the < = > key). Again, a requester window opens, asking for a name for this new bone. And again, accept the default name of "Bone." This new bone will be our *puller* for the IK chain.

Figure 2.7

Note:

Figure 2.8

You'll notice that even though you accepted the name "Bone" as the name for the second bone, it shows up as "Bone (2)" in the Current Item list (and in Schematic views and Scene Editor windows).

When there are two similar items with the same name in a scene, LightWave automatically adds temporary, sequential numbers to the similarly named items. These numbers go away if/when you choose to rename the item (which you can do by choosing Rename from the menu that opens when right-clicking on the item in a Schematic view or Classic Scene Editor window, or by choosing Items|Replace|Rename).

4. Use **Items|Add|Null** to create another null object, but this time, name the null **Goal**. This will become the goal object (target) of our simple IK chain.

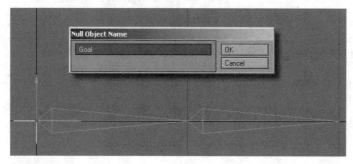

Figure 2.9

Note:

If you're not yet familiar with animating in LightWave, a hint to make your life a lot easier is to have Layout automatically create keyframes for you whenever you move, scale, or rotate an item (as opposed to having to press Enter or click Create Key every time you want Layout to remember an item's scaling, rotation, or translation on a particular frame — *keyframe*).

Figure 2.10

You activate Auto Key Create by *first* telling LightWave that you want Auto Key active by making sure its button is activated at the bottom of the screen.

Then you need to tell LightWave whether you want keys created for *all* channels (scaling, rotation, and translation), even when you have modified only one of those channels, or if you want LightWave to remember changes only for the specific channel type that has been modified.

You make this choice under Edit│General Options│Auto Key Create.

Both settings need to be active in order for LightWave's Auto Key Create function to be active.

5. Working in a Right viewport, move the null object you've just created and named Goal and to the left a bit as seen here. Select **Bone (2)** by clicking on it (you'll find it easiest to select items by clicking on the item's node in a viewport set to Schematic). Pressing <m> (**Window│Motion Options...**) opens the Motion Options window for the selected item. Select **Goal** as the goal object for this bone, and check **Full-time IK**.

Figure 2.11

Note:

If you have Display Options|Show IK Chains active, then the moment you set an IK chain's goal object, a teal line appears along the length of the chain in Layout's windows. Even viewports set to Schematic show a line connecting the puller with its goal.

Note:

What's the difference between full-time IK and IK that isn't "full-time"?

Way back when IK was new, its calculations not yet streamlined, and 40 MHz was mind-bogglingly fast, the friendly folks at NewTek thought it'd be a help for animators to have the option of only solving for IK when the chain's goal object was moved, requiring keyframes to be set by hand for the items in the chain. This saved the computer's CPU from constantly having to think about IK calculations, and in turn, sped up the process of animation significantly.

Nowadays, CPUs are so fast, and the calculations for IK so optimized, there's *almost* no reason to not have all IK chains full-time. I say "almost," because who knows...maybe you may find a need for part-time IK you can't live without that nobody else has thought of.

It's for those instances that NewTek still gives you these and similar options.

Setting the chain's goal object is just the first step in setting up IK. The chain will be pulled toward the goal, but only when the parent items in the chain are told that they can use IK to solve for their rotations.

6. Selecting **Bone (1)**, click on the **Controllers and Limits** tab in the Motion Options window. Choose **Inverse Kinematics** for its Pitch Controller. The moment you do this, LightWave begins using IK to solve for the pitch axis for that item and the bone swings upward, bringing the base of the puller item as close as it can get to the goal item.

Figure 2.12

Note:

Figure 2.13

The best way to remember LightWave's conventions for its axes of rotation is to think of your hand like an airplane. *Heading* changes where the "plane" is heading (represented by a red circle in Layout). *Pitch* changes its altitude (green). And *bank* would be the amount of "roll" (blue).

That's a quick and easy explanation of standard IK and how to set it up. The same basics hold true as you add more parts to the chain, but the math grows ever more complicated for the computer to figure out.

For IK chains of more than one item, if you want to be able to depend on IK to behave predictably in complex situations, you've got to help the IK solver as much as possible. This means putting some restrictions on what you ask IK to do.

"Standard" IK Hazards

Good, old-fashioned IK is a nifty and time-saving tool, but it's not perfect. So, here are some things to bear in mind when working with IK.

Pre-bending

Figure 2.14

An IK chain that has two (or more) joints laid out in a straight line is as apt to swing the child item in the chain *up* as it is *down*. While this is good for things like whips and chains, it's not so pleasant for things like elbows and knees.

Figure 2.15

If you need a child item to favor bending in one direction over another, it is best to set up the IK chain so that it is "pre-bent" in the direction you want the item to favor.

Note:

Figure 2.16

Some have had great success with using limits to restrict how far a bone will bend in a given angular direction. However, without the ability to "cushion" these limits, the resulting motion when an item reaches its limit is often sharp and inorganic. So I tend to shy away from using limits whenever possible, opting instead for well-planned models and cleanly executed animation.

Number of Axes Solved

When you have two or more joints in an IK chain within a three-dimensional space, the level of complexity of the calculations that IK must figure out rises dramatically. If you're going to want things to work dependably, you're going to have to limit what you ask of the IK solver.

Figure 2.17

If you take a look at your own arm or leg, you'll find that it's built much the same way as the above illustration. Your bicep and thigh can swing back and forth, and up and down (two axes: heading and pitch), while your forearm and calf move only around one axis of the elbow and knee, respectively.

I've found that referencing real life in building riggings helps more than nearly anything else in making character setups that do what you'd expect them to do.

Figure 2.18

While it may be tempting to want to have the shoulder or hip joints use IK to solve for all three axes (heading, pitch, and bank), I find that often (though not always) this makes for a loose, "swively," hard-to-control arm or leg. Most often, character riggers will leave the bank axis to be controlled manually by the animator with FK. This lets you precisely control the position of the elbow or knee joint just by rotating the bicep or thigh!

So, the rule of thumb for good, solid IK chains in character riggings is: *The topmost item can use IK to solve for a maximum of two rotation axes, and the child item in a character IK chain should use IK for only one axis.*

> **Note:**
>
> I don't recommend asking IK to solve for any more than two joints. Using IK on a chain of more than two joints creates too many opportunities for the complex math to give you something you neither expect nor want. IK Booster is the tool for the job if you have something like a tail, tentacle, whip, or rope you need to animate.

Rotation Order

Character riggings are complex things. Riggings use a lot of heavy-duty math we animators take for granted when we're doing our jobs. Usually, we don't care *how* something works, so long as it *does*.

But, if you're curious about the more complex details that make for a good, dependable character rigging, these next two sections will fill you in on a lot of the stuff that goes on behind the scenes.

> **Note:**
>
> These next two sections are mainly for the technical directors and the heavy-duty math-oriented folks who really want to understand why things happen and why certain decisions are made in the crafting of my riggings. If this isn't your cup of tea, don't worry (there won't be a quiz on this later); just skip this and the next section, moving on to the section called "Flipping."

LightWave has a fixed order in which it calculates the rotation of an item:

1) Heading
2) Pitch
3) Bank

You can think of this rotation order as if your object ("Arrow" in this illustration) were parented to a hierarchical series of null objects, each null handling *one* rotation axis. Rotate one null, and all its children rotate right along with it.

Figure 2.19

Using this logic, I've set up a scene in which we've got two arrows as children of a hierarchical series of nulls.

Figure 2.20

Figure 2.21

In Figure 2.21, notice I've selected both arrow objects and rotated them H=20, P=40, B=60.

If an object is rotated H=20, it would make sense that to reset its *applicable rotation* to H=0, its parent object would need to be rotated H=−20 ($0 = n + [−1 \cdot n]$).

When you want to "unwind" an object, reset its applicable rotation to 0, 0, 0. When its rotation is being controlled by a system that solves heading first, then pitch, then bank, the order in which the rotations were applied must be *reversed*. (LightWave does this automatically when you simply reset an item's rotation to 0, 0, 0 — but if you have a hierarchical system creating Steadycam®-like "floating head" movement, then rotation order becomes very important.)

Figure 2.22

I've left the arrow objects at H=20, P=40, B=60, and I've rotated the parent nulls labeled Heading by −20, Pitch by −40, and Bank by −60. The only difference between the two hierarchies is the *order* in which the rotations are applied: The arrow on the right applies bank first, then pitch, then heading, essentially *reversing* the rotation order applied by LightWave.

Among other things, rotation order is responsible for the phenomenon known as "gimbal lock."

21

In each viewport, the left-hand arrow is rotated 0, 0, 0. The right-hand arrow is rotated 0, –90, 0. The bank axis is a *child* of the pitch axis, and so when pitch is rotated +/– 90°, the bank axis swings into the same plane as the heading axis. In the top viewports of Figure 2.23, you see two concentric circles representing the heading (larger) and the bank (smaller) around the right-hand arrow. The right-hand arrow is in a condition where rotating in heading and bank produce the same applicable results. This is *gimbal lock*.

Figure 2.23

If you feel you've had a hard time wrapping your mind around this problem, don't feel bad; you're not alone. Even the best IK solving engines have a difficult time with this.

When the rotation axis that is recorded *second* (pitch) nears/exceeds +/– 90°, IK can start to have problems. As the pitch angle nears/exceeds +/– 90°, the item can instantly "spin" around to face the opposite direction. Often, this will happen suddenly, over the course of a single frame. This is called *flipping*.

Note:

There are as many ways of setting up a character rig as there are peo-ple to do the setups. Everyone will find his own sets of rules that work for him.

Later on in this book, when we're actually setting up a rigging in Layout, I'll ask you to record pivot rotation for your bones as they exist in their "rest" ("zero" or "base") pose. The reason for this is that this gives me the widest array of motion before a bone nears $+/- 90°$ in any axis, and so gives me a much broader range of control.

Over the course of your career, you will hear many opinions about the "best" way of doing things. In my experience, there is no "best way." There are only ways that work more easily for the ways in which your mind solves problems. Try what sounds interesting, keep it if it works for you, and always keep your mind open to finding new and better ways of working!

Joint Compensation and Muscle Flexing

Note:

This section on joint compensation and muscle flexing also gets into some pretty heavy-duty LightWave and mathemati-cal concepts. If you're just starting out, or if you have little desire to get into the "hard-core" aspects of character rig-ging, please feel free to skip this section, moving on to the next section, called "Flipping."

At the bottom of the Bone|Properties window, LightWave has a set of Muscle Flexing and Joint Compensation options for each bone. These help LightWave preserve the volume of the character's joints as bones bend and the skin flexes.

Figure 2.24

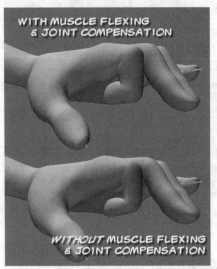

Figure 2.25

Here, you see the difference between the character's hand when Muscle Flexing and Joint Compensation are active for the bones of the fingers, and when they are not.

The thing with Muscle Flexing and Joint Compensation is that these functions *only work with the bones' pitch axis*!

Figure 2.26

Okay, so what if you want to use Muscle Flexing and Joint Compensation with a bone that is only supposed to rotate in heading, as with the forearm?

Under Modify|Rotate|Rotate Pivot, you can manually change the angle that LightWave Layout thinks of as that particular item's H=0, P=0, B=0. If you change the bank setting of an item's pivot rotation to +/– 90°, you essentially "swap" that item's heading and pitch axes.

Figure 2.27

Note:

LightWave allows you to set/record the pivot rotation for an item as a way of helping to combat gimbal lock.

A character's thigh points more or less straight downward, meaning that by default its rotation is nearly P=−90 right from the start.

By using Setup|Modify|Orientation|Record Pivot Rotation (the hot key is <P>), you can tell LightWave to store that item's current rotation as the rotation setting for that item's pivot.

The result is that the value of the item's previous rotation is stored as the *pivot's* rotation. Because the item's pivot now assumes the previous rotation information, the item itself now lies along that particular set of angles when it is set to H=0, P=0, B=0. So, the item's *rotation* is then set to 0, 0, 0, and a keyframe is created to hold the change in rotation data.

In short, using Record Pivot Rotation means that a bone can still *look* like it's pointing straight up or straight down (P=+/− 90°), but it will animate from the perception that that direction is H=0, P=0, B=0.

Note:

In changing the rotation of an item's pivot, you must do so on that item's rest pose, the frame where your character exists without any changes to his default rigging position whatsoever.

> **Note:**
> You can also use this technique of altering the bank setting of an item's pivot rotation to help control IK instabilities, which happen most often when an item using IK to solve for both heading and pitch approaches or exceeds +/– 90° in its pitch axis.
>
> If you notice that your character requires greater range of movement in the pitch axis of an item that uses IK for both heading and pitch, and that's causing you headaches with IK misbehaving, you can set the item's pivot rotation for its bank axis to +/– 90°, so then the greater range of movement occurs on the heading axis, which now falls in the same plane that used to be pitch!

Flipping

IK relies on a heavy-duty set of calculations. Even the best IK solvers still have issues when things get really complicated.

Figure 2.28

The biggest problem with even the best IK is *flipping*, where a joint will spin 180° over the course of one frame.

Foresight and planning in both your rigging and animation, coupled with a strong IK solver such as LightWave's, will usually keep flipping to a minimum.

I find that I can avoid most flipping by:

▶ Keeping the goal object at a distance of at least one-third the length of the bicep or thigh away from the bicep or thigh's point of rotation (the shoulder or hip, respectively).

Figure 2.29

▶ Keeping the bicep or thigh from nearing/exceeding +/– 90° in the pitch axis.

▶ Keeping the goal object well away from the area *behind* the bicep or thigh as that bone would lie in its rest pose.

Figure 2.30

▶ Trying to avoid having my character assume a pose that would be painful to do in real life.

> **Note:**
> I find that if I'm having problems with flipping, I'm usually trying to put the character into a pose that my own joints would complain about. If you find you absolutely, positively have to have a particular "painful" pose, you can save a lot of time by making a "special-purpose" rigging that can more easily move through that pose.

"Standard" IK Rules

These *rules* are more like *guidelines*; they can be bent and broken as you see fit to suit the needs of your particular IK setup.

However, that being said, these rules have kept my characters moving smoothly and predictably through many productions — it's always best to learn the rules and learn them well before you start seeing what happens by breaking them.

▶ IK is only dependable for solving rotations for a maximum of *two items* within an IK chain.

▶ On any item controlled by IK, let IK solve for a maximum of two axes.

▶ In a chain of two items, the child item should only use IK to solve for one of its axes.

▶ Always give your two-item IK chain a little "suggestion" in knowing which direction it should bend by pre-bending those items.

2.3 IK Booster

IK Booster is as much an advancement to the art of character animation as IK itself was back in the early '90s.

What is IK Booster? It's a whole lot of things all wrapped up in a nice, neat little package — but with respect to character rigging, it's best to think of it as something that can be used to add even more ease, power, functionality, and stability to the IK systems we've been talking about already.

Applying IK Booster

IK Booster can be applied to any object that has bones set up hierarchically. It can be applied to an existing IK character rigging, a model with bones handcrafted in Layout, or bones converted from *skelegons* created in Modeler (see Chapters 4 and 5).

1. Start with a fresh scene, and add a null (as described earlier in this chapter). Add a chain of five bones to your null (also as described earlier in this chapter).

Figure 2.31

Note:

To add these bones, once you have created your null, you can just press < = > and click OK to accept the default name of "Bone" five times in a row if you want to do things the quick and easy way.

2. Activate the IK Booster tool by clicking on **Modify|Tools|IK BoostTool** ^ **B.** Then, right-click on the **null** that is the *root object* for the bones we just created.

Figure 2.32

29

3. Once you click on **Apply IK_Booster,** as shown in Figure 2.32, you'll notice a few changes to the appearance of your object. So long as you have the IK BoostTool active, you'll see a *control icon* for your currently selected item within your IK Booster-enabled object(s). You'll also see *handles* that default to the tips of all the bones within the IK-boosted object.

Figure 2.33

> **Note:**
>
> IK Booster is a custom object function applied to the object itself. To remove it from an object, you'll need to open the Object Properties for that particular object, and remove the IK_Booster custom object under the Geometry tab.

That's it! That's all you need to do to apply IK Booster and start animating this chain of five bones far more reliably than IK alone would let you. (Read on!)

Long Chain Dependability

With IK Booster, you don't have to assign any goal objects and you don't have to tell LightWave to use IK for any rotation axes; you just grab any of the handles and move them around!

Figure 2.34

IK Booster handles "long chains" of hundreds of bones with speed and reliability. If you've got a whip, tentacle, or tail you need to animate, IK Booster lets you confidently use as many bones as you need to get the smoothest deformations possible.

You probably noticed that when you dragged your IK-boosted chain around, you dragged the whole thing around, root and all. If you want to have the root stay in place, make sure you have the root bone (or the object itself) selected, right-click on the item's control, and check ikstop. This causes the IK movements of all child bones to have no effect on any items higher up the IK-boosted chain.

Figure 2.35

IK Booster and Movement

IK Booster is a *mode* of movement unto itself. Selecting Modify | Translate | Move or Modify | Rotate | Rotate or Modify | Transform | Size (or Stretch — or any other tool) will deactivate the IK BoostTool.

Movement within the IK Booster system isn't the same as you may have gotten used to thus far in LightWave; the handles are different, and you can essentially move and rotate without having to change tools.

You've already seen how you can click and drag a handle to move the IK-boosted chain. If you need to rotate an item, select it, then click and drag on the numbers that appear beside its control. The top is heading (green), then pitch (red), then bank (blue).

Figure 2.36

IK Booster and Keyframes

IK Booster creates its own keyframes whenever you move or rotate an item in its chain (regardless of your Auto Key Create settings). And because IK Booster pushes beyond LightWave's normal way of working, the usual ways of creating and deleting keyframes (by pressing Enter and Delete) don't apply *when you have IK BoostTool active*).

Figure 2.37

When you have IK Booster active (and the Dope Track is *inactive* — see the section called "Dope Track" in Chapter 18, "Advanced Animation Tools"), a darkened area appears above the timeline at the bottom of Layout's screen. This is the IK Booster Track. There's a lot of power packed within that little track.

The display at the left of the IK Booster Track tells you which items within the IK-boosted chain will be affected by what you're doing with the chain. In this case, all the parents and children of the selected item will have keyframes created whenever I move a handle. (Clicking on this display cycles you through the different modes — you can choose to affect only the current item, only the selected item's children, only its parents, both that item's parents and children, or all items within the IKB chain.)

Right-clicking on the IK Booster Track opens up the right-click menu for that particular frame. It is from this right-click menu that you can choose to delete a keyframe or create one arbitrarily (without having to move or rotate an item). (Remember that the action you choose is applied to the Items Affected choice at the left of the IKB Track!)

Now, what if you had a whole lot of frames you wanted to delete at once?

Right-click drag-select an area within the IK Booster Track to select a *range* of frames. You can then choose Delete from the right-click menu that opens when you release the right mouse button.

Figure 2.38

Note:

Most who've used LightWave for any length of time have grown fond of LightWave's Display Options | Show Motion Paths setting that lets you see a visual representation of an item's motion, frames, and keyframes within the 3D space of its viewports.

Figure 2.39

When you have IK Booster active, if you turn off LightWave's Show Motion Paths, you'll more clearly see IK Booster's "onionskin" dots that represent the selected handle's position on surrounding frames that fade out the farther a frame is from the current one.

Pose and Motion Saving and Loading

When you have IK Booster applied to a character rigging (even if you are using none of the other IK Booster features), you can save and load poses and motions for *some* or *all* of your rigging!

Clicking on the IKB Menu on the right side of the IK Booster Track (which, as mentioned earlier, is visible when the Dope Track is inactive) brings up a menu from which you can choose to save and load the motion of your entire rigging.

From the IKB Menu|Motions menu, you can also choose to copy the motion of your entire rigging, storing it to be swapped with the current motion by choosing IKB Menu|Motions|Motion Rollback. This is very handy when you want to quickly compare two motions without having to bother with going through the extra steps of saving and loading the different motions.

Figure 2.40

Right-clicking on the control for an item in an IKB chain also brings up a menu that you can use to save and load motions *and/or* poses for that item and its children in the chain. (Be sure to right-click on the control, not the numbers. Right-clicking on the numbers will open a different set of menus that allow you to lock and/or limit motion on the clicked-upon number's axis.)

Figure 2.41

> **Note:**
>
> Using this item-based way of saving/loading poses and motions, you can quickly load complex shapes onto, say, your character's hands (clenched fists, martial-arts hand shapes, etc.). Being able to load complex poses onto parts of your characters means you can really take your time to get those complex poses perfect, knowing that you'll only have to create those poses once!
>
> It's a good idea, though, to put the name of the item you had selected when you created that pose in the name of the pose and/or motion file you create. IK Booster will let you load a pose or motion onto a different item in your hierarchy than the one you had selected to save its motion and the motion of its children, which can create some unpredictable results.

Quaternion Rotations

If you followed the information in the section on rotation order in the first part of this chapter on Inverse Kinematics and the problems with flipping that can occur because of gimbal lock, you may find it interesting to know that LightWave [8]'s IK Booster now allows for a new kind of angular mathematics that can help with the problem of gimbal lock: quaternion rotations.

You activate quaternion rotation for an item within an IK Booster chain by selecting Options|Quaternion from its controller's right-click menu.

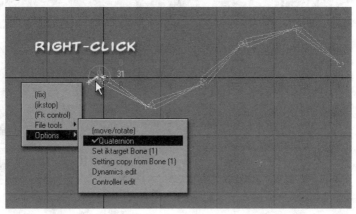

Figure 2.42

To you, the animator, you won't notice much more than a little "Q" appearing inside the controller icon, and that certain problem poses for your rigging *may* not be such a problem anymore. (Quaternion rotation only *helps* in dealing with the issues of gimbal lock — it is not a "magic bullet.")

Keyframe Move Mode

IK Booster also gives you the ability to quickly move your keyframes about without ever having to leave Layout's main window.

> **Note:**
> General Options|Show Keys in Slider turns on and off LightWave's representation of keyframes for the current item as light, vertical lines in the background of the Time Slider at the bottom of Layout's window.

37

In Figure 2.43, I'm starting off with keyframes on frames 0, 10, 20, and 30 for all the items in the IKB chain. Left-clicking on the IKB Track on frame 15 sets the center mark of the Move mode. Dragging in the IKB Track on the right-hand side of this center mark moves all the keyframes to the right of the center mark (for the currently selected Affected Items choice) by the distance dragged. (The little triangles in the IKB Track to the right of frame 15 show the start and end positions of my drag.)

Figure 2.43

In the above illustration, because Child is the currently selected Affected Items choice (displayed on the left-hand side of the IKB Track), only the selected item and its child item(s) will have their keyframes moved.

When you're done moving keyframes in relation to that particular center mark, simply click on the center mark and it will disappear.

> **Note:**
> Using IK Booster's Move mode with the parent or child Affected Items choice is a great way to quickly add the "whip-like" action known in character animation as the "successive breaking of joints" after you have made sure your character hits the key poses you want.

2.4 **Newbie Sensory Overload**

I can imagine that if you're new to IK and/or IK Booster, all the information in this chapter may seem a bit overwhelming. Don't worry. There *is* a lot to learn here.

The good thing is that as you follow the steps in Chapters 3 and onward of this book, you'll be building a character's rigging and setting it in motion by following the steps clearly laid out. You may not at first completely understand the *whys* of the reasons things are done a certain way, but you will find that once you've gone through the process, a lot more of it will make sense in retrospect.

And once you start actually using a rigging you've made, you'll experience a whole lot of "Ah, now I see why we did that."

So, remember not to worry. None of us came into this world already knowing how to pontificate on the intricacies of Inverse Kinematics — we *all* had to pick up this information somewhere on our journeys.

Your greatest asset, throughout your entire life, will be your ability to find the solutions you seek yourself.

Every question or problem can be broken down into ever more simple bits that you can more easily master.

If you find yourself feeling stuck, take a step back to where you *do* feel confident about what you know. Seek out the resources that can help you understand the smaller component parts of what you are seeking to learn (books, online resources, and exploring functional examples where these elements are used well).

Knowing you can find the way to get yourself to where you want to be is one of the most powerful realizations you can come to in a lifetime.

Prepping Your Character for Setup

You've got your character all ready to go, and you want to get started right away in making him (or her) move, act, emote; in general, you want to get him into that performance you've always known he (or she) could do. Before you can animate him, you've got to set him up. And before you can set him up, you've got to prep him for setup, and that means planning.

Planning your setup is probably the most crucial phase of CG animation (no, really). The setup you're going to create will dictate how easy it is to move your character into and out of poses. It will either follow your commands or frustrate the living daylights out of you by misbehaving just when you need the most precise control of your character.

If you build your characters with the same proportions, joints in the same places and whatnot, you'll be able to just plug this setup into your new character once you have him point weighted. Doing the proper planning and prep work makes not only this character work well, but any other character you'll use this setup for in the future.

> **Note:**
> There are very few rules of thumb when dealing with computers. If it isn't already, one of those rules should be: "The things you expect to take a long time on a computer often are the things that get done the quickest, while the things that you expect to breeze through often are the things that take all afternoon." I think one possible reason this is so is because we're paying more attention to the things we do when we think they're complicated. When we think something is easy, our mind isn't always fully there working on it. Keep focused, plan your attack, and know the result you want before you start.

3.1 **Where Is He Going to Bend?**

Most people build their characters in a kind of "da Vinci-esque" spread-eagle pose. This is great for making sure all the proportions are correct, as you can tell at a glance if something is out of whack. All joints and appendages are out in the open, so to speak, for us to see and figure out where our skeleton's bones should be.

> **Note:**
>
> The exercises in this book are tailored to using the Thinguy.lwo model, available on the companion CD. If you've got a character you're just dying to use, you may, but be aware that you might have to make nip-and-tuck alterations to the information to get it to fit your character. (This is especially so if your character has non-human proportions!)
>
> I've made the character Thinguy.lwo especially for training with this book. His poly/patch count is 1506 polygons/patches. With him, even if you're running LightWave on a 366 MHz laptop, you'll still be able to get a good, workable real-time frame rate while you're animating. Though his lines are broad and caricaturistic, he is proportioned realistically so you'll be able to get a good range of action from him and not have either exaggerated or realistic action look odd on him.

> **Advanced Note:**
>
> To all those modelers out there: The frame rate an animator gets while he's animating your character plays a large role in how well he can animate him. If you absolutely must have a character with an incredibly high pre-NURBed poly/patch count, also make a "stand-in" character for your animator to work with. This stand-in should have all the joints and bends in the same places, but at a fraction of the poly/patch count, allowing the animator to animate with ease, then swap the stand-in with your work of art at the time of rendering. (This also allows animation and modeling to go on side by side. As soon as the animator gets the weighted, setup scene with the stand-in model, he can start working, letting modeling continue almost up to the time of the final render.)

1. Copy the 3D directory from the companion CD to a place on your hard drive you'll be able to work from.

2. Start Modeler and set your content directory to the 3D directory you just copied to your hard drive.

> **Newbie Note:**
> LightWave Modeler has two separate Options panels. One is for display options (discussed later) and the other is for general options and can be found here: Modeler|Options |General Options (or by pressing <o>). General Options has important things like the Content Directory (where LightWave looks for images, objects, scenes, and the like), how many levels of Undo you have, whether polygons will default to quadrangles (for NURBial patches) or triangles, and how smooth your NURBed models will look as you're working on them. (This smoothness is the result of patch division, where the higher the number, the smoother the model will look but the more computationally intensive it will be to draw in real time. I usually use a level of 4.)

3. Load in **Thinguy.lwo** from Objects\BaseChar\Thinguy.

4. Find the places in the model where the joints will be, and turn the model around in the Perspective view. Press **Tab** to convert patches into polygons. Set the view for your perspective window to **Wireframe Shade**. Try to get an idea of what points will need to pull with what bones in order to bend his body in ways that'll look right. (Printing a screen capture of Modeler and sketching rough bone layout or pivot points can be helpful at this point.) Things to note here are the actual points from which the different parts of the body rotate. They aren't always where you might think they are, so move your own arm, fingers, neck, knees, and back and see where these movements correlate to your model.

Figure 3.1, Figure 3.2, Figure 3.3. Front, side, and top views of our character. A good knowledge of anatomy is important whether you are doing cartoonish or hyper-realistic characters. Things like scale, relationship, and rotation are stored deep in all our minds, though it isn't something that most of us are consciously aware of. Most people can't tell you exactly why something looks "right" or "wrong," but it is usually because of something being incorrectly proportioned or rotating from somewhere it shouldn't.

3.2 **Pre-bending to Help IK**

Since IK can only safely solve for a maximum of two parts, we need to look at our model and figure out what parts are going to be controlled with IK and which parts will be FK. Looking at Figures 3.1 through 3.3, the bicep and forearm will be one chain, and the thigh and calf will be another chain. I like having the neck as another chain so I can precisely control the position of the head at all times. That gives us five IK chains; the rest of the model will be FK.

IK needs all the help it can get, so we're going to modify our model a bit to give IK a hand. We're going to put in a much steeper bend at the knees so IK is more likely to bend correctly when our character is in an extreme pose. We're going to do the same for the arms, but with a bit of a twist.

Bones pull points along with them when they are moved or rotated. This is more like a magnet's pull than the way our skin slides over our muscles. This can cause problems in places like elbows and knees, and especially shoulders and under the arms. Things can pinch, bunch, and generally look wrong because it is so hard to get the points that control the model's skin to move like our skin does. A common but cumbersome solution is to build morph targets that are controlled either manually or by expressions driven by the rotation of the offending bones. I prefer a much simpler strategy: Figure the range of normal movement for that part or set of parts, and have your base pose somewhere in the middle of that range.

Most people are more apt to move their arms forward than back. Most elbows don't like being bent beyond the point where they're straight out from the bicep. So the base pose for the arms should have the bicep angled forward somewhere around 45 degrees, and the forearm angled about 45 degrees from that. This gives us our pre-bend so IK knows that elbows don't bend backward, and it also helps preserve the volumes of the elbow and shoulder when bones pull points around.

> **Note:**
> The way I like to do pre-bending is to select groupings of points (say, of the forearm and hand, for instance), and then using Modify |Rotate|Rotate, "swing" those selected points around into their new place while the rest of the model stays locked in place. By adding and removing points from your selection, you can specifically control the "bending" of your model as you rotate these groups.

1. Pre-bend your model's arms so they match those in Figure 3.4. Pay close attention to the points in the underarm area. Make sure your model looks as if there is a body there under the shirt and that the shirt hangs naturally from this frame.

Figure 3.4. Pre-bend the arms, preserving the volume of the bent elbow.

> **Note:**
> When rotating selections of points for the arms, legs, or whatever, try to bear in mind where the joints would be in an actual skeleton (Figures 3.1 to 3.3). If you rotate your point selection from these joints, you'll have a much quicker time of point pulling to make your model look correct.

Newbie Note:

Creating point selection sets (Display|Grouping|Point Selection Sets...) not only helps you know what points are what when you're pre-bending your model, it also makes things much easier when you're point weighting. (You add points to your selection from a selection set you've created by bringing up the Point Statistics window by pressing <w> with Points ^G active. You choose the point selection set you've created from the list, and click on the "+" symbol to its left.)

Figure 3.5. Add points from a selection set to your current selection.

Newbie Note:

Make use of all the tools at your disposal when doing delicate point work. Press 0 (on the numeric keypad) to make windows go full-screen to get better views of tight areas. Hide and unhide parts of your model to get a clear shot at what you're trying to manipulate. Switch between polygons and meta-NURBS to see how smoothly rings of points are lying. Alternate between Smooth Shade and Wireframe Shade in your Perspective window to see which points are causing bumps in your model. Activate and deactivate showing point selections, polygon selections, cages, guides, and whatnot in your Perspective window to eliminate clutter when you really need to see detail. (Press <d> to bring up the Display Options window. Choose the Viewports tab. Viewport 2 controls the upper-right window, the Perspective window by default. Click on Independent Visibility and you can enable and disable settings to make your modeling life easier.)

Caution:

Using Symmetry (Modes|Symmetry On/Off) can be a great help, but only if your model is exactly symmetrical before you start pulling points around. A point that is close but not exactly mirrored across the X-axis of your model won't be automatically selected when you select the point on the +x side of your model. If forget about this you can have half of your model correct and the other half misshapen. Correct this by cutting your model down the center and mirroring. Mirroring, however, copies over all point weight information, so if you mirror your character's right side to become its left, both thighs (for example) will have exactly the same weight maps targeted at the RightThigh bone.

There are several free plug-ins available that will help you fix the symmetry of your model if you need to (search the archives of www.flay.com), but the best solution is to make sure you always operate with Symmetry active if you are working with a symmetrical model.

2. Pre-bend your character's legs to match those in Figure 3.6. Preserve the volume of the knee (see Figure 3.7) when bending points to make it look like there actually is a knee inside that tube of virtual fabric. Pay special attention to the pelvic area; you'll often see deep folds in the front of the pants when you swing the legs forward. You'll also have to watch the gluteal area; it tends to get flat when legs are swung forward. Pull points to make this base pose look believable.

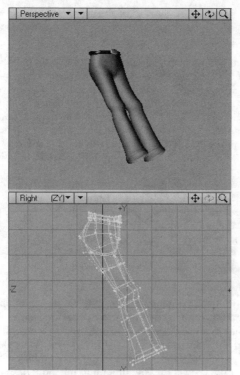

Figure 3.6. Pay attention to the pelvic and gluteal areas as the legs are swung forward to pre-bend for IK.

Figure 3.7. Preserve the volume of the knees.

3. Lower the body and head to account for the height that was lost when we bent the knees. When you're doing this, tweak the points of the pant cuff to fall properly over the shoe. You'll also need to pull the top part of the shoe to be bent by the calf section angling toward the knee.

Figure 3.8. Pull the points of the pant cuff and shoe to make the bend of this area look believable.

4. Check the alignment and position the hands. Make sure they look natural within the shirt cuffs and the fingers point straight forward.

Figure 3.9. Make sure the hands look right.

> **Note:**
>
> You may have noticed that "ThinGuy" only has four fingers. There's a convention in character design that says human characters have five fingers, animal characters have four. I break this convention in CG when I'm working with a cartoon human. This is just my personal preference, but it saves a lot of cumulative time in animation, and the clients I've dealt with would rather have better overall animation than an extra finger.
>
> If you examine the new model for this book, "Mr. Cool," you'll notice that he has four fingers, but he still works perfectly with the "ThinGuy" riggings. This is a common "cheat" where I've got both Mr. Cool's ring and middle fingers following the movements of the bones of ThinGuy's middle finger.

Figure 3.10. The model, ready for skelegons!

Chapter 4

Boning Your Character

Note:

As you continue to work in CG, you'll notice that you "hit the groove." This is when things just flow. Whether you're animating or modeling, everything just falls right into place, time seems to drop away, and you achieve a close to Zen-like state. The problem is that this is usually the time when the computer crashes, the network freezes, or any number of other problems trash what you did since your last save.

When you're in that Zen-like state, saving your work seems to be last on the list of important things to do. If you've lost your best work of the day in a crash of some sort, producers seem to think that since you did it once, it would be easier the second time. This is not the case. The only remedy to this is to save often, and make a habit of it! Not just save, but save revisions. Crashes have happened in the middle of a save, and that corrupts what might be days or weeks worth of work (if that happens to your only version of the model or scene)!

LightWave [8]'s Save Incremental features for both objects in Modeler and scenes in Layout is perfect for this task. With the press of a capital "S" you automatically save your object or scene with "_v001" tacked onto the end, and every time you do this, the number increases by one! (So, in an effort to keep my directories uncluttered, if I'm working on Blah_v003.lwo, I'll Ctrl+s (Save As) and choose Blah_v002.lwo; just in case the power goes out during a save, I've still got *03.lwo). Then, with that save completed successfully, I'll press <S> to automatically save and update my current revision to *v003. The result is that I'm *saving over* something I don't have a more recent version of, and yet I'm also not racking up a huge number of files in the object's directory.)

Always move on to a new set of revision numbers anytime you make a major change! This frees you to safely experiment, knowing you can always go back to the way things were before (regardless of whether the decision is yours or your director's).

4.1 **Adding Bones to Your Character**

We're ready to start adding bones to our character. Some of the bones will be used to pull the points of our character around. Others will be used to control the movements of these bones. We'll be using the skelegon tools in Modeler to put these bones in place. I find this saves time, lets you save the bone setup with the character, and gives you access to a whole slew of free Modeler plug-ins that make point weighting much easier.

1. Load the character you pre-bent for IK in the last chapter into Modeler. (If all you want to do is animate and you never see yourself modeling and you skipped the pre-bending, I've got a pre-bent model already made, which you can find in Objects\chapters\ch_03.lwo.)

2. Maximize the Right viewport and press **a** to Fit All.

3. Set your Foreground (Active) Layer to **Layer 2** and your Background Layer to **Layer 1**.

LightWave Modeler Layers

Clicking in the upper triangle makes that layer the foreground layer. You can view and modify items in this layer. Clicking in the lower triangle makes that layer the background layer. Items in this layer can be seen but not modified. (Holding down Shift while clicking adds or removes layers from your selected foreground or background layers.)

Figure 4.1

Note:

The order in which you create the skelegons in Modeler is the order in which they will become bones in Layout. I like to use the Up and Down Arrow keys when animating to select the next and previous bones, and have memorized how many presses it takes to get from one specific control to another. (For instance, with Spine1 selected, pressing the Down Arrow three times will select the Head control, and one more press selects the RightHand_Trans control.) This lets me keep my eyes glued to my scene without breaking my concentration to go to a Schematic view or to scroll visually through a list. This is why we'll be creating skelegons in a seemingly haphazard way; it actually makes animation much easier, for some, in the long run.

4.2 **Spinal Controls**

Spinal controls are the FK bones that will control the bending of your character's torso. These are the bones you will use first in posing your character to get a strong line of motion.

1. Create the skelegon that will be the root bone of your skeleton. Draw this bone as close to horizontal as you can and have its tip be where the spine connects with the pelvis. Remember that your spine is closer to your back than your front!

2. Create the skelegon that will be our character's pelvis as shown in Figure 4.2.

Note:

Many people create skeletons with the buttocks as the base. I create mine with the lumbar area as the skeleton's base. This allows you to swing the hips without having to counteranimate the spine. This makes animating everything from walks to slouches much faster and easier.

Figure 4.2. Angle the pelvis back, following the line of the tailbone.

3. Deactivate the Create Skelegons tool by clicking on the **Polygons** ^ **H** button.

4. Select the first skelegon we created.

5. Reactivate the Create Skelegons tool.

Creating Skelegons

To create a skelegon, click on Setup | Skelegons | Create Skelegons. Then, click and drag to create a skelegon. While Create Skelegons is active, clicking and dragging within either of the two circles at the base or head of the skelegon will drag that end to a new location. Clicking outside of those two circles will create another skelegon that is a child of the one you just created.

CLICK & DRAG ON THESE HANDLES TO MODIFY SKELEGON

Figure 4.3. This bone will be the root of your skeleton.

Note:

The viewport in which you create a skelegon will determine its bank rotation of that bone in Layout. Generally, if a skelegon is created in a Top or Back viewport, it will have a bank rotation of 0°, and a skelegon created in a Right viewport will result in a bone with a bank rotation of –90°.

Note:

Skelegons are considered polygons. You can select them with Polygons ^H active. Even though they look like they've got several polygons to them, LightWave treats each skelegon as a single polygon. Under the Polygon Statistics window (press <w> with Polygons ^H active) each skelegon is listed under its name in the Part drop-down list (the bottom line in the Polygon Statistics window).

Figure 4.4. You can manually adjust the bank rotation of the bone that will be created from a skelegon by using the bank rotation handle. (In my experience fussing with this control, trial-and-error is the only way to know what rotation handle position will yield what bone bank rotation in Layout.) Setup| Skelegons|Edit Skelegons allows you to adjust the settings of any pre-made, *selected* skelegons.

Note:

If you're ever unsure as to whether to create a skelegon in a Right, Back, or Top viewport, just look at the accompanying illustration for that step to see which viewport I'm using.

Note:

Grid Snap can help or hinder you, depending on what you're trying to do at that moment in Modeler. Activate Grid Snap by choosing Edit|Display Options| Units|Grid Snap when you need to make things snap to an invisible grid (good for aligning items), and deactivate it when you need to make fine, delicate changes.

6. Draw the skelegons that will be the first, second, and third spine bones. (Because we had our root skelegon selected, the new skelegons are created as its children instead of children of the Pelvis, the last bone we created.)

Figure 4.5. Be sure to follow the curvature and placement of the spine in these skelegons. (I've turned off points, cages, and guides so I can more easily see what I'm doing.)

7. Deactivate the Create Skelegons tool and select our root skelegon again.

8. Name this skelegon **Root**.

Naming Skelegons

Name skelegons by selecting them individually and choosing
Setup|Skelegons|Rename Skelgns. Naming a skelegon helps
us not only tell skelegons apart but also the bones and weight
maps that will be generated automatically from these
skelegons.

Figure 4.6. Making it easier to know which skelegon is which.

9. Rename the other skelegons **Pelvis**, **Spine1**, **Spine2**, and
   Spine3 respectively (Spine1 being the most immediate child
   of Root).

10. Press **Ctrl+t** to activate Drag mode, and click-and-drag on the
    base (the stubby end, not the pointy end) of our Root skelegon.
    Drag this end close to where it meets the Pelvis and Spine1
    skelegons.

Figure 4.7. Root will rotate from its base, and though it won't directly control any points in our model, it will control the bones that do. Having its rotation centered inside the body helps us much more than being able to see the bone from a distance.

11. Create another skelegon inside the character's head, making sure no other skelegons are selected before doing so. Name this bone **Head**.

Figure 4.8. The base of this bone is at the juncture where the skull sits on the spinal column.

Note:

Sometimes, even with no skelegon selected, LightWave will draw new skelegons as children of a previously created skelegon. You can solve this problem by hiding all skelegons before drawing new ones.

4.3 **Hand Controls**

Hand controls are used to move and rotate the hands. We'll also be building controls that will let us shrug the shoulders, expand or cave the chest, and rotate the elbow up or down.

1. Create and place another skelegon that reaches from the center of the wrist to the center of the middle finger's root knuckle. Name this bone **RightHand_Trans**.

Figure 4.9. This bone will control the translation of the hand and its heading and bank.

2. Copy **RightHand_Trans**, then drag its tip (the pointy end) to somewhere around the middle of the palm.

3. Paste to create a new skelegon. Name this one **RightHand_Rot**.

Note:

Now that LightWave has the ability to rotate objects in Layout based upon world and quaternion coordinates, nesting controls as we are doing for the hand isn't as necessary to control gimbal lock as it once was. Yes, it does mean that there is yet another control to consider during animation, but I find that I can more precisely control hand animation this way. So much acting comes from subtleties of the hands, and for me to be able to dictate exactly which way a wrist will unfold in a scene with complex acting is more important than eliminating a control.

Figure 4.10. This bone will control the hand's pitch. Having these bones a different length makes them easier to select without using the Polygon Statistics window.

4. Create a skelegon that follows the placement of the scapula. Place its tip where the shoulder joint will be. Name this skelegon **RightShoulder.**

5. With **RightShoulder** selected, create a tiny bone that points along the bicep toward the elbow. Name this skelegon **RightElbow**.

Figure 4.11. RightShoulder and RightElbow.

6. Select **RightShoulder, RightElbow, RightHand_Trans**, and **RightHand_Rot**.

7. **Multiply|Duplicate|Mirror** these skelegons along the X-axis *without* merging points. Rename the new skelegons **LeftShoulder, LeftElbow, LeftHand_Trans**, and **LeftHand_Rot**, respectively. (See the following Newbie Block on Mirroring.)

Mirroring

1. With your skelegons selected, press <**V**> (LightWave's hot keys are case sensitive) or select **Multiply|Duplicate| Mirror.**

2. Press <**n**> to open the Numeric input window.

3. Press <**n**> a second time to activate the controls. Make sure the X-axis is selected, and that the center is set to 0 m along the X-, Y-, and Z-axes.

4. Deselect **Merge Points.** (The Merge Points option automatically performs a **Merge Points|Automatic** function after mirroring. This is handy in a lot of cases, but we want to know that any points on these skelegons that we don't merge on purpose stay that way; it can affect hierarchy.)

5. Close the Numeric window and press the **Spacebar** to drop the Mirror tool.

Figure 4.12. Mirroring the hand controls.

4.4 **Foot Controls**

Foot controls manage the placement of the foot and the bend of the toes. We'll also be creating the control for swinging the knee in and out.

1. Create a skelegon for the right foot. Position its base in the center of the ankle and its tip in the center of the ball of the foot.

2. Create a second skelegon (a child of the previous one) that stretches to the tip of the shoe. Name these two skelegons **RightFoot** and **RightToes**, respectively.

Note:

If your character is digitigrade, meaning he walks on his toes, you'll need to use a different setup for his feet. You'll find this setup in Chapter 15, along with important notes on how to handle digitigrade and animal motion. (The digitigrade rigging I used on the characters of *Kaze, Ghost Warrior* is included on the *Kaze, Ghost Warrior* DVD available at www.KazeGhostWarrior.com.)

Figure 4.13. Positioning the foot and toe skelegons.

3. Make a small skelegon that has its tip at the center of the hip joint. (Use Figures 3.1 and 3.2 to help you.) Angle this bone so it lies along a path that points toward the knee. Name this skelegon **RightKnee**.

Figure 4.14. Positioning the RightKnee skelegon.

4. Mirror **RightKnee**, **RightFoot**, and **RightToes** along the X-axis. Rename the new bones accordingly.

67

Figure 4.15. Mirroring the foot and knee controls. All extraneous things are kept hidden to help preserve sanity.

Figure 4.16. The major controls for our character.

4.5 **Fingers**

Now that we've got the major controls that will drive the IK for our character, we'll put in the FK bones that will control the fingers. Because of my tendency to like to scroll up and down through things in Layout with the Up and Down Arrow keys, I like to build the fingers in a specific pattern. I like to start sculpting the hand position from the index finger, working my way to the middle finger, ring finger (if it's there), pinky finger, and finally the thumb. If you would rather start with the thumb or another finger, please feel free to modify this hand setup to suit your needs.

1. Create a chain of three skelegons along the right index finger. Name these **RightIndex_Base**, **RightIndex_Mid**, and **RightIndex_Tip** accordingly.

Figure 4.17. I tend to place finger bones a bit higher than the center of the finger. This gives me the most realistic finger action in bends. Notice that while the connections between RightIndex_Tip and RightIndex_Mid and their parents fall on the isoparm (isoparametric line, the lines that define NURBial patches) of their respective knuckle, the base of RightIndex_Base does not. The rotation point of this base knuckle is deeper inside the hand than what you might think. Bend your own fingers from this first knuckle, and see that the bend takes place not at the webbing but deeper into your hand!

2. Create a chain of skelegons for the right middle finger. Name these **RightMiddle_Base**, **RightMiddle_Mid**, and **RightMiddle_Tip** accordingly.

3. Create a chain of skelegons for the right pinky finger. Name these **RightPinky_Base**, **RightPinky_Mid**, and **Right-Pinky_Tip** accordingly.

Figure 4.18. The skelegons for the middle and pinky fingers. I've marked the knuckles with thick lines in this figure. I generally like to have a bend fall directly on an isoparm, and surround it with an isoparm on either side. It helps keep bulges in the right places while animating.

4. Create a chain of skelegons for the right thumb. Name these **RightThumb_Base**, **RightThumb_Mid**, and **RightThumb_Tip** accordingly.

Figure 4.19. The skelegons of the thumb. Thumbs do have three parts of articulation, just like fingers! It's just that the base of our thumb is buried deep in our hand close to our wrist! Move your own thumb about, feeling for this base joint with the fingers of your other hand.

Advanced Note:

There is actually another point of articulation in the hand that lets us fold our pinky and ring fingers over somewhat toward our thumb. So far, I haven't needed to build a setup that has this, but that doesn't mean that you won't be faced with a scene one day where you'll have to put this in. Just make a mental note that this rotation swings from the base of the palm, just on the other side of its center from where *Thumb_Base attaches.

5. Select and mirror the bones you have just created for the fingers (and thumb) across the X-axis (without merging points), and rename the new bones to reflect the fact that they're on the left.

Figure 4.20. All the IK and FK controllers have been created. All that remains for this part of the setup is to create the skelegons for the IK systems.

4.6 **IK System Skelegons**

IK system skelegons are the skelegons/bones that will be controlled by IK. Accuracy is a very big factor here, so we'll be using a few tricks that speed up precision placement. Some of the steps may seem a little odd, but they really are the fastest, most reliable ways I've found to do things.

1. Hide all the skelegons except for Spine3 (the top spinal skelegon) and Head.

2. With **Spine3** selected, create a skelegon. Name this skelegon **Neck**.

Figure 4.21. It isn't important where Neck is pointed. We'll position it in a moment.

3. Change your selection mode to **Points** ^ **G**, and select first the point at the tip of Neck, then the point at the root of Head.

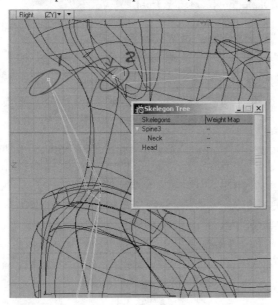

Figure 4.22. Selecting the points in order.

4.   Press **Ctrl+w** to weld these two points together.

Figure 4.23. The two points are welded together, forcing the tip of Neck to the exact position of Head. This also makes Head a child of Neck as seen in the Skelegon Tree window (Setup|Skelegons|Skelegon Tree).

Newbie Note:

The order in which the points to be welded are selected is important. All selected points will be welded to the *last* point selected.

5.   Select the single point that is now the tip of Neck and the base of Head. Press **Ctrl+u** to "unweld" this point into two points (a point for each skelegon it belonged to).

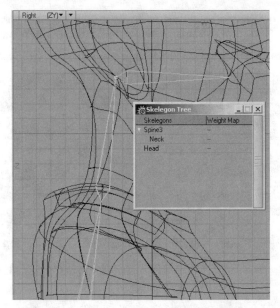

Figure 4.24. Head is now no longer a child of Neck.

6. With **Neck** selected, create a small skelegon at its tip. Name this skelegon **Neck_Puller**.

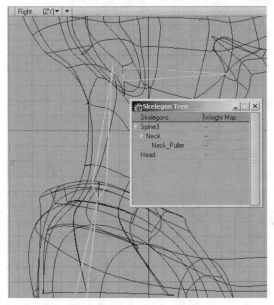

Figure 4.25. With the addition of Neck_Puller, the hierarchy of the neck is now complete.

75

7. With **RightElbow** selected, create two more skelegons that lie along the arm. Name these two skelegons **RightBicep** and **RightForearm**, respectively.

Figure 4.26. RightBicep and RightForearm, newly created and ready to be positioned within the arm.

8. Position the right elbow joint, the meeting of RightBicep and RightForearm. It should be in the center of the arm along the Y-axis, but closer to the back of the arm on the X- and Z-axes.

9. Select the point at the tip of RightForearm. Then add to your selection the points that are at the base of RightHand_Trans and RightHand_Rot (they should be right on top of one another).

Figure 4.27. Selecting the points that will position the tip of RightForearm after having positioned the elbow joint.

10. Press **Ctrl+w** to weld these points, moving the tip of RightForearm to the exact position of the base of the hand controls.

11. Select this newly welded point and press **Ctrl+u** to unweld it from the original three points, unparenting the hand controls from RightForearm.

12. With the RightForearm skelegon selected, create a small skelegon at its tip. Name this new skelegon **RightArm_Puller**.

Figure 4.28. The hierarchy of the right arm is complete!

13. Select **RightArm_Puller**, **RightForearm**, and **RightBicep**. Mirror these skelegons across the X-axis (without merging points). Rename the new skelegons appropriately.

14. Select the points that are the base of LeftBicep and the tip of LeftElbow (they should be right on top of one another). Press **Ctrl+w** to weld them together, making LeftBicep a child of LeftElbow.

Figure 4.29. Welding the mirrored skelegon chain of LeftBicep, LeftForearm, and LeftArm_Puller to the tip of LeftElbow.

15. Hide all skelegons except for RightKnee and RightFoot.

16. With **RightKnee** selected, create two skelegons that follow the line of the leg. Name them **RightThigh** and **RightCalf**, accordingly.

Figure 4.30. Position the knee joint slightly forward of the center of the model's knee.

17. Weld the point at the tip of RightCalf to the point at the base of RightFoot (just like we did before).

18. Select this newly welded point and unweld it.

Figure 4.31. Welding and unwelding to position the tip of RightCalf.

19. With **RightCalf** selected, add a tiny skelegon and name it
RightLeg_Puller.

Figure 4.32. With the addition of RightLeg_Puller, the hierarchy of the right leg
is complete!

20. Mirror **RightLeg_Puller, RightCalf,** and **RightThigh** across the X-axis, again making sure to not automatically merge points. Rename these bones accordingly.

21. Unhide everything and weld the point at the tip of LeftKnee to the point at the base of LeftThigh.

Figure 4.33. Your completed skeleton!

22. Select all your skelegons and cut them, leaving Layer2 empty.

23. Set Layer1 as your active layer and paste the skelegons into the same layer as your mesh.

24. Select **Map|Weight|Bone Weights**.

25. Enter **0 m** for Threshold Value, and set Use Threshold to **Clip**. Click **OK**.

Figure 4.34. Using these settings creates weight maps for every skelegon with the values on every point being 0%.

26. Save a backup revision of your model, and then save the model itself. When you're ready, go on to Chapter 5.

Converting, Organizing, and Aligning

The skelegons you created in Modeler are placeholders for the bones that Layout will use to deform the mesh. So now, for the moment, we can leave Modeler behind and open up Layout.

5.1 Converting Skelegons to Bones

Newbie Note:

If you just couldn't bring yourself to make the skelegons in the last chapter, there is a model that already has them created for you. As always, I strongly encourage you to go through all the steps so you have an understanding of how each part was created and how to modify them should you ever need to. If you need the pre-skelegoned model, you will find it on the companion CD as Objects\chapters\ch_04.lwo.

1. Load your model from Chapter 4 into Layout.

Figure 5.1. I find it helpful to use multiple views in Layout. You have a better feel for where something is in 3D space, and the Schematic window can be invaluable for finding a specific character control at a glance (more on this in a bit). You activate multiple views under Edit|Display Options|Viewport Layout.

2. In the Object Properties window (with **Objects O** active, choose **Item Properties p**) on the Geometry tab, set the Subdivision Order of your model to **Last** (or After Motion if you will be using Worley Labs' FPrime for real-time previsualization of your scenes) and the Display SubPatch Level to **2**. (This will allow for the fastest real-time updates as you animate your character.)

Figure 5.2. The Object Properties window.

Newbie Note:

Because "ch_04" is a meta-NURB (subdivision surface) mesh, it will come in with a default Display SubPatch Level of 3. If you have a fast computer and a GL-accelerated graphics card, this level of detail will be fine. If you are on a slower computer or don't have the real-time rendering power of a full GL graphics card, you can reduce this level of detail and dramatically increase performance. These settings let you animate at a level of detail where you can get the quickest response possible, and yet render at a complex level.

Note:

It is important to have the Subdivision Order set to, at the very least, After Motion with characters. (This is especially important if you are planning on having more than one character in a scene.) Bone influences are calculated for every point in a mesh, and when you have a mesh subdivided, that point count goes up exponentially. Updates can slow to a point where a scene becomes almost unworkable. Edit|Display Options|Bounding Box Threshold is a way of increasing screen-update speeds by telling Layout to display an object with a certain number of polygons or higher as a "bounding box" until it actually has the time to calculate its true shape.

3. With your model selected, choose **Setup|Add|Convert Skelegons into Bones.** (Depending upon your version and/or setup, Convert Skelegons into Bones may be under More in the Add menu.)

Figure 5.3. This converts the skelegons that Modeler understands into bones that Layout understands.

4. With your model still selected, under **Scene Editor|Classic Scene Editor...|Visibility**, choose **Hide Selected Items**. This will make the model invisible when it isn't selected (when a hidden item is selected, it will be visible as a wireframe) so it won't get in the way visually while we're setting up bones.

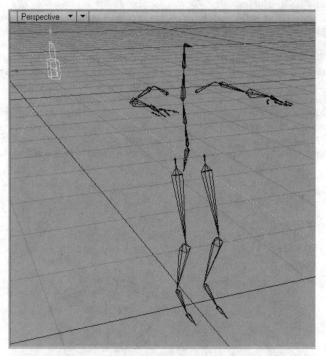

Figure 5.4. The model hidden (the camera selected). These are the bones you've just created from skelegons.

5.2 **Organizing the Schematic into Something Helpful**

Everything you can do in the preparation stage that keeps you from having to break concentration while animating is a good thing. A schematic laid out in a way that makes sense to you can be one of the greatest tools you'll encounter in 3D animation!

1. Open the Scene Editor and select the following bones: **Neck, Neck_Puller, RightArm_Puller, LeftArm_Puller, RightLeg_Puller, LeftLeg_Puller.** We'll be hiding these bones; they are used only in IK calculations and we won't need to affect them directly.

2. From within a Classic Scene Editor, select **Visibility | Hide Selected Items.** With these bones hidden, they can't be accidentally selected by clicking on them in a non-Schematic viewport when you're trying to select another control. (Layout isn't quite as good as Modeler for knowing what you're clicking on.)

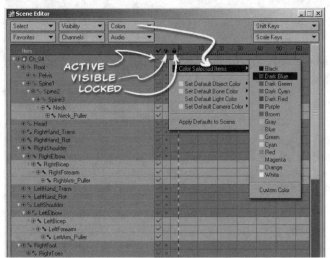

Figure 5.5. In addition to hiding the bones that are driven by IK, I like to color code all the bones to help in at-a-glance identification of them when animating gets intense. My own preference is to have red for bones on the right, green for bones on the left, and cyan for centered bones such as the spine and head. I use darker colors for the bones only IK needs to know about once we start animating.

3. Maximize a Schematic view (by pressing the numeric keypad's
    0 key, which toggles the "maximized view" mode on and off,
    just as in Modeler) and organize your character into an iconic
    representation of a human. As in Figure 5.6, I lean toward a
    classic da Vinci layout, giving the rough impression of the
    character standing spread eagle, palms up.

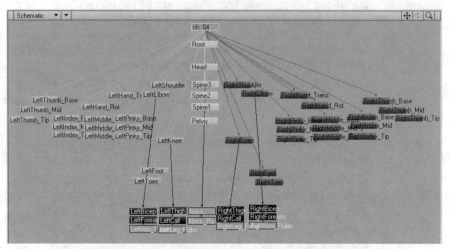

Figure 5.6. Animation can be pretty hectic. Every bit of organization you can do
beforehand helps. With the controls for your character laid out like this, you can
quickly choose the control you need without having to scroll through a list. (This
illustration is only a suggestion; it is what works best for me. Feel free to innovate
and find what works best for you!)

5.3 **Aligning the Spine, Pelvis, and Feet**

Because the skelegon "bank rotation handle" is a little cryptic to understand, sometimes you'll find that you'll need to adjust the rotation axes of the bones as Layout has created them from Modeler's skelegons.

1. Select the **Root** bone.

Figure 5.7. Pitch is what we would normally think of in LightWave as the axis to rotate an item forward and backward (around its X-axis). With the way Root is currently oriented, in order to bend the character forward and backward we would have to use heading (represented by the red circle on your screen).

Depending on the viewport in which skelegons were created, bones created from these skelegons can have a +/–90° bank rotation to them (even if the bank rotation handle was never touched). This flip-flops what we would think of as heading and bank for the bone, its children, or both! This isn't a huge problem, and we could easily work around it. But when we're deeply engrossed in a scene, and the familiar left-right mouse movement that usually means "I'm rotating in heading" instead rotates these few bones in pitch, it can feel like an unnecessary speed bump in the roadway of production. So, here's how we're going to fix it.

2. Select your character's mesh (object).

3. Choose **Items|Add| Clone** ^C and enter **1** for the number of clones. (See Figure 5.8.)

4. In a Schematic window, move this new object to a place where it won't interfere visually with the original model and its hierarchy.

> **Note:**
>
> I've found the Clone command to work more reliably than the Clone Hierarchy command.

> **Note:**
>
> Under Display Options|Schematic View, you'll find a check box labeled "Drag Descendants." When this box is unchecked, each "node" within a Schematic view can be moved independently of all the others. When this is checked, moving something in a Schematic view also moves all of its children — this is what you'll want for Step 4.

Figure 5.8. Your model will be cloned, along with all its bone structure.

5. With the clone of your model still selected, open the Classic Scene Editor and choose **Select|Select All Bones of Current Object**.

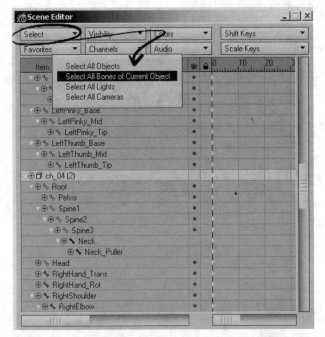

Figure 5.9. All the bones of the cloned model will be selected.

6. With all the bones of the cloned model selected, within the Scene Editor select **Colors|Color Selected Items|Orange**.

> **Note:**
>
> The bones you just colored orange will be guides for us to match as we rotate our model back into alignment. If you notice in the Current Item field that you've got an orange bone selected, stop! LightWave only has one level of undo in Layout. Make sure you have the right bone selected before making changes.

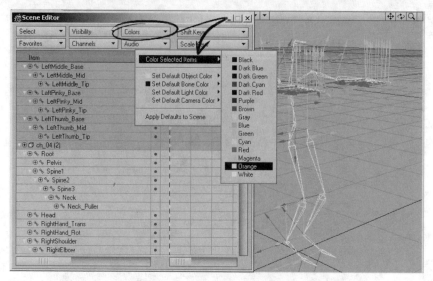

Figure 5.10. All the bones you have selected will be colored orange.

7. Select the **Root** bone of your original mesh. (It should be cyan, not orange.)

Figure 5.11. Just making sure that the correct bone is selected.

8. Change your tool (what LightWave does when you move the mouse) to **Rotate** (**Modify|Rotate|Rotate y**).

9. In the numeric input field, change the entry for bank to **0**.

Figure 5.12. The value for bank in my scene was –90. Changing the pivot's bank to 0 swings my character's spine and pelvis onto its side.

10. Select the **Pelvis** bone of your original mesh.

11. Make sure you are at Frame 0.

12. Enter **0, 0, 0** for its rotation (heading, pitch, and bank), and then manually rotate it until it lines up with the orange pelvis bone of the cloned mesh.

> **Newbie Note:**
>
> After getting each of these bones lined up, press Enter twice to create a keyframe for that bone. Even if you have Auto Key Create active, this is a good habit to get into; it reduces the chances of losing precious minutes or hours of work.

Figure 5.13. After you change the rotation values for the pelvis to 0, you should only need to rotate it along its pitch axis to line it up with the orange reference bone. Almost always, copying the old value for heading into pitch aligns the pelvis and spine bones perfectly.

13. Repeat step 12 for **Spine1**, **Spine2**, and **Spine3**.

Figure 5.14. The spine bones, back in alignment with our orange reference bones.

14. Select **RightFoot** in your original mesh.

15. Set its bank rotation to **0**.

Figure 5.15. Changing RightFoot's bank should leave it aligned with its orange reference bone (even though RightToes is now misaligned). Tweak RightFoot's heading and bank if you need to.

16. Select **RightToes** (in your original mesh).

17. Swap the values for heading and pitch, and zero-out the value for bank; RightToes should line up with its orange reference bone. Tweak as needed.

Figure 5.16. RightToes is back on track. (Nothing is parented to the toes, so they don't have to be exact.)

18. Repeat steps 14 to 17 for **LeftFoot** and **LeftToes**.

19. Check to see that the **Head**, *Hand_Trans**, and *Hand_Rot** bones also have a bank rotation of 0. Adjust them as needed.

20. Save a revision of your scene.

21. Select the cloned object you've been using as reference and press - (or click **Items|Delete|Clear Selected**) to clear it from the scene.

22. Save another revision of your scene.

Figure 5.17. Your character is done with its virtual chiropractic session; *be sure to clear the right object!*

5.4 **Bone Hierarchy**

We did a lot of hierarchy work in Modeler with skelegons, but there are some hierarchical things that can't be done with skelegons. Modeler forces child skelegons to be attached to the tip of their parent skelegon. Child bones in Layout don't have to be right at their parent's tip. We'll need this kind of relationship for our character's fingers as they attach to the hand.

> **Newbie Note:**
>
> With Parent in Place active, LightWave calculates the SRT offset required to keep the selected object in the same "worldspace" (an item's relationship to the LW world vs. its relationship to another item; more on this in Chapter 8), even though it inherits SRT data from its parent item. LightWave does a good job of this, but it can be fooled by complex hierarchies where items have had changes made to their pivot's rotation (see Section 5.5). So save revisions and always be watchful for errors in these calculations!

1. Check to make sure you have Parent in Place active (**Edit|General Options| Parent in Place**).

2. In a full-screen Schematic window, click on **Right-Thumb_Base**.

3. While holding down **Ctrl**, click on **RightHand_Rot**. This is a quick way to make Right-Thumb_Base a child of RightHand_Rot.

Figure 5.18. Parent in Place

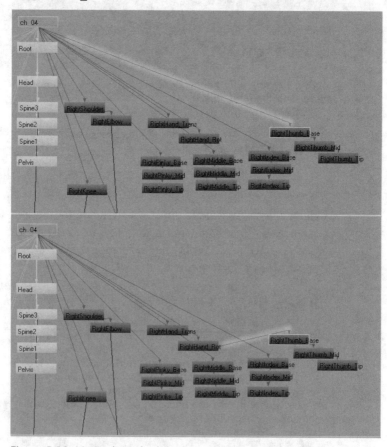

Figure 5.19. Notice how the line that once connected RightThumb_Base to ch_04 now is connected to RightHand_Rot.

4. Make **RightIndex_Base**, **RightMiddle_Base**, and **RightPinky_Base** children of **RightHand_Rot**.

5. Make **RightHand_Rot** a child of **RightHand_Trans**.

6. Repeat steps 2 to 5 for the bones of the left hand.

7. Make **RightHand_Trans** and **LeftHand_Trans** children of **Root**.

8. Make **RightShoulder** and **LeftShoulder** children of **Spine3**.

9. Make **RightKnee** and **LeftKnee** children of **Pelvis**.

10. Make **Pelvis** a child of **Spine1** (Spine1 being a child of Root).

11. Make **Head** a child of **Spine1**.

> **Note:**
> RightFoot and LeftFoot remain children of ch_04.

> **Note:**
> These are options you'll want to keep in the back of your mind for future reference. I'll go through them in Chapter 8 in the section on how to modify the setup for your personal preference, but this will get your wheels turning as to how to apply changes in setup to the needs of different scenes.
>
> With the way the hands, feet, and head are children of different items (when IK has been fully activated at the end of Chapter 6), when you move the mesh object itself, your entire model will move, statue-like, to its new position. When you move the Root bone, your character's feet will remain where they are, and his entire upper carriage will move, frozen and statue-like. When you move Spine1, your character's torso will move, statue-like, but his head, hands, and feet will stay put.
>
> You'll find some scenes to be much easier when the hands move with the momentum of the upper carriage (some martial arts katas), and some scenes much more difficult (grappling). Sometimes you'll want the head to be independent of the torso (dancing), and sometimes you'll want it to follow (walking). As you begin work on a scene, think about what kind of hierarchy of head, hands, and feet will make your work easier, and experiment. You'll find your own personal

preferences for certain kinds of work. Your solution is likely to involve reparenting these items. (The head may be a child of Root, Spine1, or Spine3; each will have a different effect on how the head inherits the motion of the body.) Nothing is wrong if it works; creativity is rewarded with a better looking scene with much less effort. Just remember that changes in parenting work best early on in the animation end of things, and that *Parent in Place only works when both items' pivots are free of rotation.* So save revisions of your scene before making changes in your character's hierarchy.

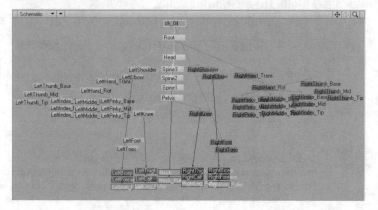

Figure 5.20. The schematic of the character's hierarchy up to this point.

5.5 Recording Pivot Rotations

Now we're going to tell LightWave to perceive many of the bones' current directions as if they were 0H, 0P, 0B. This is a big help where gimbal lock may be an issue, especially in the fingers, spine, and IK calculations.

1. Under **Edit|General Options|AutoKeyCreate**, make sure you have either Modified Channels or All Motion Channels selected.

2. In the main Layout window, make sure you have the **Auto Key** button active.

Newbie Note:

Remember that when you have Auto Key Create active, LightWave automatically records keyframes for items you move. With All Motion Channels selected, a key is created on all axes of scaling, rotation, and translation when you move the item. With Modified Channels selected, a key is only created on the axes of the channels you are modifying. Without Auto Key Create active, all changes in SRT are lost when you leave that frame unless you manually create one for each channel of each item modified. (This functionality was great when Layout didn't have Undo.)

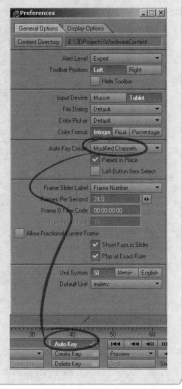

Figure 5.21. Both settings need to be active in order for Auto Key to record changes in SRT.

3. Make sure you are on Frame 0.

4. Select the bone named **Root**.

5. Choose **Setup|Modify|Orientation|Record Piv Rot** to record the Root's pivot rotation.

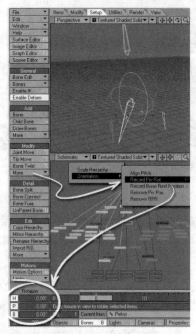

Figure 5.22. Recording pivot rotation.

Note:

In recording pivot rotation, LightWave (in essence) sets the pivot point's rotation of the current item to its current rotation. Then it "zeros" its current rotation by setting it to 0H, 0P, 0B. With Auto Key active, a keyframe is recorded at the current frame (preferably the first frame of your scene, usually 0) and LightWave perceives the item as now having a rotation of 0H, 0P, 0B. Without Auto Key active, no keyframe is created (unless you do so manually) and when you refresh the viewport (go forward a frame, then back a frame; save, then load, etc....), the item reverts to its old rotation data, but now this data is added to the new rotation of its pivot.

6. Select **Pelvis** and record its pivot rotation.

7. Repeat this to record pivot rotation for all bones.

Note:

The hot key for recording pivot rotation is <P>.

Note:

A good way to check to make sure that the pivot's rotation was actually recorded is to look at the rotation numerical input fields. If they're all zeros, rotation has been recorded! This is how I check to see if I've missed anything after doing this step. I just quickly scroll down the bones using the Down Arrow and watch the numeric input fields to see if there are any bones that still have values other than zero.

Note:

For my reasoning behind recording pivot information, see Chapter 2's section called "Rotation Order."

5.6 **Recording Bone Rest Information**

> **Newbie Note:**
>
> A bone's rest position isn't the same as its pivot rotation. *Pivot rotation* figures in rotational calculations (heading, pitch, and bearing). *Rest position* (which actually also includes a bone's rest *rotation*) keeps track of how much the bone has deviated from its initial (rest) position, rotation, and scale. The points of the object the bone is affecting are pulled along accordingly.

> **Newbie Note:**
>
> A bone should always have a scale of 1, 1, 1 when it is at rest. LightWave uses this scale of 1, 1, 1 as its point of reference to figure the deforming of the object when the bone is scaled.
>
> If you need to make a bone's rest length longer or shorter while in Layout, (i.e., the Root bone is much shorter than the Pelvis bone), you need to make this adjustment under the Bone|Properties|Rest Length setting. (Click and drag on the double-triangle button to the right of the input field.)

1. With **Root** once again selected, record its rest position, length, and direction by pressing **r** (or choosing **Setup|Modify|Orientation|Record Bone Rest Position**). (See Figure 5.23.)

2. Record the rest position for *every* bone in your model.

> **Note:**
>
> I just start at the top of the character with the Root bone, and get a nice rhythm going, alternately pressing <r> and the Down Arrow key. It won't matter if you lose yourself in the rhythm and record rest position for a bone more than once if you "wrap-around" from LeftLeg_Puller to Root.

3. Save a revision of your scene!

Figure 5.23. Record rest position.

Give yourself a healthy pat on the back! You've just completed the first half of character setup! In the next chapter, you'll finally begin to see the power of the setup you've been creating as we start to activate IK.

Chapter 6

Putting IK and IKB to Work

Everything is all set to bring the "big guns" of computer animation to bear. We're ready to activate the power (and limitations) of Inverse Kinematics, augmented with the additional power of LightWave's IK Booster! In this chapter, you'll begin to see the result of all your hard work in the previous five chapters. And after this chapter, there is only one more step until you can begin to see your character come to life by pulling, pushing, rotating, and scaling the controls you've so carefully crafted!

> **Newbie Note:**
> As always, if you feel you need a "leg up" from the last chapter, you can find the scene that has the work of Chapter 5 all done for you in Scenes\chapters\ ch_05.lws.

6.1 Terminating IK Chains

LightWave must be told where to stop using IK to calculate the rotations of the items in the chain. This is called "terminating" the IK chain (like tying off a rope that holds a string of buoys). We're going to use IK to figure rotations for the neck, arms, and legs only. This means we terminate IK at the bones that are the parents of the neck bone, the bicep bones, and the thigh bones.

1. With a freshly incremented revision of the scene you created in Chapter 5 loaded into Layout, select the **Spine3** bone (which is the parent of Neck).

2. Open the Motion Options window for Spine3 by pressing
   <m> (Window|Motion Options...) and under the **IK and
   Modifiers** tab, check **Unaffected by IK of Descendants**.
   This causes the IK calculations of the child bone, in this case
   Neck, to stop and go no further.

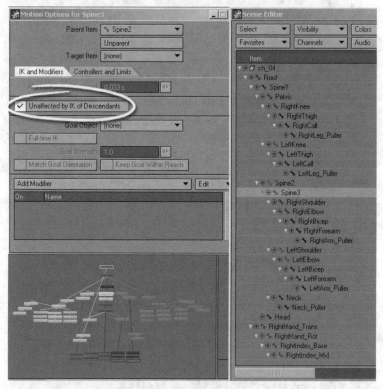

Figure 6.1. The hierarchical view of the Scene Editor is the quickest way
of selecting the bones we'll be terminating. (While working at this stage,
I find it helpful to hide the mesh.)

3. Repeat step 2 for **RightElbow** (the parent of RightBicep),
   LeftElbow (parent of LeftBicep), **RightKnee** (parent of
   RightThigh), and **LeftKnee** (parent of LeftThigh).

6.2 **Creating Goal Objects**

Because LightWave's standard IK doesn't let you use bones as goals
for IK, we have to add a few null objects (which can be used as IK
goals) and make them children of the bones we're using as controls
so that LightWave's IK can track these bones' positions. (Yes, it's
rather backward, but bear in mind, most everything cool in 3D is a
"hack" of some kind or other. "Hacking" in this sense is just working within limitations — inane as they may be — to get the result
we need. Remember, creativity is your greatest asset in doing anything with 3D. A problem or a stumbling block is simply a gateway
to untold possibilities for cleverly wrenching the systems into doing
what you think they should do by default.)

1. Click **Items|Add|Null** ^N.

2. Name this null object **NeckGoal**.

Figure 6.2. Adding the null object called NeckGoal.

3. Under **Edit|General Options**, make sure that Parent in Place is not checked. (See the following Newbie Note.)

4. Press **<m>** to bring up the Motion Options window for NeckGoal.

5. Select the **Head** bone to be the parent item for this null.

Figure 6.3. Setting NeckGoal to be the child of Head (with Parent in Place *inactive*) makes the null instantly "jump" to Head's base.

Newbie Note:

Because we deactivated Parent in Place, the moment we set Head to be the parent item for NeckGoal, it seems to instantly reposition itself to the base of the Head bone. As a child of Head, NeckGoal's world now revolves (quite literally) around Head's pivot, and wherever Head is, that is where NeckGoal perceives 0X, 0Y, 0Z, and 0H, 0P, 0B to be. From NeckGoal's point of view, it is still at 0, 0, 0. If we had had Parent in Place active when we did step 5, to our perception, NeckGoal wouldn't have moved, but if we had looked at its position in the numeric input fields, we'd have found that it now reads something like 0.1215 μm, −1.875 m, 50 mm. With Parent in Place active, LightWave calculates the offset (taking into account the parent item's rotation as well as its position) needed to have the selected object stay where it was in world coordinates, which simply means with respect to the world's 0X, 0Y, 0Z, 0H, 0P, and 0B. (More on coordinate systems in a bit!)

6. Create four more null objects, naming them **RightArmGoal**, **LeftArmGoal**, **RightLegGoal**, and **LeftLegGoal**.

> **Newbie Note:**
> Parent in Place is to remain *off* for steps 7 to 10 in this section.

7. Make **RightArmGoal** a child of RightHand_Rot.

8. Make **LeftArmGoal** a child of LeftHand_Rot.

9. Make **RightLegGoal** a child of RightFoot.

10. Make **LeftLegGoal** a child of LeftFoot.

11. Hide these objects; they are only used for IK calculations, and we won't need to touch them during animation. Color code them if you are using colors to distinguish items as to which side they belong, and in your schematic, arrange them in a way that makes sense to you. (It may seem like wasted time to have a neat, clean schematic, but its worth pays off tenfold when you're down-and-dirty in a scene and you don't have time to go hunting for something.)

Figure 6.4. The goal objects.

6.3 **Activating IK**

Now, we've got to activate IK. We'll be telling LightWave which item will be *pulling* which chain toward which *goal object*. We won't see the chains move yet; we'll still have to tell Layout which axes IK should take over on each item to be controlled by IK.

1. Select the **RightArm_Puller** bone.

2. Press **<m>** to bring up the Motion Options panel for this item. (See Figure 6.5.)

3. Select **RightArmGoal** as the goal object.

4. Check the box next to **Full-time IK**.

5. Set Goal Strength to **80**.

Figure 6.5. The motion options for RightArm_Puller.

Newbie Note:

Remember that without Full-time IK checked, LightWave only calculates IK for this chain when you're moving the goal object, and you have to manually set keyframes for each item in this chain that uses IK to figure its rotations. "Part-time" IK is a holdover from when IK was too much for most computers to continually keep on top of, but it can still come in handy if you need to lighten the load on your CPU as you work on a complex scene.

Note:

Goal Strength is a level of how much this chain will try to keep the puller touching the goal object as you animate. A low value will let the arm separate from the wrist too easily, and a high value can cause jitters. The number 80 is just an arbitrary value I've come up with that seems to keep things together, while keeping jitters to a minimum.

6. Repeat steps 2 to 5 for **LeftArm_Puller, RightLeg_Puller**, and **LeftLeg_Puller**, setting their goal objects to the respective nulls we created in the previous section.

7. Set the goal object for **Neck_Puller** to be NeckGoal, enable **Full-time IK**, and set its Goal Strength to **40**. (With only one bone in the chain, a goal strength of 40 seems to do just fine.)

Figure 6.6. The blue lines on your screen show the active IK chains from the base of the puller item to the base of the child of the Unaffected by IK of Descendants (terminated) item. (These are the IK chains, which can be shown or hidden under Edit|Display Options|Show IK Chains.)

6.4 **Activating Individual Controllers**

Next up, we've got to tell LightWave which axes will be using IK to generate rotation information for each item in our chains. This takes manual control away from whatever axes we select, handing it over to the computer. With respect to the information in Chapter 2 about IK's strengths and weaknesses, this has to be a very discriminating process.

1. Select the **Neck** bone.

Figure 6.7. We'll want this joint to pivot along both the heading and pitch axes.

Newbie Note:

With LightWave in rotation mode (Modify|Rotate|Rotate y), you can see colored circles, *handles*, representing the axes of rotation — red for *heading*, green for *pitch*, and blue for *bank*. Under Modify|General| Coord System, you can change the axes from World to Parent to Local (you can do this for translation (Move) axes too — X,Y,Z). When you do this, LightWave assumes a new method for calculating rotation and translation. With World selected, LightWave rotates (or moves) the object in alignment with the worldspace coordinates such that Y is *always* straight up, heading *always* rotates with respect to the world's Y-axis, etc. With the coordinates set to Parent, LightWave figures movement and rotation with respect to the item's parent. With the coordinates set to Local, LightWave figures rotation and movement as based solely on its own orientation (this is how LW used to figure rotation and movement before Version 6). This may seem confusing. Playing with, moving, and rotating items in different coordinate systems is the only way to really get a feel for what to expect.

Note:

LightWave's ability to switch between world, parent, and local coordinate systems (see preceding Newbie Note) comes in handy, getting you out of jams or helping to speed up precise placement. But there is a caveat about the systems: *LightWave stores rotation and translation data relative to the parent coordinate system.* You can see this by watching the numerical data update (lower-left corner of the default LW layout) as you rotate or move an item along one of its axes while using the different coordinate systems. Only the parent coordinate system always exactly matches what you're doing when you rotate or move a single axis (when rotating along pitch, only the pitch numerical input field updates; under world and local, often two or three fields can be seen to update while rotating a single controller in Layout). What this means for us *at the moment* is that in order for us to visually judge which axes we want IK to calculate for, we must be viewing rotations in Coordinate System: Parent.

2. Press <**m**> to again bring up the Motion Options panel, but this time, click on the **Controllers and Limits** tab.

3. Select **Inverse Kinematics** for both heading and pitch controllers.

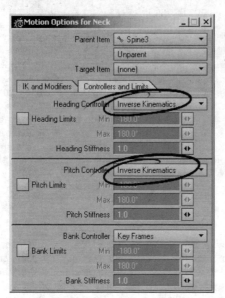

Figure 6.8. IK has been activated for controlling the heading and pitch axes of the Neck bone.

> **Note:**
>
> If you're like most people, you want to move the Head bone to see that the Neck bone does indeed track to it. (Neck will have to be temporarily unhidden in order to see it while it is not selected — just be sure to hide it again after you're done.) Whenever you do something like this to test a control or a setting, be sure to move the Time Slider away from Frame 0 (you can easily delete all keys from a frame other than 0, and get back to your character's "rest pose"). This is important even if you're *almost* entirely sure you don't have Auto Key Create active. It's always a good idea to cover your behind and give the computer as little opportunity to frustrate you as possible (an ounce of prevention and all that). This is just one small habit to get into to save you from having to utter the phrase, "What do you mean I can't Undo?" along with some choice expletives. (You need your character in this *rest pose* — where all bones are exactly where they were created as skelegons — in order to properly set skinning attributes/weight maps. And it is always best to have your character load in the same, balanced pose. If you make a modification to the key at Frame 0, you won't be able to get back to this exact pose. And if you delete the key at Frame 0, and that happens to be the only key in the scene for that item, that item has a high probability of being grossly misplaced when you reload the scene.)

Advanced Note:

If you're moving the Head bone and are thinking to yourself, "Hey, I can move the head a mile away from the neck! What gives?" Don't worry. Under moderate control, it just gives the feeling of good old-fashioned squash and stretch in action. It has been my experience that viewers don't notice if a neck, wrist, or ankle elongates a little during animation. This kind of setup is the only way I know that will allow you to lock a character's hands (which will function the same way as the head) to a surface like a tabletop and still have full range of motion for the rest of the body. You don't have to fret that the wrong twist of the body will pull the hands away from the table. As for the head, yes, it is possible to make an IK setup where the control for the head/neck simply moves the joint between the head and neck, with the head staying attached while pointing in the same direction as the control. However, if you also use IK to have the eyes point toward targets in the scene, having them in a hierarchy that is already controlled by IK (the head/neck) seems to give the solver fits. I've experienced solving errors for the eyes from missing their goal objects by a few degrees to rotating in the exact *opposite* direction from what you'd expect. (The way to be sure of this is to attach a wireframe two-point poly that is invisible to the camera and not casting shadows to the eyeball, extending in its exact "line of sight").

4. Select **RightThigh**, then bring up the Motion Options panel.

5. Set both the heading and pitch controllers to **Inverse Kinematics**.

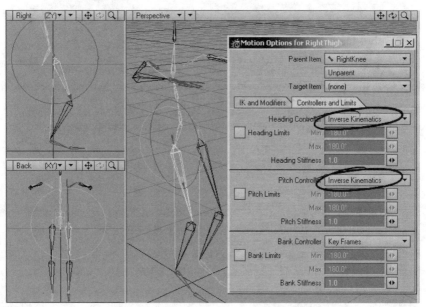

Figure 6.9. The RightThigh, set to use IK for heading and pitch.

6. Select **RightCalf**.

7. Set only Heading Controller to **Inverse Kinematics**.

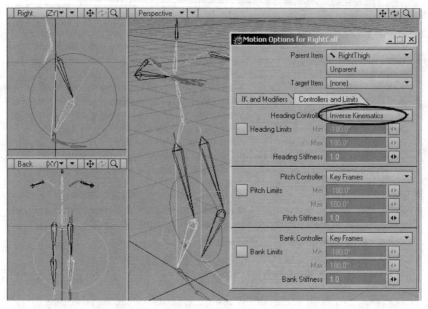

Figure 6.10. The RightCalf, set to use IK for heading.

Advanced Note:

For those of you who are wondering, "Why heading? Shouldn't pitch be the axis that the calf would rotate to swing in a normal, 'calf-like' motion?" You're absolutely right; this would be the normal way of things, except that we used skelegons to create it and its parents (the reason we tweaked the spine, pelvis, and feet in Section 5.3). Could we do what we talked about in Chapter 2, "swapping" heading and pitch? Yes, we could, but should we? Only if you want to use that bone's joint compensation and/or muscle flexing.

Note:

Your character's leg should now follow his foot when you move RightFoot. Just make sure you're on some frame other than 0 when you test it, and delete the keyframe if one is automatically created!

8. Set the heading and pitch controllers for **LeftThigh** to **Inverse Kinematics**.

9. Set the heading controller for **LeftCalf** to **Inverse Kinematics**.

Now for the arms: We're going to have to break a rule for the arms. The rule we're going to break is that rule of never having IK solve for more than two of an item's axes. It's a good rule, one that does indeed have a lot of merit. But remember, in this business, the most *creative* solutions are often the ones most strongly rewarded.

I have found, over the course of many evolutions of setups, that arms, because of their extensive and complex range of motion, need special handling. The skin can bunch or tear, and the IK that drives them is prone to flipping and solving errors. The zones that cause flipping change locations with each different base position you have for your skeleton's arms (how your skeleton's arms are in their initial pose, whether they are straight out in front, or to the sides, or a combination of the two as we have for our character). The relationship of forearm to bicep to the bicep's parent all factor heavily in how easily IK can figure rotations of these items. The setup we've created here has the bicep and forearm and their rotation points in a relationship to each other such that IK can *reliably* solve for all three axes of the bicep. With the arm bones positioned as they are, the usual problems of having a joint solve for three axes actually work for us, and the resulting movement more realistically mimics life than with any other setup I've used.

Note:

I have to mention this just to help illustrate that all-important point that you have to push beyond the bounds of being "safe" (when you have the time to fully R&D, that is), that creativity in how you solve problems is a virtue in this work. When I was R&D-ing this setup for a project some time ago, I figured that the arms of the character should be in the position we currently have them because it puts them within the average range of motion; skin would need to stretch and compress less than if the character were spread eagle. All the preliminary math also suggested that this should be an extremely stable IK setup. In reality, when I first put this together and was using IK only for the bicep's heading and pitch (as I had been taught), the setup was one of the most jittery, flippiest IKs I've ever seen in LightWave. I beat my head against the math for weeks, trying every solution I could think of to force it to work; everything I knew about IK said it should work, and yet it didn't. I was just about to scrap the whole thing. After about two weeks of fighting with the arm's IK, going through every clever varia-tion I could think of, on a whim I turned on IK for the bicep's bank. The deadline for having the characters working was looming, and I had tried everything else; I should have just gone back to an old setup I knew would work relatively well. Much to my surprise, with IK solving for H, P, and B, the arm instantly began functioning just as all the pre-liminary math said it should! The result is the setup you're building right now, one of the strongest, most realistic, and reliable IKs I've used in any package. Never be afraid to try something weird. Flying in the face of convention is often rewarded, just so long as you've got the time to backtrack to something you know will work.

10. Select **RightBicep**.

11. Set IK to control **RightBicep**'s heading, pitch, and bank (see Figure 6.11).

12. Select **RightForearm**.

13. Set IK to control **RightForearm**'s heading (see Figure 6.12).

14. Repeat steps 10 to 13 for your character's **LeftBicep** and **LeftForearm**.

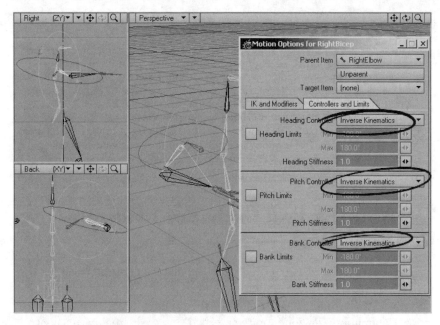

Figure 6.11. Using IK for all three of RightBicep's axes.

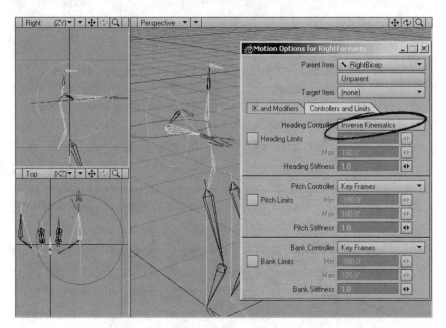

Figure 6.12. Using IK for controlling only the heading of the RightForearm.

> **Advanced Note:**
>
> There are some setup artists who use *rotation limits* ("constraints" in other packages) to keep a forearm or a calf from bending beyond its normal range of motion. I don't find there to be much need for this if there is enough of a helping "pre-bend" between the forearm and bicep, or the calf and thigh. I've actually found that it can increase the possibility of jitters or flipping because it gives IK yet one more thing to think about. Jitter or no, LightWave's rotation limits (currently) cause an item to stop like it hit a brick wall when it reaches the end of its range of movement. This is enough reason for me to strongly advise against using rotation limits in character animation.

6.5 **Deactivating Individual Manual Controls**

Here, we're going to deactivate the manual controls for items that shouldn't be moved, rotated, or scaled. This keeps you from accidentally sliding a control out of alignment while you're in that animation Zen zone (quite an easy thing to do, really). If a control does get moved, scaled, or rotated by accident and you don't notice it quickly enough to undo, sometimes you can delete the offending keys on the offending axes. You can sometimes go to Frame 0 and create a key on the offending frame for the offending axes with the SRT data of Frame 0 (by pressing Enter and typing in a different frame number on which to create the keyframe). Often, your scene is just FUBAR. This step, though slightly tedious, helps to keep these problems at bay.

> **Note:**
>
> When you are working in a coordinate system other than Parent, LightWave lets you manipulate an item on an axis by clicking on its handle in the Layout viewports, *even when that axis has been disabled*.

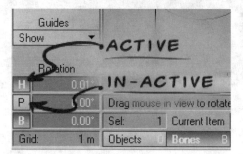

Figure 6.13. To deactivate a control, click on the button next to its numeric input field. Controls must be deactivated individually for each axis for Move <t>, Rotate <y>, and Stretch <h>.

> **Note:**
> In the case of *Hand_Trans and *Hand_Rot, I find it to be much easier to get the exact arcs of motion I'm looking for if I use *Hand_Trans for heading and bank, and *Hand_Rot for pitch and bank. You can use all three axes for a single hand control if you wish (and sometimes you may have to in order to get the exact placement you need), but this greatly limits your control of how the hand rotates between keyframes.

The following is a list of all the items in our scene that pertain to our character. Axes with an "X" in that column are axes that are to be active. Axes marked with an "o" are optional; I generally don't use them, but feel free to if you want. Those left blank indicate controls to remain inactive.

Item	Move X	Move Y	Move Z	Rotate H	Rotate P	Rotate B	Stretch X	Stretch Y	Stretch Z
Ch_04 (Character Mesh)	X	X	X	X	o	o	X	X	X
NeckGoal									
RightArmGoal									
LeftArmGoal									
RightLegGoal									
LeftLegGoal									
Root	X	X	X	X	X	X	X	X	X
Pelvis				X	X	X	X	X	X
Spine1	X	X	X	X	X	X	X	X	X
Spine2				X	X	X	o	o	o
Spine3				X	X	X	o	o	o
Head	X	X	X	X	X	X	X	X	X
RightHand_Trans	X	X	X	X	o	X	X	X	X
RightHand_Rot				o	X	X			
RightShoulder				X	X				
RightElbow						X			
LeftHand_Trans	X	X	X	X	o	X	X	X	X
LeftHand_Rot				o	X	X			
LeftShoulder				X	X				
LeftElbow						X			
RightFoot	X	X	X	X	X	X	X	X	X
RightToes				o	X	X	o	o	o
RightKnee						X			
LeftFoot	X	X	X	X	X	X	X	X	X
LeftToes				o	X	X	o	o	o
LeftKnee						X			

Item	Move X	Move Y	Move Z	Rotate H	Rotate P	Rotate B	Stretch X	Stretch Y	Stretch Z
RightIndex_Base				X	X		0	0	0
RightIndex_Mid					X		0	0	0
RightIndex_Tip					X		0	0	0
RightMiddle_Base				X	X		0	0	0
RightMiddle_Mid					X		0	0	0
RightMiddle_Tip					X		0	0	0
RightPinky_Base				X	X		0	0	0
RightPinky_Mid					X		0	0	0
RightPinky_Tip					X		0	0	0
RightThumb_Base				X	X	X	0	0	0
RightThumb_Mid					X		0	0	0
RightThumb_Tip					X		0	0	0
LeftIndex_Base				X	X		0	0	0
LeftIndex_Mid					X		0	0	0
LeftIndex_Tip					X		0	0	0
LeftMiddle_Base				X	X		0	0	0
LeftMiddle_Mid					X		0	0	0
LeftMiddle_Tip					X		0	0	0
LeftPinky_Base				X	X		0	0	0
LeftPinky_Mid					X		0	0	0
LeftPinky_Tip					X		0	0	0
LeftThumb_Base				X	X	X	0	0	0
LeftThumb_Mid					X		0	0	0
LeftThumb_Tip					X		0	0	0
Neck									
Neck_Puller									
RightBicep									
RightForearm									
RightArm_Puller									
LeftBicep									
LeftForearm									
LeftArm_Puller									
RightThigh									
RightCalf									
RightLeg_Puller									
LeftThigh									
LeftCalf									
LeftLeg_Puller									

> **Note:**
>
> The bones in the previous list are laid out in the order in which they were (or should have been) created as skelegons in Chapter 4. You can move down to the next one by pressing the Down Arrow and up to the previous one by pressing the Up Arrow.

> **Advanced Note:**
>
> As always, rules are made to be broken. If you feel that you can get the exact silhouette you need only by moving, rotating, or scaling an item that I've said shouldn't be moved, rotated, or scaled, by all means, go for it! But be sure and save a revision before doing so, just in case you find it's a blind alley. Play, have fun, be creative…and always *cover your ASCII!*

6.6 Applying IK Booster

You could leave off at this point and have a perfectly, wonderfully functional rigging. You'd have the same quality of riggings I used in getting out an average of 35 to 40 seconds of completed footage (not just "ruff animation," but clean-up, lighting, rendering, editing, and archiving) *per day* in the last months of production on *Kaze, Ghost Warrior.*

In applying IK Booster, however, you gain access to all those nifty functions we talked about in the IK Booster section of Chapter 2.

> **Note:**
>
> Just FYI, the current industry standard for how much footage is expected to come out of "ruff animation" is around four seconds per animator per week. I mention this because it's a very freeing feeling to know that if you spent 40 hours on four seconds of ruff animation, it would probably turn out looking pretty darn good too!

> **Note:**
>
> Always remember to give yourself the time *you need* to attain the level of quality *you want* out of your work. As you practice, the time required to hit that level of quality will decrease, but you must be able to attain that level of quality *first!*

1. Select your character object. Activate **Modify|Tools|IK BoostTool** ^ B.

2. Right-click on the object, and choose **Apply IK Booster**.

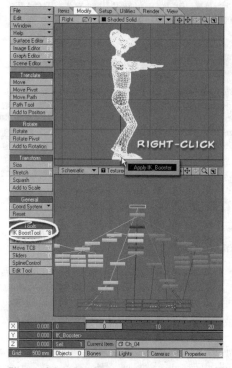

Figure 6.14. Applying IK Booster.

3. Next, in order to see the nifty little icons and handles IK Booster gives us, we've got to "unhide" our model. Since I don't want all the model's geometry to get in the way visually, in a Classic Scene Editor, set the visibility of your model to **Bounding Box**.

4. Click on the **Locked** column to lock (which hides the IKB controls for those items and makes it so they can't be selected in a non-Schematic viewport) **Root**, *****Puller**, and *****Goal** (all other items should be unlocked). See Figure 6.15.

5. Hide *****Puller**, *****Goal**, and **Neck**. (All other items should be made visible.)

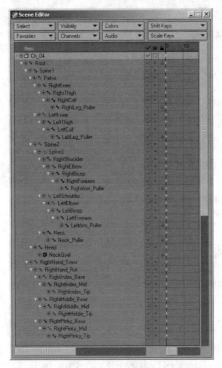

Figure 6.15. Modifying what we can see and select in a 3D viewport.

In order to keep our character from being dragged all over the place when we use IK Booster to move different parts of him, we now need to tell IK Booster where to stop IK calculations, and to fix other bones in place.

> **Newbie Note:**
>
> Remember that you need to have the IK BoostTool active in order to perform any operations on or with IK Booster.

6. Select **Spine1**. Right-click on its control icon and choose **(ikstop)**. This still lets this bone be rotated using IK Booster, but it will no longer allow itself to be moved about the scene when we're using IK Booster to manipulate its child bones.

Figure 6.16. Stopping the IK of the spine at the base of Spine1. When a bone is set to IK Stop, a diamond appears inside its control icon.

> **Newbie Note:**
> Remember to right-click on the control icon (not the numbers) when setting IK Stop.

7. Repeat step 6 for **Root, RightKnee, LeftKnee, RightFoot, LeftFoot, RightHand_Trans, LeftHand_Trans, Right-Elbow, RightShoulder, LeftElbow, LeftShoulder,** and **Head.**

Now, we need to tell IK Booster that we want certain bones to default to being moved when we drag the mouse (as opposed to being "swung about" on its IK chain).

8. Select **RightFoot.** Right-click on its control icon and choose **Options|(move/rotate).**

Figure 6.17. When a bone is set to Move, its control icon changes yet again.

9. Repeat step 8 for **LeftFoot, RightHand_Trans, LeftHand_Trans**, and **Head**.

Next, for an extra, added measure of protection against gimbal lock while animating, I like to set quaternion rotation for the biceps and thighs. (As mentioned in Chapter 2, this isn't a "magic bullet"; all it does is add an extra layer of protection.)

10. Select the **RightThigh** and right-click on its control icon. In the menu that opens, choose **Options|(Quaternion)**.

Figure 6.18. Assigning quaternion rotation to the RightThigh. A little "Q" appears inside the item's control icon, letting you know that quaternion rotation has been activated.

11. Repeat step 10 for **LeftThigh**, **RightBicep**, and **LeftBicep**.

Now I'd like to shrink the size of the unselected IKB handles so they're not overlapping one another in areas like the fingers. This will make it easier to select the control we want.

12. In the lower-right corner of the main window, with the IK Booster Track active, click on **IKB Menu**. From the menu that opens, choose **Options....** In the Options... window, set the controller size to **15 mm**.

Figure 6.19. Reducing the size of the control icons from
50 mm to 15 mm.

Next, since the control icons for Spine1 and Pelvis are right on
top of one another (those bones have the same base point), I'd like
to separate their controllers to make them a little more accessible.

> **Newbie Note:**
> I find it easier to do this step in a viewport set to Right.

13. Select **Spine1**. Right-click on its control icon and choose
    Options|Controller edit.

Figure 6.20. Entering Controller Edit mode.

While in Controller Edit mode, when you click-drag on a control icon, you move the icon's position relative to the bone it controls.

14. Drag the control icons for **Spine1** and **Pelvis** away from their shared base point, making it easier to choose each one when you're animating.

Figure 6.21. Repositioning the control icons for Spine1 and Pelvis.

15. To exit Controller Edit mode, right-click on a control icon and choose **edit end**.

Lastly, I'd like to tell the Pelvis that it isn't to follow IK Booster's Inverse Kinematics solving, controlling its rotation with Forward Kinematics instead. (Click-dragging on an FK control rotates that item normally, without having to trade the IK BoostTool for the Rotate tool.)

Figure 6.22. Exiting Controller Edit mode.

16. With the **Pelvis** selected, right-click on its control icon, choosing (**Fk control**).

Figure 6.23. Setting Pelvis to be controlled by Forward Kinematics while in IK Booster. A little "F" appears inside the control icon of a control set to FK.

Now your character's rigging is set up to use standard IK and/or IK Booster, whichever you find you prefer. You'll find in Chapter 8, "Using the Controls," that standard IK is better for some things, just as IK Booster is better for others. The important thing is that you have a choice.

Find out which tools work best in which ways for your manner of problem solving, and then use the proper tool for the job.

Chapter 7

Point Weighting

For this chapter, we'll be going back into Modeler to assign the points in our character's mesh to move with the different bones we've created. There is an art to this. And to be honest, there are people out there who are much better than I am. I'll be giving you a foundation to build on. Creativity is rewarded. Use your imagination. Observation and extrapolation are the only true keys to point weighting. (Move your own arm and see just how much of your shoulder moves when your bicep swings forward and back.) Through close observation of the "real world," you will see where the subtleties lie that will get the points of your model moving in the most believable way possible.

> **Note:**
> The most *believable* way is not necessarily the most realistic. The art of animation is the art of creating a visual representation of how it feels to do a thing, not recreating exactly how it looks to do a thing.
>   You can see this in comparing animation that has been rotoscoped (traced from live reference) and animation that is just simply good animation.
>   This is why good animation will always radiate its own inner life, far outshining even the best motion capture.

7.1 Point Weighting Basics

Point weighting is something that has to be done whenever you are using a continuous mesh model (rather than using a set of separate objects to comprise your character). Point weighting is done in many programs, including Softimage, Maya, MH3D, 3ds max, and LightWave. External programs, plug-ins, and scripts can help, but only to a degree. Point weighting always, *always* needs an observant, artful human touch.

In short, point weighting is telling which point to move with which bone. It is telling each point how much to move with one bone vs. another. (How much does a point 1 cm from your elbow move with your bicep? How much does it move with your forearm?)

Figure 7.1. The basic theory I go by is that the points that lie on the meridian where the tip of Bone 1 meets the root of Bone 2 are affected 50% by Bone 1 and 50% by Bone 2. Move a little way into Bone 1, and Bone 1 has 75% influence over the points while Bone 2 has 25%. A little more into Bone 1, and it has complete (100%) influence over these points.

This basic theory has to be adapted on a case-by-case basis. It is only through applying point weighting, bringing the model into Layout, and moving it through key poses that you can tell if the weighting is correct. In the case of a production environment, the lead or directing animator will usually put together a quick set of movements that take the character through some extreme poses or antics. The animator works only with the IK'd skeleton while the artist in charge of skinning works on the first pass of point weighting. The artist doing the weighting then puts his weighted model onto the animation, scrutinizing how the skin pulls, twists, and bunches. The point weighting artist refines problem areas, confers with the animator, and makes any notes of tight spots in this general-purpose setup that may need to be replaced with a special-purpose setup.

> **Note:**
> Often, special-case models and/or weightings have to be made for close-up shots where the model is in a pose that can't be handled correctly by the general-purpose point weighting.

7.2 Beginning the Point Weighting Process

We're going to start off with something simple — the leg from the thigh down. This is an area that doesn't have more than two bones exerting influence over any given point.

1. Load the model you used for Chapters 5 and 6 into Modeler. (For me, this is Objects\chapters\ch_04.lwo.)

2. Save this model to a directory where having lots of versions of it won't cause clutter. Name it in a way that will make sense to you if you stumble across it years later. (Objects\Work\ch07\ ch_07_v001.lwo, where "v???" is my current revision number, is what I'll be using. It can be auto-incremented by pressing <S>; be sure to use a capital letter.)

3. Center in on your character's right knee.

4. Set the rendering style for the Perspective window to **Weight Shade.**

Figure 7.2. Having zoomed in on the character's right knee, set the Perspective window's rendering style to Weight Shade.

Newbie Note:

Weight Shade is a rendering style you can set for any window. Points that have values closer to +100% (for the currently active weight map) color their adjoining polygons and patches deeper and deeper red. As points approach –100%, the adjoining polygons and patches will become deeper and deeper blue. I often activate Weight Shade for a particular viewport just to get a quick "second opinion" on how the weighting has been applied, comparing that isometric view to the Perspective window. (Sometimes, you'll find it handy to examine your model with multiple views set to Perspective and Weight Shade.)

Note:

In the way I point weight, I never set a point to have a cumulative value below 0% or above 100%. Values below 0% can make the point move in the opposite direction of the bone. A value of 200% can make that point move twice as far as the bone has moved. This can be corrected by using the weight normalization setting found in both Layout and Modeler (see Section 7.5), but I find that it is much easier in the long run to simply keep my values precise.

It is easiest to plan point weight groupings with the skelegons in the background layer to serve as a guide.

5. With the **Polygons** ^ **H** selection mode active and nothing selected, press <w> to bring up the Polygon Statistics window.

6. Click on the + next to the Skelegons field to add them to our current selection (our current selection should be empty before we add the skelegons).

Figure 7.3. Selecting the skelegons.

7. Press ^x to cut the skelegons from the current layer.

8. Paste (^v) the skelegons into Layer 2, then select Layer 1 to be your foreground layer, and Layer 2 to be your background layer. (See Figure 7.4.)

9. Hide everything in the foreground layer except the polygons of the right leg and foot. (This will make it harder to accidentally select the points of the left leg while assigning weight map values to the right.)

Figure 7.4. With the skelegons in a background layer, we can more easily see where the skelegons/bones will need to exert their influences.

Note:

If you don't have any maps listed under the weight map list selector (i.e., you're using a character of your own or the maps were cleared), you'll need to (re)create them (see Chapter 4, Section 4.6, Step 24). With both the Mesh and Skelegon layers in the foreground, select Map|Weight|Bone Weights. Enter 0 m for Threshold Value, and set Use Threshold to Clip. Click OK. (You'll also need to pay special attention to the notes in Section 7.3. If we've only just created the character's weight maps, they weren't around when skelegons were converted to bones in Chapter 5 and weren't automatically assigned to your character's bones at that time. We will need to do this manually; see Figure 7.25.)

10. With the W button active in the lower-right corner (for Weight Map mode), click on the selector bar and choose **RightThigh**.

Figure 7.5. With all but the right leg hidden, select the RightThigh weight map as the active weight map. (Windows|Vertex Maps Panel... F8 is a great way of quickly navigating all your character's vertex maps. Click on a map name to make it your active map.)

11. Select the points that lie on the junction of the thigh and calf.

12. Click on **Map|General|Set Map Value**. See Figure 7.6. (I've assigned the Shift+F10 key to this command. Because this command is used a lot in point weighting, I'd suggest that you also assign a keyboard shortcut to it.)

13. Because we have RightThigh already selected as our active weight map, RightThigh appears as the default map in the Vertex Map selector (you could change this selector to any other map, should you wish).

14. Enter **50** for Value 1. (We only need to worry about Value 1 for point weighting; LightWave automatically assumes the value to be a percent.)

Figure 7.6. After pressing Enter in step 14, the surface surrounding the isoparm defined by the points we have selected turns the shade of red corresponding to the value of +50%.

15. Select **RightCalf** as the active weight map. (The red coloring will disappear from the Weight Shade window because only RightThigh has values assigned to its points right now; RightCalf does not.)

16. Activate **Set Map Value** again, and enter **50** for Value 1.

Figure 7.7. These points will now move with 50% of their influence coming from RightThigh and 50% coming from RightCalf.

17. Select the points that influence the isoparm directly above the knee joint.

Figure 7.8. These will be influenced 25% by RightCalf and 75% by RightThigh.

18. With the RightCalf map still as the active weight map, activate
Set Map Value and enter **25** for Value 1.

Figure 7.9. RightCalf now has 25% influence over these points.

19. Select **RightThigh** as the active weight map, and set Value 1
for these points to be **75**.

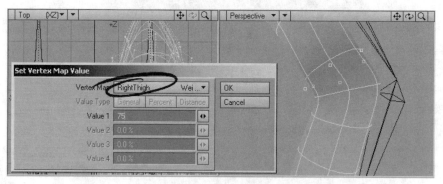

Figure 7.10. RightThigh now has 75% influence over these points.

20. Select the points that influence the next higher isoparm.

Figure 7.11. These points will be set to follow
RightThigh 100%.

21. Bring up **Set Map Value** again and enter **100** for these points.

Figure 7.12. These points will now follow 100% of RightThigh's motion.

22. Set the points of the next highest isoparm to a value of **75** for RightThigh.

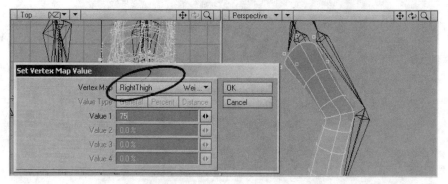

Figure 7.13. These points will move 75% with RightThigh and 25% with Pelvis.

23. Select the Pelvis weight map (in the lower-right corner), and set Value 1 for these points to **25**.

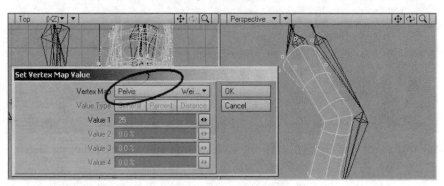

Figure 7.14. These points will now move 25% with Pelvis.

Figure 7.15. Set the points of the isoparm just below the knee to move 25% with RightThigh and 75% with RightCalf. (Two images are shown together for illustrative purposes.)

Figure 7.16. Set the points of the next two lower isoparms and the points that make up the top of the foot to move 100% with RightCalf.

24. Hide the foot so we can be sure to only select the points of the pant leg.

Figure 7.17. Using this illustration as a guide, assign RightCalf weight maps for these points.

Figure 7.18. Using this illustration as a guide, assign RightFoot weight maps for these points.

25. Press \ to unhide everything in the model.

26. Rehide everything except the right foot.

Figure 7.19. Using this illustration as a guide, assign RightFoot weight maps for these points.

Figure 7.20. Using this illustration as a guide, assign RightToes weight maps for these points.

This method is the basis for all point weighting. As you gain famil-
iarity with this process, you will develop your own ways of working,
your own tricks and shortcuts. Where multiple bones exert multiple
influences, such as in the shoulder where a point may be affected by
Spine3, RightShoulder, and RightBicep, you simply visualize how
much influence each bone should have on the point and assign the
values accordingly.

The values on each point must add up to 100%. If the combined values on a point add up to less than 100%, it will get "left behind" as you move the model. (The closer to 100% this cumulative value is, the less noticeable the lag, until the character is moved significantly from its starting position. Be very watchful of these values.) If you have the combined values on a given point add up to more than 100%, that point may "leap ahead" of the motion described by its controlling bone. (LightWave has a bit of a fix for values over 100%: activating Weight Normalization under the Bone Properties panel of Layout. It is far better to be precise with your point weighting than to depend on software to fix it though.)

7.3 **Swapping Models and Testing Weight Mappings**

The only way to *really* know if your point weighting is working is to take it for a test spin in Layout. In this section, we'll check out the weighting we just did for the right leg. To do that, we've got to swap out an old model for a new one. Using this technique, and having common bone and weight map names, you'll be able to use almost every animation you do with almost every character you make!

Note:

Figure 7.21. LW[8] has a new Setup|Skelegons|Rotate Skelegons tool that lets you test your weight mapping right in Modeler. This is exceptionally handy for tweaking problem areas. However, putting your character onto his fully functional rigging is the only way to truly know how his "skin" will behave under animation conditions.

1. In Layout, load up the scene you created in the last chapter.

> **Note:**
>
> If you need to use mine, it can be found in Scenes\chapters\ch_06.lws.

2. In a working directory set aside for Chapter 7, save a version of this scene with a name that will make sense to you if you come back to it years later. Something like "Scenes\Work\ch07\ch_07_MappingTest_01_v001.lws" will do nicely.

3. In the Classic Scene Editor, make sure that your character model's visibility is set to at least **Shaded Solid**.

4. Press <f>, and type **10** to jump to Frame 10. (We're going to be playing with the controls on Frame 10, so we can check that our character comes in properly on its "rest pose," Frame 0.)

> **Note:**
>
> If, while you're working, bending your model around, you accidentally hit <r> (an easy thing to do), LW will record the selected bone's current position and rotation as its rest position. If this happens, your model's skin will be fouled for that bone. To fix it, you need to go to the frame where the skeleton is at rest and press <r> for the offending bone. So, once again, just to drive a point well into the ground: You always need to have a frame in your scene where your skeleton is at rest. This can be at 0, –20, –100, or whatever. Just don't get caught putting the final touches on your masterwork scene (which, because of being "in the groove," wasn't saved for several hours) and accidentally tap the <r> key; otherwise you'll likely wind up exploring new and more creative combinations of expletives than you ever thought possible.

5. Select the **RightFoot** bone, and move it up and forward.

Figure 7.22. Moving the RightFoot up and forward. This scene is from the last chapter, and in it we were using the model from Chapter 4. No points are weighted, so nothing moves, yet.

6. With the mesh (object) selected, choose **Items|Replace| Replace With Object…**.

7. Select the latest revision of the model you've been working on in this chapter.

Figure 7.23. Replacing the old mesh with something newer.

Figure 7.24. If everything is as it should be, your replacement mesh loads in with the newly assigned weight maps for the right thigh, calf, foot, and toes. The points of the right leg are now controlled by the bones of the right leg. (If not, look to the following notes for troubleshooting information.)

> **Note:**
> If your new mesh isn't doing quite what you think it should be doing, double-check your mappings in Modeler to make sure that no points are mapped that shouldn't be, and that all points that should have mapping have correct values.

Note:

If your mapping values are correct, and you're still not getting the results you expect, or if the model isn't moving at all, you might need to check that bone weight maps are properly assigned for each bone. When you convert skelegons into bones, and you have already created weight maps (which we did in Chapter 4, Section 4.6, Step 24), bone weight maps are automatically assigned to the bone (skelegon) of the same name. If no weight maps exist on the skelegons at the time you convert them into bones, no weight maps are assigned. If this is the case, you have to assign each weight map to each bone manually.

1. Select the root bone.

2. Press <**p**> to bring up the Bone Properties window for Root.

3. Under Bone Weight Map, make sure that the map Root is selected.

4. Press the **Down Arrow** to scroll through all the bones and make sure that Bone Weight Map matches Current Bone for each bone.

Figure 7.25. The bone weight map should match the current bone for every bone in your model.

Advanced Note:

Another way to apply motion from one model to another is to use the Use Bones From Object setting in the Bone Properties window. (This is a fantastic way of comparing two ideas you might have for weighting a problem area, like the hips.)

Figure 7.26. A version of the character named Thinguy_F was loaded into the scene. Under the Bone Properties window for Thinguy_F, I chose Ch_07_v006, the model I am currently using to test point weighting. All SRT from all bones of Ch_07_v006 is applied to Thinguy_F.

All motion from the bones of ch_07_w03:Layer1 is applied to Thinguy_F. (This is an excellent technique for rudimentary crowd scenes.)

8. Using the RightFoot control (bone), stretch the character's leg out and rotate the foot in ways a foot would rotate.

Note:

It isn't necessary to cover all possible ranges of movement, just things that may be common positions for this character. If you need specific poses that are distant from the character's normal range of movement, you'll need to build special-case models/point weightings to handle unique instances where the general-purpose setup breaks.

Figure 7.27. Rotating the RightToes as well, watching the areas of the knee, ankle, and toes to see if the point weighting looks believable for this character. (Remember, we haven't really blended the weighting up into the hips, so we're not looking at that area yet.)

Note:

Here is where your own sense of artistry comes into play. You have to judge. A balance of your own (or your director's) stylistic sensibilities and what you think you'll eventually need this character to do determines how much the weighting needs finessing.

And that's all there is to point weighting! All the points in the model are handled in the same way. Use your best judgment when assigning weights in Modeler, toggling between subpatches and polys, then test your decisions in Layout, making changes where necessary.

Point weighting is a logician's dream. It is a process that follows the pathways of reason and empiricism. There are no magic wands or silver bullet solutions to point weighting. Thus far, I've yet to find an "automatic" plug-in that can even give you a good base from which to start. I find it much easier and quicker to just start from scratch and proceed as we have done with the right leg. (Yoichiro's Mirror Weights plug-in — a free plug-in available online at http://www.flay.com — is something I do, however, recommend. It can copy weights from one side of your model to the other and is a real time-saver.)

The following is a list of the weight maps that need to be assigned to the points of your model. All other weight maps (for control bones that shouldn't have any direct influence on the model's points) need to be left with their default influence of 0% on the model's points:

Pelvis, Spine1, Spine2, Spine3, Head, RightHand_Rot, Right-Shoulder, LeftHand_Rot, LeftShoulder, RightFoot, RightToes, LeftFoot, LeftToes, RightIndex_Base, RightIndex_Mid, Right-Index_Tip, RightMiddle_Base, RightMiddle_Mid, RightMiddle_Tip, RightPinky_Base, RightPinky_Mid, RightPinky_Tip, RightThumb_Base, RightThumb_Mid, RightThumb_Tip, LeftIndex_Base, Left-Index_Mid, LeftIndex_Tip, LeftMiddle_Base, LeftMiddle_Mid, LeftMiddle_Tip, LeftPinky_Base, LeftPinky_Mid, LeftPinky_Tip, LeftThumb_Base, LeftThumb_Mid, LeftThumb_Tip, RightBicep, RightForearm, LeftBicep, LeftForearm, RightThigh, RightCalf, LeftThigh, LeftCalf, Neck

> **Note:**
>
> *Don't use Map|General|Clear Map or Map|General|Delete Map to remove a map's influence from the vertices in the mesh. If you do, that map will be removed entirely from the character.* It will no longer be there for Layout to associate with the bone of the same name. (Even bones that have no direct influence on the character (like *Elbow) need to still be associated with a map.) Having a bone associated with a "0% influence" map (for this manner of setup) is the most efficient way to keep it from exerting unwanted influence on the model's points.

7.4 **The Use Weight Map Only Option**

There are many and differing views on whether or not to let LightWave's mathematical falloff for bones play a part in skinning. Letting LightWave use its falloff to influence the points affected by bones can indeed help quickly smooth problem areas, and can sometimes give a point that doesn't have its values add up to 100% that extra oomph it needs to stay on track. My issue with using falloff is that it is very difficult to control details where bones are close together, as in the fingers. It can also make it very difficult to troubleshoot problem points with values less than 100%. Most importantly, depending on falloff to clean up after you can make for sloppy weighting habits. If you can make something work without computer assistance, you really understand what you're doing.

My general MO is that when given a choice to do something right by hand or to depend on a computer system that might fall short when you need it most, I always opt for the more controllable of the two. (If the system needs adjusting under a deadline, you can spend more time trying to find and fix a problem in which the computer intervenes heavily than it would have taken to do it correctly by hand to begin with.) You will have to decide for yourself which works best for you. (If you are building animations for a video game, chances are the game engine won't have the spare clock cycles to calculate falloff, so you *must* use the Use Weight Map Only option.)

If this is your first time point weighting, I'd strongly suggest using the Use Weight Map Only setting. With this option, there's nowhere to hide errors. When you have a weighting that works, you know you did it right.

Figure 7.28. Use Weight Map Only and Weight Normalization.

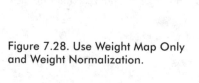

> **Note:**
>
> When you activate Use Weight Map Only, Weight Normalization is automatically checked as well. As much as I am against using a subroutine to cover for untidy weighting, I'd suggest leaving this active (unless, of course, you are working on a video game, in which case you'll have to ask your core programmer how he has the game engine deal with cumulative values greater than 100%).

Under Item Properties for all bones in your character, activate Use Weight Map Only (if this is how you will be working).

7.5 Finding Stray Points

So now you've got all your points weighted, or at least you're pretty sure you do. You swap the model into Layout and, using the Schematic window to select Root, RightFoot, and LeftFoot, you drag your model a couple of meters –Z. You notice, as in Figure 7.29, that some parts of the skin aren't looking quite right.

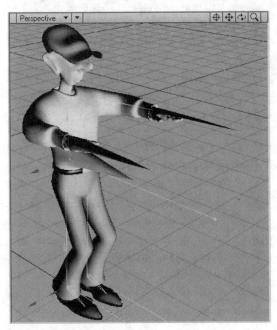

Figure 7.29. The points that are "left behind" have cumulative weighting values that don't add up to 100%.

This is a technique for letting the model itself tell you where the problem points are:

1. Switch to Modeler. (If you're not running LightWave with the Hub active so that Modeler and Layout can pass information between each other, you'll have to manually save and reload the model where appropriate.)

2. From the Current Object pop-up button (to the left of the layer buttons), make sure you have the mesh you are currently working on in Layout selected. (For me, this would be ch_07_w07.lwo.) See Figure 7.30.

3. With the mesh layer active, press **Tab** to convert subpatches into polygons.

Figure 7.30. The character's mesh, in polygons.

4. Switch back to Layout. With the Hub active, you should now be looking at your scene with your character as a polygonal mesh instead of subpatches. If this doesn't happen, you may have to save the object in Modeler, then reload in Layout to update the changes.

Figure 7.31. The polygon version of our character now in Layout.

Note:

If Layout and Modeler seem to not be passing information back and forth properly through the Hub, I'd suggest saving a revision of your scene, closing both Layout and Modeler, and forcing the Hub to quit as well. When the Hub becomes unreliable, Layout and/or Modeler are often not far behind. Closing everything, the Hub including, and reopening Layout and Modeler is often the best preventative against a nasty crash.

5. Choose **File|Save|Save Trans Object….** A dialog box will come up, warning you to "Select a different filename for the transformed object if you want to keep your original object geometry."

Figure 7.32. Saving transformed geometry.

6. Name the transformed object **BadPointFinder.lwo**.

7. Switch back to Modeler and load **BadPointFinder.lwo**.

8. Copy the mesh and paste it into Layer 3 of your current working model. (See Figure 7.33.)

Figure 7.33. With Layer 1 visible in the background, the mesh of BadPointFinder.lwo points directly to the points that need weighting adjustments!

7.6 **Straightening the Feet for Animation**

I saved this part for last because while point weighting, I like to see bones stretching from where their real-life socket would be to where their real-life tip would be. The feet have a notable "L" shape to them where the ankle is and where the toes connect. Because of this, when we built the foot control bones, we built them at a bit of a downward angle. This works great for getting a visual bearing on point weighting, but in order to animate well, the foot control bones have to be realigned to 0H, 0P, 0B.

> **Note:**
> Were we to leave the feet at this angle, it would be hard to keep them flat on the floor when we rotated them in worldspace H. Even using world coordinates, the feet dip a bit as they rotate in H because LightWave uses parent coordinates to store animation data, regardless of what coordinate system we use to manipulate the controls.

1. In Layout, make sure you are on **Frame 0**, that all parts of Auto Key Create are active, and that Parent in Place is active.

2. Change one of your viewports to **Right**, and set its Rendering Level to **Bounding Box** (so we can easily see through our model to our bones).

3. Select **RightToes**.

4. In a Schematic view, Ctrl-click on the node representing the object to (temporarily) reparent this bone to the model itself.

Figure 7.34. The RightToes are now a child of the model itself. Because we have Parent in Place active, they stay in place. (In addition to setting one view to Bounding Box, I've also set one to Bone X-Ray to see the bones that would normally be hidden by opaque geometry.)

5. Select **RightFoot**, and activate **Modify | Rotate | Rotate Pivot**.

6. Set the pivot rotation for RightFoot to **0H, 0P, 0B**.

Figure 7.35. When you change the RightFoot's pivot rotation to 0, 0, 0, LightWave automatically compensates by adjusting its rotation settings — its orientation appears unchanged.

7. Press <**y**> to switch to Rotation mode, and set the rotation for RightFoot to **0H, 0P, 0B**.

Figure 7.36. Now, when the rotation of RightFoot is set to 0, 0, 0, we see it "line-out" along the Z-axis of the world.

8. Select **RightToes** and, in a Schematic view, Ctrl-click on **RightFoot** to reparent the toes to the foot.

Figure 7.37. RightToes are once again a child of RightFoot. And of course, with Parent in Place active, they are still in the same worldspace place they were when we started this section.

9. Repeat steps 3 to 8 for LeftToes and LeftFoot.

7.7 Putting Him Through the Motions

All the points are weighted, and nothing lags behind. But is the weighting going to work for the animations the character will be performing? Does he form the silhouettes you want as he's put through a series of poses? Ankles, armpits, buttocks, elbows, knees, shoulders, toes, and wrists have to be critically evaluated, tweaked, and reevaluated.

In a production environment, you would normally have the lead animator for the character or the animation director do a little animation for the character so the motion technical directors (the guys in charge of skinning and a great deal of other things as well) can scrub through the animation frame by frame to see if and where their point weighting could be improved. To this effect, there are two scenes that you can load and swap your model into:

▶ Scenes\chapters\ch_07_PoseTest.lws is a series of poses to see how your character's skin stretches when in common and extreme poses.

▶ Scenes\chapters\ch_07_MotionTest.lws is a short animation for you to see how your character's skin stretches as it moves through a quick bit of action.

> **Note:**
> In the following chapters, I'll go over the animation controls, and you'll be putting your character through a series of poses. If, as you work, you notice something that doesn't quite seem to be working in the point weighting department, you can always go back into Modeler and finesse the weightings, updating your "final" model at any point of the production process.

7.8 **Tidying Up**

Just a few more "housekeeping" kinds of things remain before we move on to animation training itself. Don't worry: They're quick and easy, and they'll be over before you know it.

1. In Modeler, cut and paste the skelegons back into Layer 1 of your character. Clear away any unused data in subsequent layers so you've got everything all neat and tidy on Layer 1.

2. Save a version of your model in a "finals" directory, naming it so that you know it is the final version of your character. (Objects\Final\Thinguy_F.lwo works for me.)

3. If you're working on an OS that lets you set "protection bits" (read-only properties) for a file, activate this bit so you don't accidentally delete or write over it. (A backup copy in a separate archival folder is always a good thing, too.)

4. In Layout, swap out the model on which you've been working with your final model.

5. Delete all extraneous keyframes from the scene that you may have been using to test your rigging and weighting. I like to set a keyframe for my object and all its descendants (which LightWave takes to mean all of its bones as well) at frame –100, just so I can always go back to this rest pose if I need to reset a bone's rest information for any reason.

6. Save this scene in a Final directory, designating that this is your setup scene for this character. (Scenes\CharacterSetups\Thinguy_Setup.lws is what I use.)

7. Set the protection bit (and/or make a backup copy) for your setup scene so you will always have something clean and familiar to start all your animations.

And that's it! These are the secrets to character setup (or at least some of them). Everyone has their own way of doing things; everyone finds ways that work best for them. You can use this information as is, or you can blend and mold it to fit your specific needs. Hopefully, even if you're new to LightWave and/or character setup, this section has given you the tools and the understanding to be able to take the mystery out of this all-important foundation of computer animation.

Computer animation is in a constant state of evolution. New riggings are constantly being devised, revised, and abandoned, evolved upon, and stripped down. If you happen to stumble upon (or forge through sheer effort) something great, share it with others. You'll be helping the world of animation as a whole, and bettering the impression of animators and technical directors in general!

Chapter 8

Using the Controls

You've done a seriously respectable amount of work on this character setup stuff, from pre-bending to point weighting. (It almost makes modeling seem easy in comparison, doesn't it?) You rolled up your sleeves and got "down-and-dirty" with a lot of technical stuff over the last couple chapters, but what does it all do?

If you're like most creative people I know, your motto is similar to Rikki-Tikki-Tavi's, "Run and find out!" You've probably played with the controls already and put our guy through some poses. But I'm sure some questions arose, like, "Why do things this way?" or "How do I get it to do this?" or "What's the best way to do that?" In this chapter, I'll show you how to work the controls we've created. And this is simply my favored way of working, nothing more. Now, granted, it works smashingly for me, but remember, you are not limited to this way of working. After going through this chapter, play with what you've learned and see what works well for you. Based on what you've learned about how setups work, you can modify anything and everything to create the controls that work exactly the way you wish to work!

The first fourteen (yes, fourteen) sections of this chapter will get you acquainted with driving this character with standard IK. The last section will show you how to use the IK Booster settings we brought to bear in Chapter 6.

Newbie Note:
If you would like to work from my setup, it can be found in Scenes\CharacterSetups\Thinguy_Setup.lws on the companion CD.

Note:

If things do not work as described, there may be problems with the character's hierarchy or IK settings (i.e., chains not terminated or IK set to solve for the wrong axis). If you are finding errors, and you wish to understand what went wrong, you may have to backtrack as far as Chapter 4 to find where the errors are. Double-check your scenes and hierarchies with the final scenes for each chapter provided on the companion CD. Usually, when something is behaving screwy, it's the result of something extremely simple that was just overlooked and is therefore easily fixed (once it is found).

8.1 The Model Itself

When I first started building setups, I would build in a special control for moving the character to where he was going to start his scene. I gave this up because it is just one more thing to build, one more thing to keep track of. I now just use the model itself for the gross positioning control.

Figure 8.1. Using the model itself (Objects\Final\Thinguy_F.lwo in my case) to orient and position the character to where he will start his scene.

▶ The model may be moved and rotated on all axes.

> **Note:**
> For translations, it is usually best to have the coordinate system set to World. For rotations, I generally work in the parent coordinate system, but switch to World or Local when gimbal lock makes things tedious.

8.2 Root

The Root bone will move everything but your character's feet. (See Figure 8.2.) You can use this bone to get general upper carriage movements while your character's feet stay rooted firmly to the "floor."

Figure 8.2. Moving Root in −Y, you get the character's upper carriage to move downward. The character's feet stay locked in place.

▶ Root is designed to move and rotate in all axes.

8.3 Pelvis

The Pelvis bone is what you will use to swing the character's hips about.

> **Note:**
>
> Even if you're not planning on having him do Middle Eastern dancing, this is an important control. Most people stand with more weight on one leg than the other, "popping" one hip up; the shoulder on the same side swings down. The technical term for this is *contra-posto*. The ancient Greeks were the first to use contra-posto in their sculpture. Having the hips and shoulders rotated in opposite directions is an easy way to add life to any pose.

Figure 8.3. Rotating the Pelvis bone along its heading axis.

▶ Pelvis is designed only to be rotated. It may be rotated in all axes.

8.4 **Spinal Bones**

The bones of the spine do pretty much what you'd expect; they rotate to curve the spine of the character into the shapes you need.

Spine1 does double-duty, however, in that it also is used to position the character, leaving the hands and feet rooted in place. (This is useful in a scene where you've got his hands planted on a tabletop and he is getting up from a chair; his hands and feet won't move until you move them with their separate controls.)

Figure 8.4. Moving Spine1 in –Y lowers the character, but his hands and feet stay where they are.

Figure 8.5. Rotating Spine1, Spine2, and Spine3 in heading.

▶ Spine1 may be rotated and moved on all axes.

▶ Spine2 and Spine3 may be rotated on all axes.

> **Note:**
>
> Head is a child of Spine1; it will move when you rotate Spine1 but will remain in place when you rotate Spine2 and Spine3. I've made the setup this way so that the head can follow the larger movements of the character's *center of gravity*, but remain unaffected by the finer detail movements of the upper two spinal bones. This holds the head more steady when you've got a lot of expression in the shoulders for a walk or antic. I've found it easier to move the head to keep it on top of the neck than to try to counterrotate it to keep it from wobbling as the shoulders swing about. (Often, I'll have Head as the child of Root or of the model itself so I have absolute control over it in a powerful scene.) Feel free to experiment with having Head as a child of different controls to find what is most intuitive for you.

8.5 **Head**

The head is pretty straightforward. You can translate and rotate it to your heart's content. You can pull it away from the body for a frame or two to give the quick-and-easy impression of old-fashioned squash and stretch.

Figure 8.6. Moving and rotating the head control.

▶ The Head may be moved and rotated on all axes.

8.6 **Hand Translation Controls**

RightHand_Trans and LeftHand_Trans take care of moving the hands, and they control the hands' heading and bank rotations. It is better to have a completely separate control for pitch (*Hand_Rot) than to fight with the gimbal lock that is possible when you have H, P, and B all on one control. Even with LightWave now implementing world, parent, and local space coordinate systems, I still recommend a "nested" setup like this. Sometimes when using world or local coordinate systems, odd values get fed onto an item (where something was 0H, and by rotating it just barely in worldspace, it suddenly has –360.5H). With nested controls, you can more precisely control what axis gets rotated, when it rotates, and how much. With so much expression carried by the hands, I feel this small inconvenience of dealing with two controls to rotate the hands is well worth it.

Figure 8.7. Moving and rotating the hand translation controls.

▶ RightHand_Trans and LeftHand_Trans may be moved in all axes, but they should only be rotated in heading and bank. (In a pinch, you can rotate in pitch, but only sparingly, and get pitch back to 0P as soon as you can.)

8.7 **Hand Rotation Controls**

RightHand_Rot and LeftHand_Rot rotate the hands in pitch and bank. They fine-tune the hand rotations.

Figure 8.8. Rotating the hand rotation controls in pitch and bank.

▶ RightHand_Rot and LeftHand_Rot should only be rotated in pitch and bank.

8.8 **Shoulder Controls**

RightShoulder and LeftShoulder allow you to shrug your character's shoulders and cave or expand his chest. Rotating these controls in heading will raise and lower the shoulders. Rotating these controls in pitch will swing the shoulders forward and back.

Figure 8.9. Rotating RightShoulder in +P and rotating LeftShoulder in +H. The character's right shoulder swings back while the left shoulder drops down.

▶ RightShoulder and LeftShoulder should only be rotated in heading and pitch.

8.9 **Elbow Controls**

RightElbow and LeftElbow raise and lower the character's elbows. It is equivalent to the rotator cuff within our own shoulders. This control is limited in how much it can do. Try not to rotate these controls too far; it can be easy to accidentally get a value of +/–360 or more and not realize it. If the elbow rotates from 0 to +/–360 over the course of an animation, it will flip.

Figure 8.10. Rotating RightElbow and LeftElbow in +B swings the right elbow up and the left elbow down. They are mirrors of each other, so you have to watch this when animation gets fast and furious.

▶ RightElbow and LeftElbow should only be rotated in bank.

Note:

I find that if I'm having problems getting the elbow into the exact position I'm trying for, I'm probably trying for a pose that would break a real-life arm. There's usually a way to work through a problem pose by taking a look at how my own arms would most naturally strike that particular pose.

8.10 **Foot Controls**

RightFoot and LeftFoot take care of all rotations and translations on the feet. Because foot motion is usually much less complex and demanding than hand motion, it usually isn't necessary to nest controls as we have for the hands.

Figure 8.11. Moving and rotating RightFoot and LeftFoot.

▸ RightFoot and LeftFoot may be moved and rotated on all axes.

8.11 **Toe Controls**

RightToes and LeftToes rotate the toe section of the foot. Don't just use these controls to keep the traction section of the foot in contact with the ground; play with them to give some added expression to otherwise stiff poses!

Figure 8.12. Just using the feet and the toes.

▸ RightToes and LeftToes may be rotated in all axes (though usually pitch and bank will get most jobs done).

8.12 **Knee Controls**

The knee controls work almost identically to the elbow controls. The same considerations should be taken into account not to rotate them too far.

Figure 8.13. Swinging the knees wide.

▶ RightKnee and LeftKnee should only be rotated in bank.

8.13 **The Fingers and Thumb**

The base of all the fingers can be rotated in both heading and pitch. The other two bones of each finger, mid and tip, should only be rotated in pitch.

Figure 8.14. Rotating Index_Base and Pinky_Base in H to spread the fingers wide.

> **Note:**
> Because LightWave now allows you to select multiple items at once, you can grab all the finger bones and quickly bend them around an object. Be careful, however, because if you have one of the base bones selected too, the base bones can and will rotate in H, even though the mid and tip bones will not. You have to keep an eye on this so you don't make more work for yourself. (Watching the rotation from multiple views as you bend the fingers can help keep everything as it should be.)

Figure 8.15. Rotating the mid and tip bones for the index, mid, and pinky fingers.

The thumb's base can rotate on all three axes. This is to mimic the somewhat complex action of our real-life thumb's base joint close to the wrist. You will almost always need to use a combination of pitch and bank to properly simulate the way our opposable thumbs work.

▶ The base bones of the fingers may rotate in heading and pitch.

▶ The base bone of the thumbs may rotate in all axes.

▶ The mid and tip bones of all digits only rotate in pitch.

Figure 8.16. Swinging the thumb down and around with pitch and bank to get that good ol' opposable thumb action.

Figure 8.17. The other two bones of the thumb work just the same as the mid and tip of the fingers.

8.14 **Notes on Modifying the Setup**

Those are all the controls you'll need to make your character walk, dance, act, emote, and pretty much everything else you can imagine. After playing with them a little, you will probably take to them like a natural — most people do. However, some bits of the setup may seem foreign no matter how much you use it, always expecting a control to do something other than what it does. That's okay, too!

This setup is simply my way of working. It has evolved over many years, since my first feeble setups on an Amiga, long before LightWave implemented IK. It has been streamlined to balance control, speed, and intuition. Still, this is only what *I* consider to be intuitive. You are all individuals out there, and if something seems redundant or overly complex for how you want to work, modify it! With what you've learned over the last seven chapters, you now have the ability to craft the setup you've always wanted.

Some people don't like the nested controls for the hands; I can't live without them. (I actually prefer to nest the feet as well.) Some like the spinal controls to have their pivot rotations aligned differently. You've got the tools now to do almost anything you want. Experiment! Play! Learn!

This is *your* show now. Above all, this animation stuff is supposed to be fun!

> **Note:**
> Some possible setup modifications include:
> ▶ Making Pelvis a child of Root so it does not rotate with Spine1.
> ▶ Making Head a child of Root or of the mesh itself to have it hold very steady during martial arts or sensual walks.
> ▶ Making Head a child of Spine3 so it never pulls away from the torso when posing the spine.
> ▶ Making *Hand_Trans a child of one of the spinal bones so the hands inherit the torso's movement.
> ▶ Removing *Hand_Trans, so *Hand_Rot is the sole control for all movement and rotational axes of the hands.
> ▶ Making one of the hands a child of the other's rotation control (useful when swinging a bat or a broadsword).
> ▶ Realigning Pelvis, Spine1, Spine2, and Spine3, just as was done with the *Foot bones at the end of the last chapter. This makes the spine more intuitive by letting the bones of the spine, head, hands, and feet all lie along the same worldspace axes.

8.15 **IK Booster Controls**

In my exploration and experimentation with IK Booster, I've found that it works best as a "supplement" to the standard IK way of working. IKB is insanely fast for some things, yet it can still behave strangely or be extremely sluggish if asked to do things that are beyond the realm of what it can handle with easy power (just like IK itself).

The great thing is that the things that IKB has a hard time with are the things at which the standard controls we've just explored excel! Flipping quickly between the now *four* modes of manipulation open to LightWave users (**t** Translation mode, **y** Rotation mode, **h/H** Stretch/Scale mode, and now ^**b** IK Booster mode), you'll find that posing your character has become almost like working directly with an artist's wooden mannequin!

I use IK Booster to tweak my pose after I've gotten the "broad strokes" laid in using the standard IK controls.

> **Note:**
> Remember, even if you don't connect with the IKB way of working your character, you can sill take advantage of all IKB's motion and pose saving and loading, and its keyframe manipulation. IK Booster is a phenomenal tool, but it's also new — even IK itself took about six years for professional animators to trust/know it well enough to feel comfortable using it.

Fingers/Toes

Just grab a fingertip and start pulling it around in 3D space. You'll find the fingers bend and flex just as you'd expect if you were working with an artist's mannequin.

Figure 8.18

The same thing holds true for the *Toes.

Figure 8.19

> **Note:**
>
> Back in Chapter 6, I had us set the IKB control icon for the *Foot bones to Move/Rotate so you could move them about when you clicked on them, without having to hit the <t> key, exiting IK Booster, to do so. However, if you don't mind doing this, you may want disable (uncheck) Move/Rotate for the *Foot control icons so when you're dragging the *Toes into new angles, the foot also follows.

Knees/Elbows

Using IK Booster, you no longer need to rotate an *Elbow or *Knee control to position the elbows and knees of your character. You can simply grab the calf or forearm and physically move the knee or elbow joint where you want it to be. (Doing this actually rotates the *Knee and *Elbow bones to the applicable bank setting.)

Figure 8.20

Note:

You'll want to be very watchful when you're manipulating knee and elbow joints in this manner. Just as a little twist of the bank heading on the *Knee and *Elbow controls themselves can swing that character's knee or elbow joint all over the place, so can the slightest twitch of your mouse here. It is best to work in very small moves on only one axis at a time. And if you see the knee or elbow joint swinging at a funky angle, it's best to undo your action and start again — until you click on *Knee or *Elbow in Rotate mode, there's no way of knowing if bank has just exceeded +/– 360°.

Note:

Undoing in IK Booster seems to be a bit odd at the time of publication. When I hit ^z to undo my last move in IKB, not only is that move undone, but also the last move done using standard controls is also undone. I've found, however, that by redoing (by pressing <z>) and *then undoing again*, the standard control's position is restored, and then only the IKB move is undone.

Shoulders/Hips

To shrug the character's shoulders, or cave or expand his chest, just grab the *tip* of a shoulder bone and drag it around.

Figure 8.21

By grabbing and moving the *base* of a shoulder bone, you can tilt the entire carriage this way and that. (Just remember that when you do so, if you have chosen to have the Head a child of Spine1, the Head will stay mostly in place since Spine3 does most of the moving when manipulating the model in this fashion — it's a minor tweak to move the head back squarely on top of the shoulders.)

Figure 8.22

You can swing the hips and the entire carriage about by dragging one of the *Knee bones in 3D space.

Figure 8.23

Spine/Head

You can click and drag on any of the *Spine bones, moving the character's carriage with ease. (I've also repositioned the head in this illustration.)

Figure 8.24

The Head has its control icon set to Move/Rotate so within IK Booster it is only able to be moved. (It is recommended that you control the head through the standard IK way of doing things, but if you really need to position the head quickly without exiting IKB, you can use its IKB control to do so.)

Figure 8.25

Hands/Feet

You can click and drag on the *Hand_Trans controls and move them about in 3D space (just like the Head).

Figure 8.26

You can also click and drag on the handle at the tip of *Hand_ Rot to swing the hand up or down.

Figure 8.27

197

And, if you pull hard enough on a finger control, you can also get the hand to swing up or down, following the direction of your pull.

Figure 8.28

> **Note:**
>
> The IKB controls discussed in Section 8.15 are the only ones I regularly use under IK Booster. I use standard IK to manipulate all other controls.

Control Order

I've had a lot of people ask me which controls to move first when I'm posing a character. To tell the truth, I don't think most animators think about it that much — we just move whatever needs moving.

I believe strongly that there is no "right" or "wrong" way to do anything, so long as it works for the person doing the doing, and respects those who are affected by the doing.

But I can completely relate to someone who's never seen this plethora of controls and ways of working feeling overwhelmed with the vast spread of choices, so I'll walk you through how I'd strike a simple pose.

Figure 8.29. As with all the other life drawing exercises, I'll be working from a pose created with the same controls I'll be using to do the work myself — I know I can strike this pose if I give myself enough time to do so.

"Start at the beginning, go on until you get to the end, then stop!"
— The Mad Hatter, *Alice in Wonderland*

Figure 8.30. The first thing I do, of course, is load the setup I've just completed, then save it as a file prepped for revisions (*_v001.lws) into a working directory so I can fiddle with things to my heart's content.

Figure 8.31. Then, I swap out Thinguy_F for MrCool_Facial_F, the model used in the pose I'll be copying.

Figure 8.32. Next, I load in the life drawing model from Extras\Life_Drawing\
Objects\ICanFly.lwo. (And make sure I've got OpenGL Transparency enabled in
my Display Options.)

Figure 8.33. The first thing I'll do is move the object itself to get my own character close to the position of the life drawing model.

Note:

When I'm animating, I usually leave the object alone once I've got it in its starting position — using only the controls to move the character around the environment.

Figure 8.34. Then, moving and rotating Spine1 under standard IK, I line up the waistline, using the belt as my point of reference.

Figure 8.35. Next, using Back and Top views, I position the hands with the *Hand_Trans controls, rotating the hands only on their heading axis at the moment.

Figure 8.36. Now, I get the feet into position the same way. (At the moment, I'm not concerned with perfection, I'm just getting things "in the ballpark.")

Figure 8.37. Next, I move and rotate the Head so it comes close to matching the model.

Figure 8.38. Then, I start getting more precise with the hands and feet (using heading and bank on *Hand_Trans and pitch on *Hand_Rotate).

207

Note:

I'll often use the Center Selected Item button to help me quickly jump to an item I want to manipulate in a Perspective viewport, sometimes just quickly clicking the button on, then off, to "bull's-eye" it and yet still let me adjust my view to suit my needs.

Figure 8.39. Now I start using IK Booster and drag the fingers into their proper positions.

Figure 8.40. Working on the spine comes next. Switching back and forth between using IKB and standard IK controls (sometimes even actually moving the bones of the spine if I feel it's necessary to sculpt the pose I want), I begin to get more and more precise with the accuracy.

Figure 8.41. Then, it's just a matter of settling in for the long haul, continuing to refine your "noodling," working back and forth between standard IK and IK Booster controls until the pose is what you want.

There are no "right" or "wrong" ways of doing this...so long as what you see is what you want. This is the way I usually work.

The real knack for this will come when you've done all the practice exercises in this book, and you know on a gut level what each control will do and when it is best to use it.

Like my mentor told me when I was working to get a more polished, cleaned-up line to my drawings, your line quality will get better when you know enough to not worry about your line.

Chapter 9

Life Drawing — The Next Logical Step

Life drawing? In 3D? You betchya! Life drawing is the best way to learn how to break down shapes and to understand what is actually going on to create those wonderfully complex and deceptively simple poses. As you work with life drawing in 3D, you'll begin to see exactly what makes a pose look and feel the way it does.

Why does a good animation drawing have the emotional impact it does? It has that kind of impact solely because of the poses the characters are in. Animators are often considered draftsmen; there is no more precise art form than animation. (In a standard-sized animation drawing, the deviation of a line by even 1/32" can completely change the emotional read of the drawing.) Yet, at the same time, everything must appear effortless and inevitable. You achieve this level of proficiency by mastering the sets of skills required. You master these skills to the point that they become so much a part of you, you can't do anything but execute them perfectly, precisely, and without thinking. All it takes to get to this level of proficiency in anything (animation being no exception) is simply to practice at least a little each and every day, to know where to start and how to proceed — how to get to the "next logical step."

Finding the next logical step is all getting anywhere with anything is. All of us can move steadily from one step to the next. We all start this path the same way. The troublesome thing with these next logical steps is that it is only when you begin to achieve mastery that you begin to understand what they are. Looking back from the plateaus of mastery, you can see where all the steps were and where you got lost along the way. From the plateaus of mastery, you can also see the next logical steps that will carry you to where you would like to be. (No matter how good others may think you are, you must always, *always* be looking for that next logical step. There is always something more.) This is why it is so vitally important for teachers of anything to not only care about what they're teaching and be able to communicate it, but to have achieved a level of mastery to be able to see these steps. Mastering animation takes humility, dedication, passion, and time. But with these steps, mastery should not be painful; you should always be able to see your path before you. Moving from one simple signpost to another, studying and understanding, learning how to see motion, how to understand the conveyance of feeling. Each step builds on the successful completion of the last. Each next logical step has an "Aha!" factor that is often so simple that it could all too easily hide forever in plain sight.

And so the next logical step from where you are right now is to get to know those controls you labored long to create. You need to know them so well that they become second nature to you. (And if there is something in the setup you simply cannot work with, go back and change it until it feels right to your way of working.)

If, after going through the life drawing models in this chapter, you still feel you need more life drawing experience before moving on, flip to Chapter 14 where you'll be directed to many more models to "draw" from. (Don't be afraid to go back and revisit these old models. It's always good, throughout your career, to go back and reaffirm the things you know.) Move forward only when you feel comfortable. Doing so will make the whole process of learning animation that much more enjoyable and rewarding.

9.1 The Standing Model

Posing a character is the art of translating what you have in your mind into the 3D coordinates that will make your character fit that vision.

Figure 9.1. We'll be starting with a standing model. The pose is interesting enough to keep us from getting bored, but still easy enough to be recreated with relative ease.

Now, you might be asking, "How do I know where in 3D space to put these things that I'm seeing on this flat, 2D page?" In very short order, you'll get the hang of being able to translate the subtleties of slight differences in angle and size on a page into 3D coordinates. (LW's grid lines are very helpful; I wish all life drawing classes had their plinths marked with grid lines.) We'll be starting with a technique that will have you well on your way before you know it.

On one project I was given hi-res scans of models I would eventually have to animate. The project didn't have the budget for Paraform (a program designed to make animatable NURBS models from hi-res scan data) and we knew the client was going to be a stickler for having the models perfect. After reducing the poly count somewhat with qemLOSS2, just to make the scans manageable on a 500 MHz PII, we changed the surface of the scanned model to be partially transparent. We then built our subpatch model around that framework. We could see exactly when our subpatch was passing through the scanned model's surface, and it turned out to be a rather quick way of not only getting an animatable subpatch model, but also in getting a whole lot better at modeling very quickly. (Running my own studio, I've had to learn to wear a lot of hats to get jobs out on time. I'll always be a better animator and director than I'll ever hope to be a modeler, but every new thing you can add to your set of skills is an asset.)

We'll be using that same technique to get you started in life drawing here. You'll know when you have enough angle here, enough distance there to support the character's weight. You'll know when your character carries the essence of the pose, and you'll know when your character is spot-on. You'll be able to turn the view and explore from every angle. You'll see, right there in front of you, whether your model covers the drawing model or not!

1. Load in your setup scene and then save the scene as something that will let you know this is life drawing model 01. (Scenes\Work\ch09\LifeDrawing_01_w01.lws works for me.)

2. Load in Objects\chapters\Ch_09\LifeDrawingModel_01.lwo.

Figure 9.2. Your model and the pose you'll put him into.

3. Using Chapter 8 as a reference if you need to, start moving controls!

If you find yourself in a bind, don't be afraid to scrap your work and start over (with a saved revision, of course, just in case you really were on the right track). As they say, "Animation is the art of revision." Also, don't hesitate to come back to this pose at some time in the future, using what you've learned to see if there are better, faster, more elegant ways of getting him to assume this pose.

There are a few things I'd like to point out about the pose itself before moving on. If you look at it from any angle — back, front, side, or top — the character looks balanced. Even though he's got his weight shifted back and to the right, his legs support him in a way that he could hold indefinitely without falling over. Weight distribution is a very important thing. Every stationary pose must read as balanced from all angles, not just the camera angle. The character's center of gravity must appear properly supported; he can't look like he's about to fall over.

> **Note:**
> Another thing to watch on the whole weight issue is that when you have a character moving he has to have the proper weight distribution for the speed and direction of his movement. Walking is just falling forward and catching ourselves every time we step. Running means that we're leaning forward farther to get more offset for the forward thrust. Every pose, whether moving or stationary, must be balanced or the character must be about to fall over.

The best way to assess the balance of a pose is to turn your head away from the monitor, close your eyes, and turn your head back to the monitor. Open your eyes for no more than 1/4 second. The afterimage you have in your mind will have a feeling to it; it'll either feel comfortable ("Yeah, I'd buy that") or awkward ("Man ... there's just something not quite right about that"). Do this from every angle, even if your final output will be to film or another 2D medium. Human minds work better than we might sometimes guess, and though your audience might not know exactly why something doesn't look quite right, they'll feel the difference between a pose that carries its weight properly and a pose that is off balance even slightly.

Note:

A properly animated scene should look good from all angles. (This is especially true if you're doing work for a 3D video game and you can't control the camera.) True, there will be angles that look better than others, but no angle should look unbelievable. Watching your scene from the worst angle you can find is a trick you can use to make it read all the better from the intended angle. It is like flipping a drawing over and looking at it on a light table from the other side. You disassociate yourself from what you've been thinking for the past hours or days and are able to look at it from a more objective point of view. From that unflattering angle, make the tweaks you see that need tweaking, then look at the scene from the camera angle; you'll be surprised at how much more believably it reads.

We've also got contra-posto, the reversal of angles between the hips and shoulders, going on in this scene. The character's hips are swung down and back on the *right* side. The character's shoulders are swung down and back on the *left* side (though in relationship to the shoulders' initial pose their new angle doesn't appear that different). This makes the pose read with more life than if the hips and shoulders were parallel.

Hands are important with every pose. Much of the emotional read of a pose is carried in the character's hands. This is as important with wild action as with subtle acting. When working with a run or other vigorous activity, don't forget the importance of the hands. If you were ever on a track team, do you remember your coach telling you that the way to run faster is to pump your arms harder and faster? This balance and counterbalance works throughout our entire bodies. Our subconscious minds have ways of picking up on these *non-verbals* — cues given by the way someone stands, the timing with which they do something, and many other subtle cues that have nothing to do with spoken words. Non-verbals have ways of translating themselves directly into an emotional read within the viewer. Understanding everything you can about what it is your character is doing, putting yourself into that situation, and letting all of that wealth of information flood through you as you work is the key to believable animation.

Another thing to pay attention to in this pose is the handling of the finger groupings. Rhythm plays a very important role in animation. Having the fingers equidistant, either close together or spread apart, is monotonous and boring. A common technique to break this up is to pop the pinky or index finger out from the other two by rotating its base in heading. It is a simple thing that adds a lot of life to a pose. Making sure the fingers aren't all bent the same amount is another important thing to remember. Often, you'll see a pinky bent slightly when all the rest of the fingers are straight. Watch for opportunities to add these techniques to your own poses, but make sure that the emotional read it adds goes along with the read of the pose you're trying to create.

4. Look over your scene closely. Are all areas of the life drawing model covered by your model? If so, congratulate yourself! You've just taken a huge next logical step on the path that leads toward being a fantastic animator!

9.2 **The Seated Model**

This exercise is just the same as in Section 9.1. We'll be loading a life drawing model into a fresh scene and moving our character until he "assumes the position" (as it were).

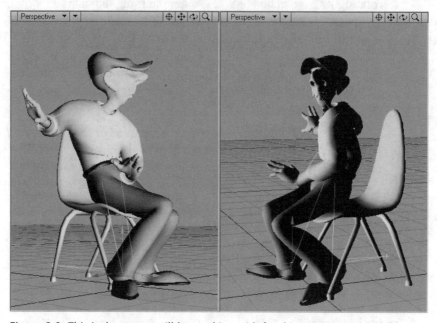

Figure 9.3. This is the pose we'll be working with for this exercise. It looks like there is a lot more going on, but it is actually just as easy to manage as the previous pose. Do watch the fingers and thumbs; there's a little more action going on there.

1. Load a copy of your setup scene, then save the scene in your Chapter 9 working directory as something that'll remind you that this is life drawing model 02.

2. Load in Objects\chapters\Ch_09\LifeDrawingModel_02.lwo.

3. Load in Objects\Props\Chair.lwo.

4. Start pulling controls until your model fits the pose held by the life drawing model.

Note:

Twinning is an industry term for anything that mirrors something in the scene, either in motion or in pose. Hands and arms can twin. Feet and legs can twin. Fingers can twin, and entire characters can twin each other in a scene. *Watch out for this!* Twinning is something that almost never happens in real life. It is easy to fall into, and it makes your pose read flat and unbelievable. Luckily, twinning is something that is easily caught and fixed if you have a watchful eye out for it, both during the creating of the scene and in watching it when you think it might be finished.

Some notes on the pose itself: The character's feet are both at different angles and positions with respect to the center of the pose. Even so, both feet are braced against the chair legs, giving a feeling of tension and readiness to bolt. Not only is the character perched on the edge of the chair, he is off center to the chair's right, adding to the feeling that something more is going on than what the audience knows. His knees are together in a way that reads of fear and protection. The focus of his torso and hands is away from where his head is turned, giving a reading that there may be separate things making him uneasy. The hands form two distinctly separate shapes that don't twin regardless of what angle they are viewed from, yet they both read of surprise and trepidation within this pose.

Everything comes together in this pose to give a reading that this guy isn't happy about being where he is. As you work, try to understand and internalize what subtleties build these feelings within you. Animation is a lot like jazz in that you build riffs that you know work well to produce certain feelings within certain contexts. You put them all together in a piece, transposing, modifying, and working on the fly. Always be on the lookout for new riffs that you can add to your repertoire. Real life, film, television, and comic books all abound with different takes on experience and response. When a scene comes along where you can use one of these new riffs, you'll feel like a kid in a candy store: "Oh man! I've been wanting to give this a try!"

> **Note:**
> Animation is supposed to be fun. The surest way to take the fun out of it is to not have the time you need to get the job done right. Whatever the situation, always strive to give yourself the time to feel good about the end result. Don't rush things. When you walk away from your desk, it is important to want to walk back.

9.3 The Reclining Model

Now we're going to do a couple of models lying on the ground, one face-up, the other face-down. It is best to get familiar with doing things as many different ways as possible. This is called "filling the well." When a situation arises and you need to do something differently from your normal way of doing things, it won't catch you by surprise.

I'm going to recommend using the model itself to lay the character onto his back for the first pose and using Spine1 to get him there for the second pose. You not only get a feeling for different controls, you get used to seeing the model all out of joint — hands, feet, and head dragging behind — but knowing that there's a method to the madness.

1. Load a fresh copy of your setup scene, then save a revision as we've been doing.

2. Load in Objects\chapters\Ch_09\LifeDrawingModel_03.lwo.

3. Using the mesh itself to lay the character onto his back, start pulling controls; see how you do!

As you work with the hand controls in this pose, pay attention to what happens when you rotate the *_Rot control first or the *_Trans first. Certain poses are easier to get when you move one first instead of the other. Also, don't be afraid to break some rules. If you see what you want, and all you need is to rotate *_Trans in pitch, go ahead and rotate it in pitch. In making this pose, I found it much easier to rotate the RightShoulder control in world H than to fight with parent H and P.

Figure 9.4. This is a pretty straightforward pose; you should have very little problem with it. It is also a bit of a standard life drawing pose; it's the pose the model usually assumes when he knows he's going to be there a while.

> **Note:**
>
> Something that will help you as you work is being aware that LightWave has a *solving order*, the order in which it calculates heading, pitch, and bank. LightWave figures heading first, then pitch, and lastly bank. This makes sense when you think of bank as being the child of pitch, and pitch being the child of heading. Rotating bank doesn't affect any of the other two axes. Rotating pitch affects the angle of bank (hence the wonders of gimbal lock). Rotating heading affects both pitch and bank. When rotating something into what may be a bit of a complex space, try working backward — bank first, then pitch, and finally heading.

> **Advanced Note:**
>
> If any of you techno-wizards out there find yourselves working on an expression that will "cancel out" the rotation of a previous item, say to have a platform always be level no matter how its support arm rotates, the solving order info will help. What you've got to do is to have a hierarchy similar to: SupportArm => Cancel_B => Cancel_P => platform. With either the LWFollower plug-in or by using an expression, have Cancel_B rotate at the bank rotation of SupportArm multiplied by –1. Have Cancel_P do the same for SupportArm pitch, and have the platform itself do the same for SupportArm heading. (I know this may seem like something out of left field, but believe it or not, this has saved my behind in a character setup.)

Something else that will help you as you go: Before you start, actually lay down in this position and see how it feels to lay like that. Doing this will help you more than just about anything else you can do. Animation is a *kinesthetic* art, an art based on movement and feel. If, while you're working, you can remember how it felt to be in that pose, it will make your work go much more easily, and you'll get a much stronger, more readable, believable pose. Animation is getting the viewer to feel what it feels like to do or to be something. When you believe in that feeling as you do the work, it will show through your art. And don't worry about appearing weird by standing up at your desk, going through a motion, or striking a pose — all animators do it! The halls of any place I've worked have at least one or two animators acting out their scenes at any given time. And because animation is all about feeling, watching yourself on videotape only goes so far. If you are using videotaped reference, try to put yourself there in that action as you watch; feel what's going on, both kinesthetically and emotionally.

4. Take a close look at your pose from all angles. Did you get everything covered?

When you feel comfortable with the work you've done, we'll move on to the next reclining pose.

5. Save your scene and load in your setup scene again.

6. Load in Objects\chapters\Ch_09\LifeDrawingModel_04.lwo.

7. Save a working revision of this fourth life drawing scene.

8. Avoiding the use of the mesh itself and the Root control, start posing!

Figure 9.5. This pose has a lot going on. There is heavy curvature of the spine, twisting the pelvis and the shoulders onto very different lines. The right side of the pelvis is raised to accommodate the right knee's angle at the side of the body; the right shoulder is pulling forward, reaching for the hand's position. The fingers aren't just flat on the ground; they spread and reach, reading of support and intent. All in all, it is a very cat-like pose, and the curves read strongly from every angle. (Poses where the curves read well from every angle are what to strive for in video game work where you don't know where the viewer's camera will be.)

9. Take a step back and look at how you did! (Hide and unhide the life drawing model. Move it off to the side so you can compare the two at once. Do they both give you the same gut-level feeling?)

Does your pose need more work? Do you need to scrap it all and start over? (Remember, you can save yourself a lot of time in the long run by doing this.) Were you able to get your pose to match the model's? Try to remember the order in which you rotate the controls. If you're having problems, zero-out those controls and try rotating them in a different order.

> **Note:**
>
> Oftentimes, when something isn't quite coming together, I find that there are usually just one or two things that keep the pose from reading the way I want it to. Taking a quick break to get a cup of tea, take a quick run around the building, or do something else that gets my mind off the ways I was thinking usually does wonders. When you come back to the scene, almost always there's an, "Oh, duh! Of course!" and you make a few quick changes and wham — everything has fallen into place!

When everything is reading well, and your character covers the life drawing model perfectly, congratulate yourself! This is one of the harder poses I could think of for you to try. Animation consists of two things: timing and posing. You're well on your way to having posing down pat!

9.4 **The Character and Weight**

How do you get a character to read as if he is carrying something heavy when all we've got are the tools of pose and timing? We have to show the audience by how the character responds to and interacts with the weight. (You never want the character saying, "Boy, Phil, this 500-pound weight is heavy." That's bad directing.)

Note:

Actually, *everything* in filmmaking (storytelling) is about showing how characters respond to things in their environments. The characters' responses will tell an audience how heavy, happy, or scary a thing is. The audience will empathize with what they see, pulling from their own experience. An excellent example of this is in the 2001 version of *Lord of the Rings*: When the ring wraiths enter the Inn of the Prancing Pony, we see a big man who looks to be a cook. His response of utter, childlike fear, hiding as the wraiths enter, lets us know beyond the shadow of a doubt that this is a very bad situation.

Figure 9.6. Based entirely on the memory of how it feels to carry a heavy household appliance, we read everything from how heavy this weight is to the character's outlook on carrying it.

1. Load in a fresh copy of your setup, saving it back out as the revision with which you will be working for this sitting.

2. Load in Objects\chapters\Ch_09\LifeDrawingModel_05.lwo.

3. Animators, start your engines!

Notice with this one how the model really feels like he's working with this weight? It's all about posture, silhouette, and how we ourselves have experienced similar things and empathize with how he looks. An interesting thing is that you can get a totally different read on this pose by swinging the knees inward to touch. Try it. The model goes from this hefty dude to someone looking like he's about to lose it. Different angles of the head give the impression of catching this guy at different points of lifting this weight. With his head tilted down, as it is, he gives the impression of someone concentrating on the task at hand. If you tilt his head up, he looks like someone just picking up this weight and trying to get it settled for the long haul.

Another interesting thing to note is (and I'll go over this again in the section on silhouette) that with good, strong poses, you've usually got one side of the character smooth, like this guy's back. The other side is all full of interesting jutting shapes to catch and hold the eye. Again, this is rhythm. This visual sense of rhythm — smooth vs. bumpy, straight vs. curved — is the key to making a pose read of highest quality.

Also note that the character's hands are beyond the reach of his forearm bones. This stretches the wrists out of the shirtsleeves and adds to the visual feeling of the hands being "pulled" by the weight. In an animation, the moment the hands were to come back in touch with the ArmPullers, the arms would pop a bit, making a quick motion that is noncontiguous with the surrounding motion. This happens any time you pull a goal away from its puller and then let it come back in contact. It's a good idea to try your hardest to make sure the goals always stay within reach of the pullers assigned to them. If, in a pose like this, it really needs to be that way, you can cover that pop by having a bit of quick action surrounding the motion or by making several, precisely controlled keyframes of the control that moves the goal so that when the joint does start moving again, it isn't so abrupt.

Note:

Strong poses are poses "drawn" with verbs, not nouns. Pose an arm stretching, a back reaching, a leg compressing, or a neck craning. Always pose with verbs, even when a character is doing nothing.

How did you do? It's a relatively simple pose when it comes right down to it, but there are a lot of subtle points to make sure you've covered. Take a step back, brew a cup of really good tea, and analyze.

9.5 The Timed Pose

Whenever you take life drawing, you usually start with a series of quick :30 (thirty-second) poses. You then move on to 1:00 poses, then 3:00, 5:00, 10:00 poses, and then to long poses of 30:00 to 2:00:00. The idea behind this is to loosen up not only your drawing arm but your mind (and heart) as well. During the quick poses, you remember to not get all mired in the minutia; you focus on the big picture, the things that get the pose to read at a glance.

Figure 9.7. This pose is simple but still interesting for this timed pose set. There's enough going on here to keep your attention for 30:00, and broad enough to get good, strong gestures in :30.

1. Load in a fresh setup; save it as a working scene revision as usual.

2. Working only from Figure 9.7, give yourself 3:00 (three minutes) and see how you do.

> **Note:**
>
> Working solely from the figure is the next logical step in what we're doing. You've already become familiar with the controls, what they do, and how to use them to pose your character from a model directly in the scene with him. Now, you've got to be able to take an image (real or imagined) and turn that visual into the 3D coordinates that delineate a character's pose.

3. Take a step back from your work. How did you do? Did you work any differently from when you had the life drawing model right there in the scene with you? Did you approach the scene any differently than when you knew you had an unlimited amount of time?

4. Save a revision of this scene, load up a fresh setup, and get ready to tackle this pose again.

5. Try this pose again, just from the figure, and this time give yourself 10:00 (ten minutes). See how you do.

   Try to start the scene the same way you did when you had 3:00. Rough in the broad gestural lines first, then work on fine-tuning the details.

6. Again, take a step back and compare the work with the figure. How do you feel about it? Did you start this pose the same way you did the 3:00 one? (If you had saved a revision as the 3:00 mark passed, would it look similar to what you had done in the last sitting?)

Note:

There will almost never be enough time for you to be completely, 100% happy with a scene while working in production. Some productions will give you more time than others, but you will always have something more you want to do with the scene. Like a painting, an animation is never finished; it simply stops in interesting places. Being able to rough in the important details first, being happy with silhouette, weight, and emotional read, and then being able to noodle the details is what will make you content with your work and yourself as an animator when you see your scene in the final product.

7. Load in Objects\chapters\Ch_09\LifeDrawingModel_06.lwo.

8. Move (only in X and Z) and rotate (only in heading) the life drawing model until he comes as close to being in the same position as your character as possible.

Compare and contrast. Your character, after 10:00, should match the life drawing model fairly well. There will, of course, be details not quite there yet, and exact positioning will probably be off. But the overall feel of the pose should be the same.

9. Save this scene as a revision.

10. Load in a fresh setup, saving it out again as a working scene.

11. Using what you've learned, give yourself 30:00 (thirty minutes) working just from the figure. While still starting the same way you would if you only had 3:00, try to get things to totally match the model.

You've become very familiar with this pose. You know which controls to move now and how much to rotate them. You know what it takes to put this guy into this pose you now feel deep in your own bones. You don't just see the pose in your head, you expect to move him into it and you plan on moving specific controls to achieve this pose. This is the Zen zone of animation. You've achieved it already. All it will take is a little more practice with posing to get that same knowing feeling about any pose you visualize.

12. Take a step back again. Get up and shake it off. When you come back to your desk, load in Objects\chapters\Ch_09\ LifeDrawingModel_06.lwo and see how you did.

Your pose should be very close to the life drawing model's. Based on where you know you deviated from the model in the 10:00 sitting, you were able to correct those parts in this sitting. You've had the time to get the fingers and all the other little details posed just right. Things are pretty darn close. If you had another chance at this pose, you know what you'd do to speed up the process and make it even more effortless.

Here's your chance.

13. Save this scene as a revision, reload a fresh setup, and save it once more as a working scene.

14. Giving yourself only 3:00 (three minutes) this time, pose this guy from the figure alone, using all you've learned from the previous three sittings.

> **Note:**
>
> Animation being the "art of revision" as it were, you will more than likely run into a scenario where you will have to go over and over a scene that was perfectly good the first time you did it. More and more often, directors of animation succumb to the notion of, "I don't know what I want, but I'll know it when I see it, and that ain't it." It's really too bad. It can be disheartening to an animator, and it really only reflects the director's own lack of vision and confidence. Sure, the scene may not be *exactly* what the director had in mind, but does it move the scene forward? Are the characters true to themselves? Is there good acting going on? Do you believe in and feel for the characters? These are the things that once mattered under the great directors of animated works. These are the things that let animators fall in love with their characters and their scenes. These are the things that let that love read fresh and bright through the screen and move the audience to tears and joy. These are things that hopefully will matter again. "Making an animated film is like workshopping a play"? Hardly! Not unless you want to dishearten your crew and blow a whole lot of dough. *Revise to improve, not simply to make different!*

15. Take a step back. How did you do?

16. Select **File|Load|Load Items From Scene**, and choose the scene you saved after your first 3:00 sitting.

17. Using the mesh itself, move the characters side by side.

18. Compare and contrast.

Your more recent scene should radiate a lot more confidence that you as an animator had in posing out the character. You should be able to see your knowledge of the things that will catch the viewer's eye in an instant — the broad strokes, leaving the finer detail work for later (or for an assistant).

> **Note:**
> When you first get issued a scene, a good idea is to spend no more than three to five minutes on each pose as you're roughing in the action. You'll be thinking in broad strokes, seeing if the silhouette is giving you the reading you wish it to. And if you don't like what you see, you won't have that much time invested in the scene. You won't feel compelled to stick with something that could be better if tackled from scratch from a different angle.

9.6 **The "Cool Walk"**

Everyone has got to have a "cool walk," right? Well, this is our character's. Even though this pose is a bit more complex than the last, it's still very straightforward. You should be able to take what you've learned in the previous sittings and nail this pose pretty quickly. Pay special attention to the shifts in weight and the multi-axis contra-posto going on. The character is walking, so he would indeed fall over if he tried to hold this pose indefinitely, but the amount he is off-balance is congruent with the perceived speed of his assumed forward momentum.

Figure 9.8. This pose has a good, clear line of motion (the line or arc that clearly defines the pose or action) running right down the character's head/neck/spine/right leg — a very prominent "S" when seen from the back view. Look for this line (or arc) of motion in all your future poses and scenes.

1. Load up a fresh setup, and save it as a working scene as usual.

2. Using only Figure 9.8, put your character into this pose, giving yourself all the time you need to do so.

You may want to stop after the first three or ten minutes, save a revision of what you've done, and start over from scratch. As I've said, it isn't uncommon for an animator to throw away his first drawings until he gets into the groove of the scene. More often than not, it'll get you a better quality finished pose than you would have had, had you kept right on going from the start.

3. How did you do?

4. Take a step back, take a bit of a break, and then compare and contrast your work with the figure.

    Do you get the same emotional read from your pose as the figure? Do you have the same feeling of a jaunty, rakish lilt to his step?

5. Load in Objects\chapters\Ch_09\LifeDrawingModel_07.lwo. Compare and contrast.

How closely did you match the curvatures of his spine, the placements of his appendages? In the sections on animation, we'll get into improvisation, but right here, we're trying to build your ability to see and to interpret that information into as precise 3D coordinates as possible. Make notes and do the pose again, if you feel the need!

9.7 **Clickin' Them Heels**

This is another relatively simple pose with a strong arc of motion. Work with this the same way you worked with the previous life drawing model. When you're ready to compare and contrast, the model can be found in Objects\chapters\Ch_09\LifeDrawing-Model_08.lwo.

Figure 9.9. Notice how the model's left side is all about stretching. You can almost feel the pull along your own back muscles. The model's right side is all about compression. You can almost feel the pressure along your own rib cage. This gives us a strong, definite arc of motion. We also have one side that is relatively smooth, the model's left, and the other side that is quite interesting. Rhythm and arc of motion make this pose one that reads in an instant.

Pay close attention to the lines of the shoulders and feet. A lot of the strength of this pose is carried in the ways these angles balance straight lines against curved lines.

9.8 Batter Up!

This is the hardest pose we'll get into right now. It has a lot of complex weight balancing going on: Some compound curves and a very tight angle for the right shoulder require a lot more attention to get him into place. The positioning and angle of the pelvis can make the knees a bit vexatious as well.

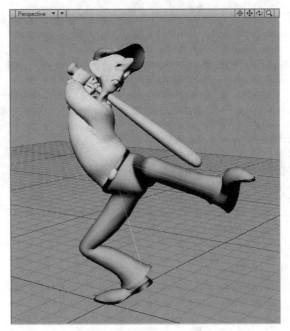

Figure 9.10. I want you to work with just this one perspective angle first. See how far you can get before using Figure 9.11, which has the other two angles you have become accustomed to using.

Turn this model around in your mind first before jumping right in. Try to visualize where the different body parts are in relationship to the others. Do this for a good three minutes before starting to move controls. Look at the figure, close your eyes, and see if you can turn the model over in your mind. Based on what you know of the pose and your experience with the controls, where do they have to be to get the character into that position?

After you've gone as far as you can go just looking at Figure 9.10, compare what you've done with Figure 9.11. Keep working a bit if you need to. Try to get that same moment-before-he-swings kind of feeling to your pose. Break down the angles in your mind, and dissect what combinations of angles and curves, stretches and compressions, arcs and balance make this pose read the way it does.

Figure 9.11. The right and front views of the pose.

When you feel you've got this guy as close as you can by just looking at the illustrations, load in Objects\chapters\Ch_09\ LifeDrawingModel_09.lwo. Compare and contrast how closely you were able to hit the pose. Make mental notes, hide LifeDrawing-Model_09, and make changes. Unhide the life drawing model and see how close your changes brought him to the model's pose.

9.9 **Life Drawing**

Animation truly is only two things: posing and timing. Working with posing the character in this way (life drawing in 3D) is integral to becoming a quick and intuitive animator. It is the only way to get the guesswork of figuring how to get the pose you're looking for behind you. The more life drawing you do, the sooner you will find this stuff internalized, ready for use without even thinking about it. When all of this has been internalized (and when timing has been internalized, too) is when animation can become this wonderful foray into imaginary worlds where you and the character are one for as long as you're working on the scene. This is when animation is pure magic.

Always keep on top of your life drawing. When you have downtime, flip to Chapter 14, where you'll be directed to other poses to work from. Go through magazines and books, and "draw" from both photographs and animation drawings. Take a course on life drawing and bring your laptop! Pose your characters from the people you see around you every day. Movies, television, real life — there is a wealth of knowledge waiting in experiences that don't stand still.

No matter how good you get, always keep up on your basics. Life drawing is a plinth from which the masterworks of animation rise up.

Reviewing Animation Basics

Every animator, no matter how accomplished, always goes back to studying the basics at different times throughout his career. These are the foundations that support all the techniques of advanced animation mechanics. Actually, you could probably get through an entire career just on these basic principles alone, and you could do quite well. Having them at your fingertips, ready to use at a moment's notice without the burden of thinking about them, is what to work for in your studies.

10.1 Timing

As I have mentioned before, animation is really only two things: posing and timing. Timing is the placement through time in a scene of when events occur. Understanding timing is simply understanding how things appear to happen as actions play out over time.

As an animator, you will need a stopwatch. Go out and get yourself a good one (if you haven't already got one). Keep it with you always and just start timing everything around you. Find out exactly how long it takes to do everything you see. Time different people doing the same thing. Time someone getting up from a chair. Time people looking at their watches. Time someone giving you a mean look for being so intrusive. (Time how fast you can run away.) You get the idea.

The only way to understand timing is to take notice of it as it exists all around you. When you get up from a chair, you don't just stand straight up; you lean forward, putting your center of gravity over your feet, and then you straighten. Each of these motions requires some amount of time to complete. There is a pause between the lean forward and the rise. That takes time, too. Explore and understand real-life timings. Once you get a feel for them, start to modify and play with them.

Animé, Japanese animation, makes great symbolic use of modified timings to convey different feelings. Characters hang in the air much longer than they "should" before crashing back down to the ground with an impact that belies their apparent mass. This obvious departure from reality crafts feelings of great power and otherworldliness. Animé uses timing to sculpt how you, the viewer, feel about what you're seeing. Something just barely perceptibly outside of reality makes a viewer feel uncomfortable. Slowed timing appears dreamlike. Often, when timing is artfully used to sculpt feelings, the audience only gets the impact of the feelings, and is unaware of the reasons why.

Timing is also a rhythmic device. Just like music, animation has beats, rhythms, and tempos. You want to keep things interesting for the viewer and not have everything fall on the same timings. This makes a scene read dull and flat. If your scene has keyframes every eight frames, it will read like mush. You have to break up the keys, stagger them, and syncopate them. Get the audience to expect something by setting up a pattern, and then break that pattern (ONE, two, *three*, four, one, two, *three*, four, one, TWO, three, *four...*). Keep them on their toes, when their toes need to be kept on. Slow, languid scenes need this special attention to timing even more than frenetic scenes to keep the audience from losing interest, yet maintaining their dreamy flow.

Timing is also important to get across the relationships between objects and mass. Massive objects don't get moving as quickly as slight ones do, but when they do, they're quite a challenge to stop. A light object or character can leap up from the ground more quickly than a heavy one. Lighter items can seem to float a bit more before gravity begins to exert its effect. Heavier items can seem to be pulled greedily back down to Earth.

Everything you do with timing helps the audience to differentiate between the shapes they see on screen.

Note:

Animation is experience. If you don't live it in your heart, it won't come out of your scene.

Note:

Since stopwatches are such physical objects, and you may leave for work and forget it, I've included a small animation timer on the CD under Extras\AnimationTimer\. There are two files that are, in essence, the same thing. One is just the bare .swf (Flash4 file), and the other is an .exe (executable program) exported as a stand-alone from Flash to run on Windows machines. If you're on a Mac, open up your Internet browser (with the Flash4 plug-in installed from http://flash.com) and drag the .swf file into the open Internet browser window. You can also choose File|Open and browse to the .swf file. You can e-mail this tiny .swf (only 68K) to yourself so you'll never be without a way to time animations! It does frames, feet/frames, SMPTE, and seconds. It converts between these formats, and you can use it to do some rudimentary frame-offset calculations. (Click on the "Help?" icon to find out more!)

10.2 Squash and Stretch

Squash and stretch is one of the keystones of good animation. Even the most realistic of animations needs to have some element of squash and stretch in it. Animation is all about the emotional impact of experience; you alter the outline of a thing (not the volume) to give the audience a visual interpretation of the forces impacting it.

1. Load Objects\Props\Ball.lwo into Layout.

2. Make a 21-frame sequence (from 0-20) where the ball bounces similar to Figure 10.1.

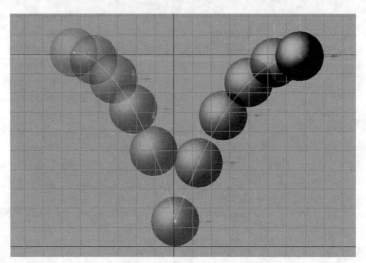

Figure 10.1. This bouncing ball has good timing to it: It accelerates toward the ground, springs back up, then decelerates as it nears the top of its rebound. The timing may be good, but it has no squash and stretch to it. (You can find the scene to study in Scenes\chapters\ch10\Figure_10-01.lws.)

In order for the ball to really give the impression that the force of gravity is pulling it down to the ground where it impacts and springs back up again, we have to push reality a bit.

Figure 10.2. Just using stretch and rotate to put rudimentary squash and stretch on the ball gives a visual read to the forces acting upon it. (See Scenes\chapters\ch10\Figure_10-02.lws.)

> **Note:**
>
> A more believable take on this would be to use bones to flatten the ball around the area of impact where it hits the ground. I also like to stretch objects into wedge-like shapes with the point of the wedge leading the eye into the coming motion.

3. Now, using whatever techniques you'd like, add some squash and stretch to your bouncing ball scene.

> **Note:**
>
> LightWave, having introduced Bezier interpolation for splines, has made it a whole lot easier to get nice, smooth motion curves. Don't be afraid to drop the old TCB splines in favor of these more controllable curves. However, because you have more ability to noodle with the Bezier handles, you can more easily throw things out of whack. I've also noticed that Bezier splines almost always need some kind of adjustment and are rarely interpolated correctly (for my tastes) by default.

Compare what you've got with Scenes\chapters\ch10\Figure_ 10-02.lws if you need to. *Always remember to preserve the volume of the object*. When you squash in Y, the object has to expand in X and Z in order to preserve the mass we perceive it to have. We're not getting rid of mass, we're displacing it. (Think of a water balloon. When you squeeze or stretch it, there's still the same amount of water in it — until it pops, that is.)

Note:

Something to be said about working with spline curves is that they should have the absolute minimum number of keyframes needed to keep the item moving, and they should be as elegant as possible. "Elegant" is a relative term and does not necessarily mean "smooth." The curves should be a linear interpretation of the action. I like to think that the curves should be pretty if the motion is to be flowing and beautiful, or harsh if the motion is to be percussive and violent.

Figure 10.3. Here are the scale curves for my bouncing ball.

> **Newbie Note:**
> Squash and stretch doesn't just happen with entire objects; it happens with parts of objects separately, too. It happens with legs, hands, arms, torsos, fingers, heads — any part of the character that can visibly have a force acting upon it. Drop a weight into our character's arms and his legs should squash to show the impact the sudden introduction of the weight has on his body as a system. As our character's hand whips up to catch a fly ball, his hand and fingers elongate over the course of the frames. The hand travels the greatest distance to accentuate the feeling of speed. (You can think of this like handcrafting motion blur.)

The way our character is set up, stretching the neck, arms, and legs is easy. We pull the controls for the head, hands, and feet away from where the IK chain can reach and things stretch. You can squash individual parts of his body by scaling that individual control; all children of that control will be equally affected (squash the hand and the fingers will also squash). You can even squash and stretch the bones controlled by IK, like the thighs, calves, biceps, and fore-arms, but be careful when doing so. IK calculations are complex, and adding stretching into the mix can make normally dependable IK chains unpredictable.

As always, when you're done squashing and stretching and your character is at rest, make sure you return him to his original, at rest proportions. Multiple instances of squashing and stretching can be going on simultaneously in a complex and explosive scene, but you always need to return the parts that aren't being acted upon by extreme forces to the proportions the audience has come to expect.

10.3 **Gesture and Line of Motion**

Gesture is the most important part of an animation drawing (or pose). Gesture is what makes a silhouette read with purpose and intent and helps the viewer understand the motives behind the character. Gesture is the ultimate distillation of an idea into form (2D or 3D). *Line of motion* is the path that flows through and defines the gesture.

Figure 10.4. Some poses we've visited before, and the *thumbnail drawings* (quick, loose drawings to get the gesture, idea, and feel of a pose — not the anatomy of a pose) that inspired them. Notice how clearly the line of motion (represented by the thick line running through the center of each thumbnail drawing) reads through both the thumbnail and the finished pose.

The line of motion is the "big picture" read we get from a pose. It tells us what is going on and where we should look. It gives us an idea of what has happened a moment before and what to expect to happen next. This line of motion should be clear and readable in all your poses. The more simple and readable it is, the stronger it will be. You can think of it like a graphic design element with arms and legs. It has to telegraph as powerfully as any sales pitch you've ever had. The line of motion has to read clearly, even on the *break downs* (the main poses you have to put between the key poses that keep a character's motion true to the vision you have in your mind) and inbetweens (all the frames that come between keys and break downs).

Lines of motion should be clearly readable and have at least some curve to them, unless you are using that straight, rigid graphic concept for effect (like using the character as an arrow). Lines of motion should also be no more complex than an "S" shape. Our minds generally don't bother to figure out the complexities of a super squiggly line; it just reads as chaos. Unless you're using that chaos for effect, it will have much less power than a strong, simple shape.

Reversing the line of motion keeps it interesting and builds strength in the pose. You can also have parts of your pose reverse their arcs, too, like an arm that reverses the direction of its curve as the hand rises from rest. Reversing a curve is a powerful graphic element; the audience's eye will be drawn to it. Because of this, you should carefully orchestrate these reversals, like a symphonic conductor. Too many reversals in a short span of time will exhaust the viewer. Too many reversals happening all at once over different parts of the character will splay the audience's focus and lose their interest. Through an animation, line of motion is like the bass beat that drives the scene.

> **Advanced Note:**
> The concept of curves and reversals can be extended throughout multiple characters in a scene, paying attention to how each interacts with another to create an overall line of motion that moves over the visual plane of the screen.

10.4 **Anticipation**

Anticipation is leading the eye with motion. You are using a preceding action to lead the audience's eye to what is going to happen next or to an important area that they will need to be focusing on. The concept of anticipation really comes from stage magicians who need you to look at their right hand while their left puts a pigeon into a wineglass.

Filmmaking has always been about leading the audience's eye. (When we take the 3D information and squeeze it onto a 2D plane, the audience needs help so they don't miss what's important.) Lots of motifs have been developed to help catch the audience's eye, from carefully planned editing, to a splash of color in an otherwise dull set, to a breeze that ruffles the curtains right before the hero enters.

> **Note:**
>
> Motion leads our eye. In the wild, a fox can seem to disappear in a field not three feet away if he stands still. When he moves, our eyes lock onto that movement. Anticipation is moving an important part of the character's body to draw our eye to that spot so we don't miss the action that follows. Before some fast action happens with the character's hand, flex his fingers just a little while the rest of his body remains still or in a moving hold (see Section 10.8). You can use "leading the eye with motion" (anticipation) as any other rhythmic device at your disposal. You can tease the audience with it, building patterns and getting them to look in a certain direction expecting more of the same, then wait until their expectations have died down before hitting them with that big knockout punch! (This is classic horror movie timing.)

1. Load your setup scene.

2. Save it as a revision for Section 10.4 in your working directory for Chapter 10.

Note:

The exercises in this book are about to get a lot more subjective. For the exercises that follow, there is no "right" way and there is no "wrong" way. There is only what looks good for the scene. It isn't my goal to turn you into a clone of me. I'm going to do my best to give you the tools and let you decide what you do with them. What it will take to let the exercises truly do their best for you is for you to honestly and humbly appraise what you see in your finished scenes. You have to ask yourself, "Is this something that would fit flawlessly into the best animated feature I've ever seen?" You have to be honest with yourself about the answer. If the answer is "no," then you have to go through both the animation basics and the advanced animation mechanics as checklists to see if your scene has everything in it that it needs. Evaluate your animation from as many different viewable angles as you have time. When all angles read convincingly for your character's intent (and being), your scene should give you a bit of a shudder and an innate knowledge that if you saw this on the big screen, sandwiched by the best animation you've ever seen, it would fit right in.

Figure 10.5. This composite image shows my take on our character anticipating, jumping, and landing. (He "jumps down" before he jumps up.)

Figure 10.6. This is an image sequence of the same animation. (Shown on *twos*, a new drawing for every other frame, running at 24 fps.)

Pose Copying

I'd like to make a concerted effort to not leave anyone behind, even if you've never animated before. There are a few scenes included on the companion CD where you'll be able to do a kind of "moving life draw-ing in 3D," which will get you further ahead in understanding animation than any amount of reading ever will. Remember, though, this is simply *copying* animation. In order to get the full impact of that particular section, once you've done a spot-on copy of the animation, take a short break and go back and (referencing only your imagination) do the animation from scratch. Make it *your* animation. Take what you've learned by copying and push it farther; explore and experiment. You will be building confidence by going through the motions (building "muscle memory") and then using the experience to make your own decisions. Do this with as many of the exercises as you need; you can cover a lot of ground this way.

To do this exercise as an exploration of moving life drawing:

1. From your working revision (created in step 2 of this section), select **File|Load|Load Items From Scene....**

2. Choose **Scenes\chapters\ch10\Figure_10-05.lws**. (In response to the request to load lights as well as objects, choose **No.**)

3. Select the **Thinguy_F (2)** object.

4. Choose **Items|Replace|Replace With Object File....**

5. Select **Objects\Final\Thinguy_LifeDrawing_F.lwo** and click **Open.**

6. Under **Display|Display Options|Schematic View**, make sure **Drag Descendants** is checked.

7. In a Schematic view, with Thinguy_LifeDrawing_F still selected, drag it and its hierarchy away from Thinguy_F's hierarchy so it doesn't get in the way as you work.

8. Change the end frame to 29 (assuming you're working in 24 fps, as both my setup and animation are) and you're ready to start matching my animation, pose for pose, frame for frame.

9. Scrub through the animation. See where the extremes are and copy those poses first.

10. Scrub back through the animation and reposition him to the model where he drifts farthest from the model's animation. (This is in essence what a break down is.)

11. Repeat this process until your character matches the model's animation perfectly.

As you copy the poses, look for the other animation principles going on in the scene as well. There's squash and stretch, drag, follow-through, circular motion, overlapping action, and there's even altering realistic timing to get him to snap up from the ground as he leaps. As you go over these points in this and the next chapter, think back on what you did here. Think not only of how things in my scene worked but how you can make them better!

3. Animate the character anticipating, jumping, and landing.

Note:

If you choose to have your character's fingers clench into fists as I have done, you'll run into that lovely issue of gimbal lock. I had to switch to local coordinates in order to get the *Base bone of the two outer fingers to not leave a gap between themselves and the character's middle finger. The problem is that when you go back to parent coordinates, you find yourself presented with a problem: There are some huge numbers (+/– 90 or more) in heading and bank. If you have already created other keys for these bones where heading and bank are more reasonable (+/– 80 or less), those fingers will look wrong when they inbetween from one keyframe to the other. My solution was to click in the numeric input box for heading, and leaving the value intact, type in "180 – " to the left of the current value (say 117.00). When you press Enter, LightWave figures what 180 – 117 is and leaves "63.00" as the value for heading. I repeated this for bank, and got something that was a pretty darn close approximation of what I had gotten using local coordinates. The only difference between the rotations is that this set inbetweens just fine with a keyframe of 0H, 0P, 0B.

Note:

Before I animate anything, regardless of whether it is for money or just practice, I try to come up with a reason for the character to be doing the action. It helps to get personality into the scene so it doesn't read as a flat and boring (even if it is a well-animated) bit of purposeless action. Before getting into this scene, ask yourself, "Why would this guy be jumping?" Is he startled? Did he win a lottery? Is he avoiding a sweep kick, and why is someone throwing a sweep kick at him (how does he feel about having someone throw said sweep kick at him)? When you're comfortable with the answers to these questions, those answers will read through the scene as the character's intent and purpose. Even if this little snippet is all the world ever sees of this guy jumping, there will be a feeling that this guy has a life, a soul, an opinion about and a reason for jumping. (Think Degas — a slice out of time. You want the audience to feel that the character came from some moment before, and that he's gone somewhere a moment after the scene ends.) Doing this will leave your audience wanting more.

" …which is a kind of integrity, if you look on every exit, as an entrance …someplace else."
— The Player, *Rosencrantz and Guildenstern Are Dead*

10.5 **Drag**

Drag is a pretty simple concept. Hold up a (clean) shirt. Move your hand moderately fast to the right. The bottom of the shirt lags behind your hand. This is drag.

Figure 10.7. As the wrist moves up, the fingers and palm drag behind.

Drag happens on nearly everything in animation. You can make a scene look multitudes better by making sure drag is appropriately applied to hands, fingers, toes, elbows, and heads. It's like squash and stretch in that it may not happen in real life quite as much as we show it in animation, but it gives a visual representation of how an action feels.

If you were to see someone next to you in the café acting with the amount of drag that feels natural on a cartoon character, you'd probably seriously think about changing tables (or restaurants). Drag isn't about what looks real, it's about what looks good.

Sensuous villains tend to let drag and follow-through unroll their every action. ("Oozing charm from every pore, he oiled his way around the floor... " — Professor Higgins, *My Fair Lady*)

Cartoon items can show their mass with respect to other cartoon items by how much drag (and follow-through) they have as they animate.

Almost every animated action, even the most realistic acting, needs to have some element of drag in order to make it read well to an audience.

Figure 10.8. We'll be using this scene to practice drag.

1. Load in Scenes\chapters\ch10\Section_10-05_Setup.lws.

Note:
All of the scenes I'll be handing you to work with are at 24 fps. If you need to practice at another frame rate, feel free to make adjustments accordingly.

Newbie Note:
Newbies, my take on the scene is: Scenes\chapters\ch10\Section_10-05_F.lws. Load items from the scene and copy if you need to!

2. Paying special attention to drag on the fingers and palm, animate ThinGuy reaching up with his left hand and grabbing that floating handle.

As you work, here are some suggestions to bear in mind: Raise the character's hand above the handle first, then let it settle down upon it (don't just go straight for the handle; that's boring). Take a quick read ahead in the next section on follow-through to help you refresh your mind as to what happens when the hand reaches the top of its arc and begins to settle onto the handle. Let the fingers unfold with their own follow-through, but make sure they don't do it all at the same time; try to keep at least a one- to two-frame difference between each digit.

Give your scene as much screen time as you need to have your character's intent play out. Is he scared of the handle? Does the handle represent some kind of long-sought-after goal? Is he going to save the world with this handle (if it were part of a switch assembly) or destroy it?

> **Note:**
> You'll notice that this scene starts on Frame 0. The character's rest pose is on frame –100. With the rest pose at –100, I can still go back to it in case I need to straighten anything out, but it is far enough away from Frame 0 that it won't have too much of an adverse effect on the motion curves (causing the character to inbetween in an unwanted way from 0 to the first keyframe). If you do notice the motion paths going off their intended course between 0 and the first keyframe, you can always set the frame counter at 0, and make a keyframe for all items at –1. (This works best if you're using TCB splines. It doesn't work quite as well for hermite or Bezier splines.) Remember, though, to rekey –1 if you make adjustments to the pose on Frame 0!

3. When you're satisfied with your work, load in Scenes\chapters\ch10\Section_10-05_F.lws and compare your solutions with mine.

Are there any ideas that come to mind as you're watching and comparing the scenes? Can the solutions I came up with for drag, anticipation, or timing help you in making your scene better?

4. Take another pass through your scene. See if there are ways in which it can be *plussed* (pushed beyond where it is) to make it more entertaining or read better.

10.6 **Follow-Through**

Follow-through is the counterpoint to drag. When you hold up that (clean) shirt, and move your hand to the right, then stop, the shirt flows beyond the stopping point of your hand. This is follow-through. (The shirt then settles gently back to where your hand stopped. This is *settling*.)

Figure 10.9. The wrist moves upward, beyond its settling point, then comes back down to rest. The palm and fingers continue to flow upward (they follow-through), even as the wrist begins to settle back down. (The palm and fingers then drag behind the wrist to settle slightly after it does.)

> **Note:**
>
> Some of the subtlety of the animation is lost in the above figure. (There are many things about animation that can be best understood when seen as animation.) Load in Scenes\chapters\ch10\Figure_10-09.lws. As you watch it as a preview or scrub through the frames, watch the graceful, fluid nature of the hand. See how the motion almost unfurls but still has some snap to it as the fingers follow-through. Notice also that the pinky settles first, then the middle finger, and finally the index finger and thumb. (This variation in timing keeps the fingers from twinning and is almost unnoticeable unless you go looking for it, but adds a wealth of life to the motion.)

Figure 10.10. Here's the scene we'll be working with for this exercise. The character's initial pose is almost identical to the previous exercise, but his intent is entirely different.

1. Load in Scenes\chapters\ch10\Section_10-06_Setup.lws.

> **Newbie Note:**
>
> Newbies, between the last couple of exercises, you've learned a lot. I want you to work this scene from scratch with the rest of us. If you're really unhappy with how you do on it, you can always go back and work with posing to my scene. But I think you'll surprise yourself with how well you actually do on your own here.

2. Giving yourself three seconds of screen time to complete the action, I want you to have our character place both his hands on the crystal ball.

We're going to be working with some acting here. The scene is still very much open to interpretation, but I want you to make his movements very fluid and mystical. He is moved by an irritable power he doesn't quite understand but doesn't fear; the blood of his gypsy ancestors runs deep in his veins. He raises both his hands over the scrying sphere and lays them gently, reverently, almost sensuously along its sides to gaze deep into the mists of time.

> **Note:**
> An animator is an actor with a pencil, stylus, or mouse. In this sense, being an animator is the best job in the world.

As you work, focus on all that you know, all that we've gone over so far. Make sure there's appropriate anticipation, drag, and follow-through. With the exception of the scene length of three seconds, you have carte blanche as to how much action to put in there. Make sure that whatever action you do put in reads clearly; that there is enough action to keep the scene interesting (by the end of the scene, the audience will want to see what happens next), but that there isn't too much going on and we overwhelm the audience. (You don't want total sensory overload; people lose interest very fast when they're overwhelmed.)

After you've finished the scene and you're watching it play out before you, ask yourself if your character reads with the same personality you envisioned him to have before starting the scene. Has he remained true to your vision? If not, has he improved? Did you find new ways of making his characteristics show through even more?

This is a scene that should have a lot of fluidity to it. It should really play up the drag and follow-through, not just on the fingers and hands but on the elbows, back, and head, too. You're allowed to go over the top with the whole "mystical" thing on this scene. Ham it up!

> **Note:**
>
> It's a lot easier to pull something back from the edge of over-acting and tone it down than it is to try to get something that is dry and straight to read with more warmth and richness. When in doubt of what the director wants with a scene, I usually err on the side of subtle intensity. I can always pull it back if the director thinks it's too much.

3. Before you go on, jot down on paper some notes about your scene and where you feel things could be improved (there should always be at least some areas you feel can be improved). Take note of the good things going on, too, the things that read well and touch on what we've gone over so far.

4. Save a revision of your scene.

5. Take a look at what answers I came up with for this scene in Scenes\chapters\ch10\Section_10-06_F.lws.

As you watch what I did, keep in mind that there are no "rights" and no "wrongs." There is simply my take on things and yours. Since there is no overall story arc to which we are adhering, we don't have to worry about our guy being in character; all we have to concern ourselves with is: Does the action look believable? Does the action look good? Are there any areas in which things can be improved?

> **Note:**
>
> Scenes\chapters\ch10\Section_10-06_F.lws is just to give you ideas and another viewpoint on how things can be done. The greatest thing you can do for yourself as an animator is to explore as many ways to do a thing as possible. Find as many different solutions to problems as you can. Talk with other animators, get their ideas on things, find new angles and insights, and share what you have learned. The broader the range of experience you can bring to your work, the more deep, rich, and fulfilling it will become, not just to do, but to watch as well.

In watching my take on the scene, are there any ideas you get about things you can do to your scene? Are there bits of the ways I've used drag and follow-through that give you ideas on how you can plus your scene?

> **Newbie Note:**
>
> Newbies, if you feel you could benefit from posing through my animation, take time to do that now. Then retry this scene from scratch.

6. Take another look at your scene. Work from the notes you've made about your scene to bring this animation to a level you feel would fit seamlessly in a collection of the best animation you've seen. Take as much time as you need before moving on.

> **Note:**
>
> As far as quality goes in animation, you only get as good as you let yourself. By that I mean you have to give yourself the time it takes for you to do feature-quality work before you can pare that amount of time down to that which might be given on a TV series. If two weeks is what it takes to bring a certain complexity of scene up to feature-level quality, do your best to make sure you have that time given to you. Eventually, after working and streamlining your processes, you may be able to get a scene of similar complexity done in one week. But being given only one week to do scenes of that complexity time and time again, you can work forever and never reach that level of feature-quality animation. Our brains give to us what we ask of them. We have to ask for that level of quality, and give the amount of time it takes for feature-quality habits to be formed.

10.7 **Easing In/Easing Out**

We've already been doing this in our practice scenes. *Easing in* or *easing out* is simply slowly bringing our character into or out of a motion. We saw easing in in the gentle settling of the fingers in Figure 10.9 and its corresponding animation. The wrist, palm, and fingers eased in to their resting point. In Scenes\chapters\ch10\ Section_10-06_F.lws, the character's hands eased out of their initial pose at the beginning of the animation.

Easing in and easing out are ways of taking the sharp "edges" off of an animation. Care must be taken so that the "edges" aren't smoothed so much that the animation becomes "mush." Use varying amounts of easing in and easing out to build rhythm in a scene. You can allow one part of the character to take more time to slowly enter or exit a motion than another to prevent your character from twinning.

Note:

The best kind of spline curve for easing in and easing out is a Bezier curve. Working with Bezier curves means that you often spend as much time working in the curve editor (motion graph) as you do actually animating. The hard work pays off with a scene that has the barest minimum of keyframes needed to keep the animation on track; you have absolute, precise control of how the curves enter and exit a keyframe.

Note:

You can get a pretty good ease in and ease out effect with TCB splines, too, by moving the Time Slider one or two frames before the keyframe into which you want to ease. You create a key for that item one or two frames before the frame the slider is currently on. The drawback to this method is that you can end up cluttering your keys. Unless you remember which keyframes are the poses and which are the ones you've created to ease in or out, you can accidentally delete the wrong one while making changes to the animation. (Save revisions of your scene to CYA!)

Easing in and out isn't just used for keeping an item from "slamming" to a dead stop; use it to add texture, rhythm, and flavor to a scene. As you act out a scene before settling into animation, note how you enter and exit moves. Bring that kind of characterization into the easing your 3D actor performs in the scene!

10.8 Moving Holds

A *moving hold* is where the character is stationary and one or two parts of him are moving (like an ear or an eye), or when the character moves almost imperceptibly to another pose after settling into his key pose. These are ways in which a character can be kept alive while he isn't performing a *storytelling action* (an action which furthers the story or scene).

To do a moving hold in traditional animation, you had to either animate the parts that did move on a separate layer (the ear or eye that continues to move) or trace back (redraw from the first drawing of the hold) the parts that didn't move. In traditional animation, this can be time consuming. In 3D animation, it is simply a matter of adding a little offset to a control on a future keyframe so the character appears to continue to live while he's "stationary."

One of the biggest criticisms of computer animation, however, is that the characters never stop moving. It is so easy with the splines we have to work with, and the computers to (relatively) quickly handle the inbetweens, that knowing when to lock down a character has now become an issue.

> **Note:**
>
> "Splineyness" refers to the problem of a 3D character always being in constant motion or to the problem of the motion not having enough "crispness" to it. ("I dunno. The motion looks a little spliney.") Don't just accept the computer's interpretation for the spline curves; make sure they are exactly the way you want them to be. Make sure that there is a good balance of "texture" to your animations: soft, sharp, quick, slow, tiny, and broad. Make sure that the storytelling actions read clearly and don't get lost in the moving holds.

Pay close attention to the style of animation you're doing. It may look stylistically best to have your character visibly freeze for a bit or to have most of him freeze while an ear and his whiskers droop as smoke rises from his head. Remember that animation is all about the conveyance of feeling. Stylistic symbolism is a powerful tool for doing so. Make an effort to understand what kinds of symbolism have been used before. Understand the "language" of symbols that audiences have come to accept. This is a language that has been explored and refined since before the 1920s!

> **Note:**
> You may even try setting all your splines to interpret as stepped, so your character stays frozen until you put in a keyframe, break down, or inbetween. This gives your motion the same feel as traditional animation; it's handled in exactly the same way!

If you are working on a more realistic piece, take a look at how real life handles its moving holds. Sure, when we stand, we're not perfectly still, but how much do we actually move? How visible is the motion on screen? If a particular motion is visible, where and how does it affect the form? Remember that movement attracts the eye. You want to make sure that the audience's focus is where you want it at all times. Don't let an overactive moving hold distract your viewer from important action (or lack thereof)!

Study all the great actors you can. Watch how things are done on stage, and compare this with how the best film actors of today use their motion or lack thereof to sculpt an emotional performance. Compare this with the greats of the Silent Age of filmmaking. Masters like Chaplin (who at times did more than 50 takes of a scene to get it exactly the way he envisioned it) made sure that every character on the screen was moving exactly as they intended.

> **Note:**
> Watch films with the sound off. This helps you focus on the action and really see what is going on and how the scenes were crafted. As you watch, ask yourself what these actors were doing to evoke the feelings they do. What were they doing with timing and pacing? How is their delivery of thoughts and ideas? How do they use anticipation, drag, and follow-through?

Use all the resources at your disposal to gain an understanding of how to best use the tools before you. Always make sure that every aspect of your final scene adds to the feeling you want your audience to read, that nothing detracts from it, and that everything that needs to be read, reads clearly.

"Music is the silence between the notes." — Unknown

Chapter 11

Advanced Animation Mechanics

11.1 Silhouette

Silhouette is the first thing our minds read when we look at anything.
This is why it is so vital to pay very close attention to our character's
silhouette as we work and as we evaluate. Not only must it read
strong and true to every feeling and opinion of our character, it must
also clearly carry the intent of his action. (You have to be careful, too,
that parts of the silhouette can't be misconstrued for things they
aren't.) From the silhouette alone, you should be able to tell what's
going on and how the character feels about it.

In terms of reading the character's intent with the silhouette, if
the character is evil, every line of his silhouette should radiate with
villainy. If the character is a lovable goof, every line should read with
pleasant silliness. If the character is sweet and inculpable, every line
of the silhouette should emanate innocence.

The silhouette should have appeal. Audiences have to identify
with a part of what they read in the silhouette and like what they see.
Even if your character is distilled badness, he still has to appeal to
the audience; otherwise, they're not going to relate to him or care
about what he's doing. This does not mean toning things down, not in
the least. This means making sure whatever you do looks cool. The
audience has to read the silhouette and think, "I want to be that" or
"I want to have one just like that!" Granted, appeal can be pretty
amorphous, and what has appeal for one person may not for another.
As ethereal as appeal can be, you know when you've nailed it when
you see your scene and think, "I gotta get one of those!" (Or at the

very least, you feel as if there's a part of you that can connect with what you're seeing on screen.)

Note:

Milt Kahl said it best about appeal: "If you're working on a scene and you either want to be that character, or be with that character, you're doing it right." The magical thing about this is that if you're true to yourself, and you do feel this way while doing a scene, the audience will too.

Newbie Note:

Appeal is a tough quality to nail down. What makes something look appealing and something else look like a "transporter" accident? You could have an entire book on this quality alone. Yet, one thing is certain: When you try your hardest to make something appeal to everyone is when you most often fail. To start off in gaining an understanding of appeal, watch high-quality animation and take note of when something strikes you close to your heart. Try to exactly copy what you see with your own work. The more you do this, the more you will build "muscle memories" for how to achieve certain specific results. This is important because when you're working, you need to turn off the "thinking" part of your brain, and just go by feel. (My mentor, Tom Roth, said that to get a good quality line, you had to stop trying.) As you're working, you have to watch for the moment your control passes a part of your character through a pose that feels right (maybe you've seen something like it before and it worked in that context). You'll quickly build "riffs" you know will work for certain situations and you'll be able to put your brain on "autopilot" and just enjoy the work. Remember, the key is to understand what makes things great by consciously understanding great things!

The strength of the pose still has to ring, crystal-clear, through the silhouette. There has to be enough visual information — *landmarks* (internalized cues all mammals seem to use to identify based on shape, perceived relative distance, and angle) — that the viewer will be able to identify what is going on and relate to his own experience. Landmarks are the shorthand we use to identify a situation at a glance. In a silhouette, they are all we have.

Figure 11.1. Three views of the same pose in silhouette; each has varying degrees of success and drama.

The image at the upper left is a straight-on shot. You can't really tell what is going on. Things are just a mass of rounded shapes. If you didn't know this was a human character, you might not know what you're looking at.

The image at the lower left reads better, though there is still a bit of confusion about what is going on with the character's hands. We get the idea that this is an *up-shot* (a shot from a low angle pointing upward, also known as a *worm's eye view*). (I'm guessing that it isn't a down-shot (over the (left) shoulder) because of the size differences in what I can make out to be the hand masses. Also, his shoulders appear straight; in order to get the extension of what would be the right arm, he would need to rotate his right shoulder in.) We get a feel of the angle of the character's head from the outline of the character's left ear, what we can discern to be the character's right ear, and what we know of the kind of hat it looks like he's wearing. From there, we're able to pretty quickly guess that the character's left hand is outstretched with the palm upward. We get this because of what we assume to be the thumb, the bump above the plateau of the hand, which would most comfortably be created by the thumb being to the left of the hand mass. (We can guess that this is the left hand because for it to be the right hand (palm down to have the thumb on that side) we would need to see indications of fingers along the bottom line of that hand.) The left index finger appears to be outstretched, and the other fingers appear to be curled slightly because of how the angles meet on the underside of that hand. What's going on with the right hand is a bit of a mystery. We can't really tell its placement in relationship to the other hand; its silhouette doesn't give us enough information to accurately guage its size. The right fingers don't give us much either; their definition is hidden in the mass of the hand.

The image on the right has the most information of the three. We see exactly what is going on. The only question we have by looking at the silhouette is which hand is right and which hand is left (something that's fairly minor in the grand scheme of things.) We can all relate (we've all probably done something similar in our lives). So even though we don't know quite what he's got between his fingers, we can see that it must hold some interest because all his attention is focused on it. Because of the landmarks, we can identify in an instant what is going on, and we get immediate ideas as to how this character feels about what he is doing.

Rhythm plays a huge part in how good a silhouette looks. It has to be interesting. It has to hold your attention. There have to be engaging little nooks and crannies, and strong expanses of gently curving lines. (We are referential beings; smooth is only smooth because we have something to compare it with.) And there has to be variance in how big these interesting details are. You need details big enough to grasp the very instant you look at the silhouette, and little particulars that you begin to notice only after several moments.

These rhythmic details will determine how successful your silhouette (and your pose and animation) will be. The idea is that you want to have the viewer want to explore the piece. There have to be large, smooth areas to balance the tiny details. There have to be curves balancing the straight lines. Balance, rhythm, straights, curves, big, small — there's a lot that goes into just this one aspect of silhouette. Remember that the best thing you can do is to find what works (you can hold up a frame from an animated feature and clearly see the difference between that and the average bang-it-out Saturday morning cartoon) and look for what you know should be there making it work.

> **Note:**
> In painting and drawing, the different levels of detail are called the different *reads* of the piece. The big details catch your eye from across the room. The medium-sized details are noticed as you move across the room toward the piece, and there should also be wonderful little details like brush strokes that you only see when you have your nose almost touching the canvas. *None of these sets of details should interfere with the others.* Your ability to integrate elements like these into your own work comes not only from looking *at* other pieces with successful levels of detail, but looking *for* them.

As far as rhythm goes, there's not much to mention about the image at the upper left in Figure 11.1. It's all about semi-definable curves, with only a few straight lines thrown in here and there. There's nothing to catch and hold our attention; as silhouettes go, it's quite forgettable.

The silhouette in the lower left has some great areas of bumpy details, balanced and offset with large smooth areas. The *negative space* (the area surrounding the character which is interpreted to be contiguous even if broken up by background) is carved into interesting shapes by the jutting hands and head. There's a great balancing of the straight line of the (character's) right forearm where it meets the gentle, broken curve of his right upper arm/shoulder at an almost right angle. That strong, pronounced angle is balanced by the wide, powerful curve on the underside of the elbow. (Notice also that the large shape of the bottom of the elbow is actually a curve that becomes a straight line.) There are many smaller, interesting details as well — fingers, ears, curves of the hat. The balance of large details and small, curved and straight lines, angles and arcs makes for interesting and enjoyable rhythm.

The image at the right of Figure 11.1 again has large, languid curves and flats balanced against the quick little curves of the fingers and mouth. There are lots of great little points where curves and straights meet or blend. And the line of the back reads as a powerful straight against the equally powerful curve of the tummy (made up of two lines that themselves could be considered straight). The rhythm of this angle is more complex than the previous two. It is interesting; it has many areas to explore and large, smooth shapes to balance and carry the finer details. But even so, it doesn't quite have the drama that the silhouette in the lower left does. We read what's going on, do a quick exploration of the details, and stop. Our eye doesn't want to re-explore the details, traveling through the composition again and again as it does with the silhouette in the lower left. This is because of the way wedge shapes are used in both compositions.

Wedge shapes are powerful design tools. They lead the eye from their widest part to their tip. In the image in the lower left, the large mass of the torso and arms is a wedge and shoots our eyes over to the detail work of the hands and fingers (especially that pinky). From there, we're caught by the brim of the hat and wedged back into the torso, and our eyes start taking that journey all over again. It is a triangular composition, made up of smaller, directional wedges.

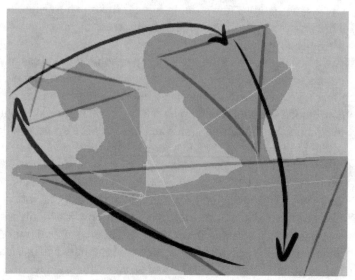

Figure 11.2. The triangular composition, made up of smaller, directional wedges, accelerates our eye around the composition.

The image on the right has wedge shapes as well, but they're less pronounced. The large wedge of the torso mass has its narrowest part down toward the bottom of the screen, leading our eye out of the picture. The head is triangular shaped, but equilateral; we don't perceive a direction in which to be led. The space between the arms is the strongest wedge shape (created from the negative space outside the character); this leads us from the eye-like silhouette of the hand back into the torso, but there is nothing in the torso to hold us there.

Figure 11.3. This composition just doesn't work as well as the previous one. We read what is going on with the character, but after a cursory exploration of the parts, our eye "just sits there."

Note:

The concept of triangular compositions and using directional elements to lead the eye was brought front and center by the Renaissance masters. Look to the works of Rembrandt, Gentileschi, da Vinci, Caravaggio, and Peter Paul Rubens. See what you notice first; turn away, close your eyes, and when you turn back to the painting, what do you see first? Where does your eye move next? Why? Is it a hand pointing? An arm leading toward another area of interest? The way light cuts a silhouette through the darkness or light? Heads that are turned, leading us toward other characters, and pools of light and shadow are subtle, brilliant ways of drawing the audience in and keeping them moving around the two-dimensional plane of the screen. Look for what you know to be there! Understand because you begin to see what was so elegantly hiding in plain sight!

There's a lot more to silhouette than just making the action read clearly. Every scene should be staged and animated so that the silhouettes are instantly readable, dramatic, rhythmic, and executed with attention given to how their design elements impact the viewer.

Newbie Note:

All this information on silhouette may seem like esoteric, artsy-fartsy stuff, but understanding, internalizing, and applying it is what will make your work stand worlds above the rest.

Note:

The view I'd stage the scene from is the one on the lower left. Aside from the strong design and compositional elements, the silhouette doesn't give away everything about the scene at once. It gives enough information that it captures the audience's interest the moment it comes on screen, and the playing out of the scene (through character motion and/or camera motion) will reveal the rest. I like there to be a little mystery in what I do; it draws the audience in, makes them wonder — and in that wondering (if they already care about what's going on), they are in essence participating in the scene. This is the name of the game in any kind of storytelling; get the audience to *want* to know what happens next!

11.2 Exaggeration ("Bad" Poses)

How far can you push a silhouette and still have it work in a scene? It depends on how "realistic" the animation, but it is always more than you first think.

Good animation often has many so-called "bad drawings." These are drawings where the character is exaggerated so much that were you to see just that one frame, it would look seriously wrong. Even the tightly rendered classics have characters moving through poses that are pushed so far that they look weird out of context.

With most of us, it is harder for us to really push something into exaggeration than it is to take something that is a little too broad and pull it back. (And when we first start out in animation, most of us are so self-conscious of doing something "wrong" that a lot of our

Figure 11.4. Extreme poses.

scenes look stiff and boring.) It's okay to push things; we're show-ing the *impression* of experience, not the photographic representa-tion of an action.

There are two basic kinds of exaggeration: extreme poses and "super-mega-ultra-extreme" poses. (We'll just call these "ultra-extreme" poses.) With both, you need to get your character back to his original proportions and expected silhouette as soon as possible. (The audience will buy into a lot, if there's a bit of relative normalcy for them to cling to as madcap action plays out.)

Extreme poses can be moved through for two to three frames. (Anything on screen for four frames or longer tends to cement in the audience's mind.) They heighten the visual impact of the force acting on the character. (This force doesn't have to be physical — remember the Avery cartoons!)

Figure 11.5. Ultra-extreme poses.

Ultra-extreme poses should only be left on screen for one frame (one frame at 24 fps — you may be able to push an ultra-extreme to two frames at 30 fps, but use caution). Ultra-extremes are meant to be felt, not seen! They are meant to run right by, without the audience even being aware that they were ever there, with only the elusive sense of bright, snappy animation in their wake. They can almost be thought of as subliminals. Their power is in the emotional impact, not in their cognitive retention.

Extremes and ultra-extremes show the intense impact that really gets your character moving. You can have crazy shapes and proportions, insane squash, incredulous stretch; you can have your character stupendously off balance. You can break all the rules for the sole purpose of driving a point home (and have fun doing it). Extremes and ultra-extremes can also be used as *smeared* frames (exaggerated motion blur) as a character turns his head ultra-quick. Use them to add sharp, percussive rhythm and snap to your actions; they are the breve of the animated world.

Figure 11.6. This is the scene we'll be working with for this section; we'll be animating him doing a wild take as something spooks him from off-screen left.

1. Load up Scenes\chapters\ch11\Section_11-02.lws, and save a working revision.

2. Animate our character doing a take, but keep him from going into any extreme poses; keep all his poses strictly believable.

The direction for this scene is: Our character is in a haunted house. He can barely see in the gloom and has lost his companions along the way. He's just paused to better hear something behind him when, without warning, a loud crash explodes from off-screen left. The character needs to end the scene facing screen left.

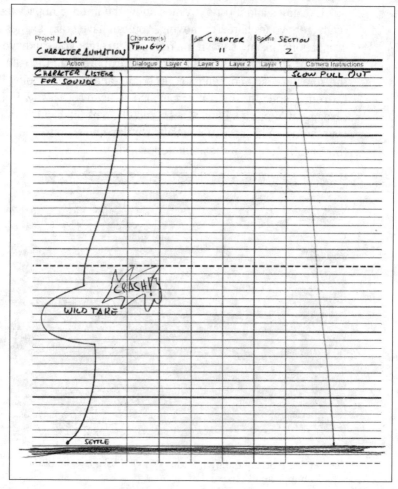

Figure 11.7. The X-sheet (exposure sheet) for scene 11.2.

Note:

X-sheets are mostly used in traditional animation where draw-ings may be repeated or reordered, and different characters (or parts of characters) may be on different levels (or layers) of paper. I still use them for 3D animation because the action line is a great way to get a visual feel for how the rhythms of the action will play out over time.

Reading X-sheets

Reading an X-sheet becomes second nature pretty quickly. Every com-pany you'll work for will more than likely have a different variation on the X-sheet's layout, but the information you need is always there. Project, character(s), act, and scene are self-explanatory. (I've changed "act" to "chapter" and "scene" to "section" to make these headings apply to the exercises we're doing right now. Some animation compa-nies use "sequence" in place of "act.") Every new camera setup (different angle, cutaway, etc.) is a new scene (scene 1, scene 2, scene 1B, or scene 1B-1, if you need to add a scene between scene 1 and 2). Plan your animation well in the storyboarding phase so you don't have to insert a lot of scenes after the planning phase is done and scene numbers have been assigned.

Next, we've got sections for action, where the action is described and (usually) represented by a meandering line. (Usually the action isn't cast in stone; you can push it and pull it to make sure everything reads well on the screen.) Then the dialogue is phonetically spelled out in the dialogue section. (Since dialogue isn't being covered in this book, I'm putting in sound effects, SFX, cues here.)

Then we've got different layers for individual characters (parts of characters) or objects. You can use this area in 3D animation to repre-sent the motions of individual characters or scene elements within the scene. You can also use these layers to choreograph elements to be worked on in a separate scene file to be composited later in post-production if a scene is just too complex to be held in memory all at once.

Farthest to the right is where the camera instructions go. If you were going to have to *dolly* the camera (i.e., move the camera as if it were on a wheeled cart (a dolly) on a track) around the character, *truck in* or *out* (push the camera in or pull it out, again, as if it were on a wheeled cart), zoom in or out, or *rack focus* (pull the focus of the camera using either depth of field controls or with an external post-processing program so that it goes from being in focus to being out, or vice versa), all this information would be here.

This X-sheet is geared for 24 fps. There's a thick, dashed line after every 24th frame, letting you know where each second ends. There are thicker lines every eight frames. These thicker lines help visually break each 24-frame second into three, equal, tractable sections. These eight-frame divisions also help by breaking the scene down into 1/2 foot segments; many studios still measure an animator's output in feet and frames. (Each foot of 35mm film is 16 frames long. This scene is 2' 14 f, it lasts :01.22, or 1.91 seconds, and is a total of 46 frames long.)

Looking at the X-sheet for this scene, we've got the character listening for sounds until the "crash" happens exactly at Frame 27. He does a wild take until about Frame 34. Then he settles until the scene ends at Frame 46. (The folks whose job it is to make X-sheets usually scribble a thick line where a scene ends so you, as an animator, know where to stop. If you find yourself timing X-sheets (also known as "slugging"), remember that you have to take into account any "heads" and "tails" (additional time that is needed to make transitions between scenes when dissolving or using another kind of transition that doesn't instantly cut from one scene to the other) that those in charge of editing the film may need.)

As you work on the scene, examine it from every angle to make sure the character is reading as he should. Make extra sure that the camera view reads solidly (work from the camera's predefined motion).

3. When you get done animating your scene, compare what you did with my version: Scenes\chapters\ch11\Section_11-02a_F.lws.

See if there are any ideas you can work into your scene, such as ideas on timing, posing, drag, follow-through, and silhouette. Take another pass through your scene if you feel you can push its entertainment value farther. Remember to keep things from exaggerating. Keep the silhouettes strong and "realistic."

4. Now, save a working revision as 11-02b; we're going to take what we just did and add a little exaggeration to it!

5. Go back through your scene and push the poses farther. Exaggerate them to the limits of what your eye will believe. (Remember to let the character return to his rest proportions after the impacts that exaggerate him have passed.)

Really push the poses you did in the first pass of this animation; keep them from being ultra-extreme, but really see what you can get away with. Exaggerate everything you've learned so far — drag, follow-through, silhouette, squash, and stretch; make interesting visual shapes that flow well into one another.

6. Again, when you're comfortable with what you've got, compare it with my barely restrained bizarreness: Scenes\ chapters\ch11\Section_11-02b_ F.lws. See if there are any more ideas you get about how you can push things.

If my scene does help bring about ideas of ways you can exaggerate things, go back and work them into your scene before moving onward. We're exploring how far you can push things and still have them read as "believable," which is very different from "realistic." Now's the time to play and have fun! Push and pull, and knock yourself out!

7. When you're content with your scene 11-02b, save a working revision as 11-02c and get ready to really nail a far-out, super-mega-ultra-extreme pose!

Ultra-extremes work best as an accent to a quick bit of action. In our scene, the only place a "bad drawing" extreme would work is in our guy's wild take, around Frames 30 to 32.

Ultra-extreme poses are islands unto themselves. They push what you've already got to the nth degree. They shouldn't affect any of the surrounding frames, so they (usually) can't be inbetweened into; you have to isolate them so they are there-and-gone before the audience has an inkling of their existence. The best way I've found to put in an ultra-extreme is as follows:

8. Scrub through the action to find the place where you want this ultra-extreme; this is where the character either moves the farthest between two frames or comes to the apex of his action.

9. Select the mesh object itself, and create keyframes for Current Item and Descendants on all position, rotation, and scale axes on the frames on either side of the frame that will be the ultra-extreme. (If I wanted to have the ultra-extreme pose on Frame 30, I'd go to Frame 29 and create keyframes for Current Item and Descendants, then go to Frame 31 and create another keyframe for Current Item and Descendants.)

By having the mesh selected, you're creating for it and all of its children, bones and all, keyframes to lock in these poses. You're telling LightWave that even though (in my case) Frame 30 will have a bizarre keyframe, make sure everything still passes through these pre-established poses. You may even need to create these "anchoring" keyframes on (in my case) Frames 28 and 32 as well, just to be sure this bad drawing pose doesn't affect the splines in our animation as it currently is. Be sure to save a revision of your scene before putting in your ultra-extreme pose!

10. Go to the frame that will be your ultra-extreme pose and start pulling controls to throw our guy into the most extreme pose you can think of. Move, rotate, and scale things far beyond where you think they would rationally hold up in an animation.

11. Play your animation through, and check it out. Does that ultra-extreme pose add extra snap to the animation!

12. Load in my version of the scene: Scenes\chapters\ch11\Section_11-02c_ F.lws and give it a play through.

13. Go back and modify your animation if watching mine has given you any ideas as to how to make the ultra-extreme in your animation read better.

Ultra-extremes can take a bit of finessing to get them to work within animation. They need to read as a bit of subliminal smack. They shouldn't jump out of the animation or hold your eye. They should flow right by you, only leaving a sense of added energy in their wake. Once you get the hang of extremes and ultra-extremes, you have yet another tool at your service that can bring added life and entertainment value to even the most mundane scenes.

11.3 Snappy Animation (Modified Timings)

There are times when an extreme or ultra-extreme just doesn't quite give your scene the right plussing you're looking for. Consider altering the timing of things to make them snap! You can remove frames, and you can replace an inbetween with a copy of the held-frame from the immediately preceding key. The name of the game is to get your scene to have the feel of what you're trying to get across, and in this game, there are no rules! If it works, go with it!

Remember the animation in Section 10.4 (Scenes\chapters\ch10\Figure_10-05.lws)? I had the character spring up from the ground a bit more quickly than would be considered "realistic." I've pulled a frame from the part of the animation where he would be pushing off from the ground. This gives him the feeling of snapping up from the ground, like something was there that made him want

Figure 11.8. We're going to be animating a punch for this scene.

to pull his feet from the ground as quickly as possible. ("Yipe!")
Now let's try animating a punch.

1. Load in Scenes\chapters\ch11\Section_11-03_w01.lws, saving
   it as a working revision for this section in your Chapter 11
   working directory.

Figure 11.9. This is the X-sheet we'll be animating to.

As you animate, I want you to try something. Don't have a
keyframe showing the actual impact of the punch. Instead, put a
keyframe a little bit before the impact, and then on the following
frame, key a pose a little bit after the impact. You can have ThinGuy
2 either already arcing backward or still being propelled by ThinGuy
1's fist.

2. Working with the above X-sheet, animate the scene.

Even though we don't actually see a "drawing" of the impact,
we as viewers don't have any problem interpolating what happened.
We see the lead-in and the follow-through, we see the effect
ThinGuy 1's swing had on ThinGuy 2, and by omitting the one
frame detail of actually showing the impact of the punch landing, we
maximize the perceived impact and thrust!

3. Compare what you have with the animation I did (Scenes\chapters\ch11\Section_11-03_F.lws). Even though our styles may be different, the impact of the animation should be very close!

11.4 **Circular Animation**

The concept of *circular animation* says that everything in animation happens along some form of circular, flowing arc. This follows along the same line of thinking as arc of motion and getting the most powerful reading out of a gesture. You can think of circular animation as an arc of motion through time. It is a way of getting the strongest four-dimensional gestural "drawing" from your work.

Figure 11.10. Turning the head from screen left to screen right; linear and booor-ing.

Figure 11.11. Just by adding one break down pose, tilting the head down so that it follows an arc as it turns, you add feeling, heighten interest, and increase the entertainment value of the animation.

Everything (that isn't making use of an intentional linear graphic element) can be plussed by introducing a circular movement to it. Care must be taken to ensure that motions still retain their textures and rhythms; don't let things get so fluid that they turn to mush. You want fluidity that is comfortable for the eye to follow and retains all the elements of good animation.

> **Note:**
> Most motions produced by living beings (on this planet at least)
> are constructed around an arc of some kind. These arcs have a
> kind of smoothness to them because of an inherent desire to
> conserve the energy required to generate that motion; it is a
> needless exertion of energy to apply force to redirect or modify
> the trajectory of an object when you don't have to. When some-
> one throws a punch, the motion of the punch is controlled by
> the unfolding joints of the elbow, the shoulder, and the position-
> ing of the body. When that punch reaches the end of its motion,
> it is pulled back into the body by the same rotational joints; the
> mass of the fist causes the motion to be smooth and (from a
> motion analysis point of view) elegant. Everything is a balance
> of rotation and counterrotation. Our minds accept and under-
> stand circular movements more readily than angular or
> unexpected movements because our minds have evolved to
> quickly read a situation based on silhouette and movement. We
> analyze motions in an instant, projecting where they will go
> next; it is a survival adaptation all animals have. As animators,
> we need to play to this adaptation, unless we are using our
> knowledge to intentionally startle our audience or throw them
> off balance.

Heads, hands, and feet aren't the only things that have circular motion to them. Elbows, knees, torsos, hips, shoulders, every part of the body that moves should be handled with respect paid to circular motion as you create, finesse, and examine your animation.

As you examine your animation, glue your eyes to one part of your character's body, say a knee. Watch that part play through again and again. Does it flow? Does it look believable? In its fluidity, does it still have textures that make it an interesting and balanced part of the whole? When knees compress for a jump, they can start out wide, then swing inward slightly as they propel the character upward, describing a slight ellipse. This is much more interesting than a knee just going straight up and down. Like all things in animation, though, subtlety is the name of the game — subtlety with intent.

> **Note:**
> If you're having a hard time tracking a movement, or if something doesn't read quite right along a series of frames, grab a dry erase marker and put tiny dots on the monitor's glass tracking a specific body part's progress from frame to frame. (Don't do this on a laptop screen, and do make sure that the marker won't hurt the monitor first!) These dots will show you exactly where that body part deviates from the smooth arc of motion, where it accelerates and decelerates, and where it jumps, pops, and wavers. It is a good idea to do this not just from the camera's view but from side, front, and top views as well.

Remember circular motion with every character, but especially when you're working on those characters with poise and polish. It can make both villainy and gallantry read with heightened impact!

11.5 Successive Breaking of the Joints

Back in the early days of animation, when an animator wanted an arm to bend or flex, he simply treated it as if it were a rubber hose. This sort of animation was entertaining for the time, but audiences had to have a high level of suspension of disbelief. As artists became more comfortable with the underlying anatomy of their characters, they began to achieve fluidity with their motions not by treating bones like rubber, but by successively bending the joints connecting the skeletal structures in a fluid, whip-like manner. This is known as the *successive breaking of the joints*.

What this means to us (where it's harder for an arm to bend like rubber than to have it retain its bone structure) is to concentrate on letting motions unfurl, paying attention to all the joints that make that motion possible.

1. Load up Scenes\chapters\ch11\Section_11-05_w01.lws, and then save it as a working revision in your Chapter 11 working directory.

2. Animate the arm in a 40-frame loop (at 24 fps) so that it flows in the same successive breaking of the joints as in Figure 11.12.

Figure 11.12. A wave-like motion undulates through the arm. The curve is led by the elbow, which "drags" the rest of the arm down, then "pulls" the rest of the arm back up. All the joints operate well within their normal ranges of motion; this is the successive breaking of the joints.

3. Compare your work with my final scene when you're done (Scenes\chapters\ch11\Section_11-05_F.lws). Make adjustments to your scene until the motion is smooth and fluid.

Successive breaking of the joints fits into the same category as circular motion. It helps things read better, it shows attention to detail, and it heightens the entertainment value of your scene. These finesse points give "high-dollar" animation the feel it does. By understanding how to artfully incorporate them into your work, the animations you create will read with that level of class too! (Observe, dissect, understand! Continue with the practice scenes in Chapter 14 and watch as the subtle complexity of your work grows in leaps and bounds!)

11.6 Overlapping Action

Overlapping action is an extension of the principles of follow-through. Not all the bits of a character start moving at the same time, and not all of them come to rest at the same time. Each part of a character has its role to play in balance, momentum, and acting. Having each part of a character following its own natural timings adds up to a convincing, overall fluidity of movement.

Figure 11.13. Here is our character doing a bit of a take as he turns around. Technically, these poses would work, but because all his parts strike their extremes at the same time, this appears robotic.

Figure 11.14. This is the same action but with different parts of the body pulling others into motion in their own time.

In Figure 11.14, the hips start the movement, dragging the upper torso which, in turn, drags the head and hands. The torso then rolls upward as he straightens then settles back to look. Each part of his body reacts in accordance with its own mass, dragging and following through with respect to its own points of rotation. This set of frames reads with more life and fluidity than that in Figure 11.13.

All animations, even the most realistic, will require attention to at least subtle overlapping action. Acting through a scene beforehand and really getting a sense of how it feels to perform the action will help you to understand the order in which things move and settle.

1. Load in your setup scene, and save it back out as a working revision for Chapter 11, Section 6.

2. Giving yourself 20 frames (in 24 fps), recreate the animation from Figure 11.14.

3. After you're done, compare it with the animation from that figure (Scenes\chapters\ch11\Section_11-06_F.lws).

4. Make any refinements to your scene you might need to get your motion to express the same fluidity of overlapping action.

11.7 **Entertainment Value (Presentation)**

Entertainment! That's the business we're in, isn't it? Whether it be video games, television, or films, our job is to tell the story we've got to tell in the way that is going to be most interesting to the viewer. Even a "ready animation" (just some idle movement a character in a video game does while "waiting" for the player to decide what to do next) should be interesting to watch.

We must do what we do not only to the best of our technical ability but also present it in such a way that it leaves the viewer wanting more! This is entertainment value. Viewers must feel that they've gained something by sitting through and watching what we've done. (Or as Frank Thomas said, "Would anyone other than your mother like to see it?")

> **Note:**
> A good storyteller can make even the most humdrum of stories riveting with the way he tells it.

When you get a scene to work on, go to a quiet place and think of all the unusual ways to get that story idea across that will be entertaining to watch. You, the animator, are the storyteller. You have to make sure that the characters continue to develop and show insights about themselves as your scenes progress. You have to make sure that the acting is believable and approachable. You have to make sure that the audience will want to know what happens next. You have to make sure that what you're doing is entertaining! And you have to do all of this and still make sure that your scene fits in as a seamless part of the unified whole, choreographed, cast, and orchestrated by the director.

In the exercise for this section, we're going to take a bit of ho-hum action (the character removing a bit of lint from his sleeve) and present it in three completely different ways. Give yourself as much screen time as you need to get the idea across. You may pose the character any way you like; I just want three of the most unusual, entertaining ways anyone might remove lint from his sleeve. These can be three completely different characterizations for each of the three takes, but I want this guy's being to show through every move in which he gets at that bit of lint!

For the first two passes, go as hog-wild as you'd like, but for the third pass, I want you to have his attention elsewhere, not on the lint, and still have the removal of said lint be unique and entertaining. This last foray will be an exploration into what is called secondary action. *Secondary action* is something a character does that doesn't really tell the story of what's going on in the scene. The scene could function perfectly well without it, but how the character does this action speaks volumes about his personality. In live action or theater, it would be considered a "throwaway" line or action. If the audience catches it, great, but it should in no way overtake the primary storytelling intent of the scene. Subtlety is power! Your strength and confidence as an animator, and the character's life and energy will show through more clearly if your action reads with subtlety. Think easy power! Think, "Yeah, sure... if you get it, you get it. I know I'm good. I'm beyond having to prove myself."

It will help in this final take to have some sort of mental story or dialogue going on. Think of some reason for him to be focusing elsewhere, brushing at a bit of lint as he does so. You've got to get inside his head, get inside the scene itself. You've got to act it out in order to better understand the whys of his actions. You've got to understand his feelings about his actions — what he's trying to show, what he's trying to hide.

1. Load in your setup scene, and save it as a working revision for Chapter 11, Section 7.

2. Do two separate takes on our character removing that bit of lint from his sleeve, making them the most unique and entertaining ways for getting at a bit of lint you can think of.

3. Do one more take on the lint removal thing, but this time let it be secondary action, something that isn't the primary storytelling point of the scene, but lends depth and detail to who this character is and how he feels.

How do your scenes hold up? Do they have entertainment value? Are they presented in ways that make their storytelling strong? How's your action? Is it good animation? Does the character feel like he's got an opinion on things, a reason for being, a soul? Can you read an inner dialogue through watching your character's actions? Do you care about seeing what happens next?

Rework your scenes if necessary, honing points and making them as strong as they can be.

11.8 Acting, Not Action

What we're working for is acting, not action. It is important for you to hone and finesse all the finer points that make animation great. But these things are learned, then forgotten so that the character lives and flows freely through you, not from you.

> **Note:**
> Good animation comes through you, not from you.

At first, you'll have all these things to remember — squash and stretch, drag, follow-through. You'll be asking yourself, "Is my character twinning?" Often, it's easy to lose that crystal of magic amid what really amounts to a lot of focused work. It's like learning a piece of music or a dance. You go through a period of time where you're just worried about not hitting a wrong note or making a misstep. Then, after you get all the bits and pieces of it down, you can go on "autopilot" and let the feelings the piece fills you with flow out through you as you do what you do. You become simply another observer to the beauty your hands or feet just happen to be creating.

Note:
This is actually the secret to all art, really (if art did have such things as "secrets"). You learn a piece of classical music. You hear it on the radio and you think, "Man...that doesn't sound anything like what I'm doing. I know I'm hitting all the right notes, but..." What you have to do is to pay attention to how the music you're hearing on the radio makes you feel as you're listening to it. Then, when you're back at the keys playing, replay those feelings you felt while listening to the concert pianist. Your music will suddenly sound a lot more like what you heard on the radio.

When you get done with a scene, take a break. Heave a sigh, and walk away for a bit. Get a latte or a cup of herbal tea. Do something that will take your mind off the long, tense time you just spent on this labor of love. When you feel like you've "walked it off" sufficiently, go back to your scene and look at it as if you're seeing it for the first time.

Ask yourself the all-important question, "Is this character alive for me?" Does he follow the direction of the scene and add to the story in ways that seem as believable as they are inevitable? When you acted this scene out, is the feeling you got inside the same feeling you're getting now as you watch it?

Remember, animation being the art of revision, if something isn't working, if the character isn't emoting, breathing, and living, break down what the issues are and revise. (Usually there's just a couple of things that when they do drop into place, the animation seems to do a 180; what was "just not coming together" suddenly is "totally spot-on!")

Animation is forever. The beings we're creating will live on long after we're gone. They'll continue to touch people with the dreams we dreamt while they were being brought into this world. Do everything you can to make their lives worthy of living.

11.9 The Importance of Thumbnails (Planning Your Scene)

When you get a scene, whether it has been storyboarded or not, before you start animating you need to take the time to do small thumbnail drawings of all the poses that will tell the story of your scene. These quick, loose drawings don't have to mean anything to anyone but you. They only need to show you what's going on during the scene, how the character feels about what's going on, and his outlook on making it through (hopefully) in one piece.

Try to think like a comic strip artist as you do these quick little drawings. You're trying to distill an expression or an attitude into a single drawing. These drawings will have a strong line of action running through them, and their silhouettes (it is often a good idea to shade in the thumbnails) will read with the full impact of the idea being portrayed.

Figure 11.15. Here are some thumbnails for a scene in which the character is running with a flashlight, slips on a banana peel (does anyone slip on banana peels anymore?), and lands flat on his back.

Yes, the drawings in Figure 11.15 are rough; they are just a loose collection of circles and lines that don't have to mean anything to anyone but me. Yes, this is how loosely I work when I'm doing my thumbnails for my scenes. It took less than two minutes for me to run through three different takes on this scene; there's so little time invested in the drawings that I have no qualms about scrapping the whole idea and starting over. In doing three (or more, if necessary) versions, I break through the "Man, I have no idea how I'm going to handle this" phase of ideation. The first set was a mark on the wall. The second was closer, and the third was what I wanted; it feels like I felt when I acted it out. (Ow ... just kidding!)

Figure 11.16. These are the thumbnails I'd show to a client. (I redrew what I had done for myself, tightening up in the process. Like I say, thumbnails don't usually mean anything to anyone but you; this set should clarify what's going on in the previous set.)

Note:
Thumbnails (storytelling drawings) aren't the most extreme drawings; they're the ones most comfortable for the eye to settle on.

Note:

No matter how "artistic" a client may think he is, never show him anything he would have to use his creativity to figure out. This goes for thumbnails, animations-in-progress, whatever. Most often, clients just won't get it and start complaining about how it just doesn't seem to be working the way they'd hoped. Never mind that you told them this is just a rough draft. Or, on the other side of things, they could get grandiose ideas that there's no way you would have time to implement. It's a good idea to only show the client things that leave as little room for interpretation as possible.

These thumbnails help make sure you have the best presentation possible and the most entertainment value to your scene. (It's so much easier to erase a quickly scribbled line than it is to rekey a pose.) You're thinking out loud, throwing ideas out to see what sticks. Do a couple of quick versions and see which one reads best. (For some reason, I find it's either the first set or the third set that works best.)

Make sure your character's attitude reads through every thumbnail. Even if he's only walking across the room to get the door, his attitude and his opinions about getting the door should remain front and center. Act your scene out. Sit. Ponder. Doodle. Let yourself open up to the flow of good ideas that come through you.

Thumbnails will also vastly reduce the time it takes to get a good pose in 3D. When you do sit down with the software, there'll be very little guesswork as to how this guy should be posed out. You'll probably find ways of pushing that loose, little drawing further, making it read better, stronger, and more on character. In that quick little scribble, you have a signpost that tells you how to quickly get to where you want to be. When your character reads with the same vibrancy as in that loose collection of circles and lines, you'll know you're there and you can move on!

11.10 **Pacing**

As the number of things you can do as an animator increases and as you add "riffs" to your repertoire, it is only natural to want to show as many of these awesome little things as you can in a scene. Remember … easy power. If you give to the scene what it needs, and you do this with ability that looks effortless and natural, people will just assume that you could do anything you wanted to. You just (wisely) chose to show only what you needed to and you left your audience wanting more.

You don't want to rush the scene. You want to give the acting poses (the storytelling poses you thumbnailed, the poses that are comfortable for the eye to settle on) enough screen time for the audience to read them. You want the audience to be able to see the expressions change. You want to give the character time to think, and the audience time to digest.

You want to have the flow of action in a scene be strong enough that you keep your audience's attention too. (If you will eventually have music scored to your work, music can extend an audience's attention, as can waiting for the music to return — the "silence between the notes"). Achieving this balance between keeping the scene moving and giving the acting time to connect with the audience takes practice. Doing the work and revising until it fits within the scene length requirements and still carries this power is what will help to hone your own internal sense of pacing.

Watch animation from the great masters of the art. See what kinds of rhythms they use and what kinds of emotions those rhythms create. Fill the well. Practice and make it yours. You are working in a medium where rhythm drives everything. Know beforehand the kind of rhythmic feel you want for the piece, and then stay true to your vision. Let that vision read clear and strong to the audience.

Taking a Scene from Start to Finish

Okay, so now you've got a scene assigned to you; what do you do? We're going to work here as if it came through the channels of a large production, where you've got departments, PAs (production assistants), PMs (production managers), APMs (assistant production managers), and the whole nine yards. But you can make these steps work whatever the size of your production, even if it's just you and your trusty computer at your side. It's all about breaking what can be a formidable task into small, manageable, "bite-sized" bits.

12.1 Do Your Homework...

Whether this is your first scene in this production or your one-hundred-and-first, you need to make sure you do your homework before jumping in with both feet. There are few things worse than doing some beautiful, brilliant work and having the director come by and tell you that, yes, it is beautiful but it doesn't fit with what the story needs, or that it doesn't link up with the previous and/or following scenes.

By "doing your homework," I mean "research." Go back through and reread the part of the script that contains this scene. Walk around and look at the storyboards. Find out what got the character(s) into this place to begin with. Find out how they feel and think about being in the situation they are in. Find out how they plan to move onward, out of your scene.

Look at animations that have been completed and approved that go around your scene, and watch the *Leica reel* (the timed story-boards made into a movie, also known as an *animatic*). Get a feel for the timings and pacings of scenes that have already been finalized. Understand your character's timing, pacing, posing, and acting so you can begin to feel the same things he does.

Get a clear picture of things before going to the director. If you have any questions about the scene, curiosities, comments, whatever, write them down! A meeting with a director can be a whirlwind. Make sure all the questions you can think of pertaining to your character's development through this particular scene are asked. You don't want to get back to your desk and remember those one or two (or ten) vitally important questions that just happened to slip your mind during the conversation.

12.2 Talk with the Director

After you've got a clear vision and feel for the scene, sign up for time to talk with the director. Have your list of questions handy, and check the items off as they get talked about. Make notes! Do everything you can to retain what you learn about the director's vision for the scene. The director is counting on your abilities as an actor and an artist, but in order for the show to succeed, it has to have one, clear (good, confident, worthy, etc.) point of focus from which the entire story radiates, and that is the director.

Listen to what he has to say. If you don't understand something, ask him to explain it another way. (Did I already mention taking notes? Unfortunately, you may need to *ahem* "remind" a director of an agreement on characterization or planning the two of you made earlier.) A good director will always listen to what you have to say, too. Talk through your feelings about timing, pacing, and acting. Make sure the two of you are seeing the same vision for the scene and its place within the film.

12.3 Scene Planning

If there is a background already built for you, or if your character is going to be interacting within pre-shot footage, talk with the scene planning people about how your character will interact with and within it. Get a clear vision of how you see your character moving within the background. Make sure that the elements that are there permit his freedom to interact and emote in character and to fulfill the requirements of the scene. If it looks like your acting and the background may clash, talk to the scene planning people about it.

If you're the one who has to build the background yourself, sketch out a floor plan and notate your character's blocking. Find out where the camera will stand and where you're going to have to hang lights to get the desired shot and lighting. Look to see if there are going to be any elements of the background conflicting with the character's movements or drawing attention away from his acting.

> **Note:**
> The rule of thumb I use for nearly everything — animation, character design, set design, lighting design, you name it — came from a character in the film *L.A. Story*. Trudi (Marilu Henner) was telling another woman how she coordinates her fashion accessories. (Bear with me now.) She said that when she thinks she's ready to go, she turns away from the mirror, then turns back quickly. The first thing that catches her eye, she removes. (I would suggest doing this several times.) What she ends up with is a complete, contiguous ensemble with everything working together. As weird as it may sound, this is the very best technique I've found for analyzing nearly anything artistic. If it jumps out at you, if it stands out abruptly, it is like a jitter in an otherwise smooth curve. Everything should work as a unit — even the things that are meant to draw your attention!

If you are setting up your own background, there's one key bit of advice I'd like to give you on lighting and setting up your camera: Pretend you're on a practical (real) set. Pretend you've got to light it with real lights and that you're bound by the same physical limitations with which to shoot. We, the audience, have grown accustomed to certain conventions established by both still photography and motion pictures. Working within these conventions, we more easily form a connection with the viewers because they are preconditioned to understand the "language" you're using. This can be said for "steadycam" shots, too — save the flying camera for the high-dollar, mega-impact shots! (Hitchcock shot most of his suspense films from medium and long setups. When he hits you with the one or two close-ups in the film, those shots make you jump out of your skin because you haven't been numbed to close-ups!)

> **Note:**
>
> If you can tell a story with the camera left, unmoving, on its tripod, you really understand storytelling and the story you're telling.

> **Note:**
>
> I use mostly shadow-mapped klieg lights (spotlights) to light my scene; they're what I'd have if I were on a practical set. I use spotlights and distant lights (set to not cast shadows) as if they were *shinyboards* (also known as *skimboards*), bouncing diffused lighting where I need it. I'll use the occasional light with a negative intensity to tone down an area, as if I'm using a flag to block light from hitting an area. I use intensity falloff for lights and an almost imperceptible bit of black, nonlinear fog to enhance drama and "realism."

Note:

There's only one real trick to understanding good lighting: Watch what works, and figure out what makes it do what it does. I love *chiaroscuro* (a method of painting with strong lighting and shadows) and film noir, and my lighting styles reflect this. In beginning photographic portraiture, you learn that in order to make any object look three-dimensional, you hit the subject with a warm light on one side and a cool light on the other. (Subtle variations of "white" will do; you don't have to punch the saturation unless you're going for a specific effect.) One light should be brighter than the other. That's it! That's all you *need* to do, but there is more you *can* do. You should hit your subject with a light that makes one part of his outline brighter than the background he'll be in front of (a "rim" or "kick" light). Keep in mind the color of the "ambient" light, and use a shadowless klieg to fill in any overly dark areas. (I turn ambient lighting off unless I'm using radiosity.) We expect ambient light from above to be blue, reflected from the sky. We expect ambient light from below to be golden or green, reflected from the ground or grass.

Now that LightWave has radiosity and caustics, we can think a lot more like a traditional director of photography when constructing our sets and lighting them. Make sure that the final imagery (colors, tonality, "pools of light," sharpness or softness of design elements, curves, angles, shapes, and compositional balance) works as a whole to convey the mood and direction of the scene. Pay attention to silhouette and design elements, just as you will with your character when he starts interacting within this environment. Areas of highest contrast (value, color, and saturation) should be where the character will move, drawing the audience's eye to these areas instantly. The composition of the background alone should give you an instant feel as to what is going to happen in the scene.

When you're satisfied with how your background will work with your character to facilitate the best, most riveting presentation of your scene, it's time to move on!

12.4 **Visualize**

Okay, now's the time to go to that quiet place and let yourself slip into the world of your character ... into his thoughts ... into his life. Turn off the phone. Put out a big "Do Not Disturb, Under *Any* Circumstance .... THIS MEANS YOU!" sign and let the rest of the world go on without you for just a little bit.

This is where you get in touch with the character as he exists *inside* of you. Yours is a unique viewpoint on his existence, his thoughts, his feelings, his actions, his dreams, his desires, his plans for the future, and his laments about the past. Within the quiet space of your own mind/heart, you can let go of your own past and take up his. Let your mind wander ...

Imagine the first thing he did when he got up that morning. How long has it been since he's eaten? Has he ever been in love? How does it feel to have those hands, that face? Why do you dress as you do? Does it make you feel safe? Does it remind you of someone you looked up to in your life? These may seem like esoteric questions, but questions like these are the keys to opening the doors inside yourself and letting you live as your character for the length of time you are working on this scene. And that is *exactly* what you must do! You have to live his scene. Every subtlety you feel, every nuance that would touch your own actions having lived a life like that, being in the surroundings he is, every minute detail breathes volumes of life into this character and this scene. It is through these details that the audience will share their own private selves; it is through these private details that the character gains his own life.

Wander back in time, back in his time. Live the days of his youth, his explorations, his sorrows, his joys. Experience the entirety of his being as a cloak that you wrap around yourself and get lost in. Know the decisions in his life that have brought him to the point where your scene begins.

Now, allow the scene you will work with play out before you. As you let the scene unfold before you, remember how you feel about what is going on. Remember how it feels to move as you do. Remember your ideas, your thoughts — both those open to others and those open only to yourself. Remember how the whole experience feels to live, continuing out the end of this scene and slightly into the next.

> **Note:**
>
> There's a thing about actors, especially good stage actors. I'm not talking about the grandiose ones who fill an auditorium with their overblown presence. I'm talking about the ones who make you believe they're really there in that moment. There are many, *many* things you can learn by studying these actors (and studying acting itself), but what I'd like to make note of is that no matter how many times a day they may have already gone through the same material, you feel as if it is only just now happening to them. You feel as if this set of events is only now coming into being, and that their responses to these events are natural and inevitable. They are merely continuing to make the same kinds of decisions (on a moment-by-moment basis) that they've made all their lives, the same kinds of decisions that have brought them to this point right now. The "actor" may know what happens at the end of the line or at the beginning of Act 3, but the character lives in this one moment as we all do.

The reason I'm asking you to remember how it *feels* to experience his life is that for most people, it is hard to remember every nuance of things that happen as they happen. But feelings, kinesthetics, and empathy carry much more than just positional or temporal information. They are the doorways through which we can live again, in all the detail, the experiences in our past. When you're looking at your thumbnails, your action line on your X-sheet, and at your animation as it takes shape before you, you know if what you're looking at gives you the same feeling as what you experienced in your visualization. All the myriad of subtle cues, the volumes that would fill shelves upon shelves with information, all boil down to a single thing: a feeling.

There's not enough room in this book to cover all the different techniques for letting yourself live as the character with which you work, and still cover all the other information that needs covering. I can, however, recommend two books to you that have helped me more than words can ever say. They are: *To the Actor* by Michael Chekhov and *Audition* by Michael Shurtleff. I cannot recommend these books enough. If you are serious about becoming the best actor/animator you can be, get them, study them, and practice them.

"…they are two sides of the same coin…or, being as there are so many of us…the same side of two coins."
— The Player, *Rosencrantz and Guildenstern Are Dead*

12.5 Thumbnail

While your "Do Not Disturb!" sign is still out, sketch out your ideas. Do this as quickly as you can, still preserving as much of the echoes of your visualization as you can. When you get done with one set, do another and another. In the process of doing this just-being-in-the-moment drawing, not trying to "get it right" or "perfect," you again link with the feelings you felt as you lived that character.

All you're trying to do is to put into a kind of shorthand the things you'll need for your mind to travel back to that place where you walked with his feet, touched with his hands.

> **Note:**
> Small, fluid, strong, these drawings are your pitons; they'll keep you from falling.

12.6 **Exposure Sheet**

Before you go take down that "Get lost, Punk!" sign, reach for your exposure sheet. Use the action line to make a visual notation of the timing of the actions you've just been living. (If your project doesn't use X-sheets, I've included a 24 fps sheet in Extras\X-Sheet.jpg.)

Jot down this four-dimensional shorthand for the character and any other items that may be moving or interacting with him. Notate any camera motions you envisioned (clear them with the director, and the scene planning and editorial departments before putting them into play though). When you run your eyes down the sheet at a presumed 24 fps, you should get a feeling that rings true to what you felt in your visualization.

> **Note:**
> The action line of your exposure sheet is your four-dimensional thumbnail.

12.7 **Animate**

Using all you've learned, all your skills, and all your easy power, hold the feelings you felt when you lived this scene close to you as you work. With your thumbnails and your action line, you've got a lot of the work of animation done already. You can let your mind wander back to that visualization, and let the feelings you remember help you to fit the hands into just the right shapes, sculpt the spine into just the right arc, and swing the knees into just the right angle. When what you see before you resonates with what you feel inside you, you know you're there.

> **Note:**
> You are an actor. You are the character. Enjoy the luxury of being him for as long as you're working on this scene!

12.8 Examine

Look at your animation from all angles, not just the camera angle. Make sure that each part reads plausibly and that the feelings you get when you watch it are the feelings you felt when you visualized how it would be to live that situation.

Let the animation play at speed, looping again and again. Let your eyes focus on one part of his body as the scene repeats itself. If there's something in the motion of that part that catches your eye, slow it down and examine it. Track its movement with dry erase markers; is the motion exactly as it should be from all angles? (Sometimes a "pop" is caused by a part of your character moving improperly in Z, with respect to the camera, when the other two axes are fine.)

Focus on each part of your character in turn, and then watch your character as a whole. Are all the parts adding up to a sum that radiates life and believability? Walk away from your scene for a while; take a break. When you come back, look at it with fresh eyes. Does anything jump out that didn't before?

Examine, revise, repeat. Do this until the scene fits the criteria both you and the director agreed upon. Do this until the feelings you get from looking at the scene ring true with what you felt when you, yourself, lived the same experience.

12.9 Critique

So, now you're at a point where you want to get comments on your work, comments from a fresh point of view. Make sure that you seek comments from someone who knows what they're talking about, and that this someone knows how to look at partially completed animation (if your work is still a work-in-progress). Hopefully, these are all the same person, and hopefully, this person is the director.

Note:

Learning how to accept criticism is important. It is an acquired skill, but it is one that everyone can learn. Remember that animation is a team effort; what matters is the piece as a whole. But also remember to consider the source. If you just asked your cube-mate for a critique, and he mercilessly shredded all your hard work, ask yourself if your animation, which you thought was pretty darn good, threatens him or his position within the company. (Unfortunately, the more you stick your head out, the harder some people try to lop it off.) Seek criticism only from those people qualified to understand what they're looking at. Seek critiques only from those who genuinely have your and the production's best interests at heart.

Have your notes ready for when the director (and his entourage of yes-men and yes-women) comes to call. Refer back to your notes if something doesn't quite jive with what you thought he said the last time you spoke. Be prepared to talk about where you are with the scene, where you see it going, how you feel about where it is. Talk with him about how it makes him feel. Jot down any notes, and make sure you understand what he's saying. If you feel you nailed this scene spot-on, and the director isn't quite happy with it yet, talk about his vision for this scene and how it fits in with his plan for the sequence. (Compromise is not capitulation, but it is he, the director, who must be accountable for the vision of this production after all is said and done.)

If your studio doesn't incorporate *dailies* (where they call together all the animation staff or the entire company to watch what was completed the previous day or week), see what you can do to encourage the powers that be to implement them. This is the best way I know of to boost the quality of a production. Not only is everyone more inclined to do their absolute best on the work they did that day because everyone they work with is going to be seeing it, but everyone shares ideas on how to solve problems from watching each others' works-in-progress. If you do have dailies every single day, you really get to see how a scene evolves, you get to see how the other animators think and solve problems, you see how they develop their ideas. (I've also found that things I might not have noticed to be wrong just make my skin crawl when I have others watch my work in dailies. This is a great flag for problem areas!) The morale boost, the camaraderie, the learning that goes on in the showing of dailies is something worth looking into.

12.10 Revise

Make it as perfect as you can. Don't let anything that isn't your absolute best effort leave your desk. (Now and then, everyone does something they aren't completely happy with, but make sure you put every effort into making it the best you can.) Compile the comments you've gotten, put them through the "Do they know what they're talking about" filter, and revise.

They say a painting is never finished, that it only stops in interesting places. The same can be said for an animation. Even so, scenes must move on, production must continue. Learn to work your piece as a whole, exploring finer and finer details as the entire scene reaches contiguous levels of quality; don't fixate on the minutia of a single slice of time. Allow the entirety of your scene to carry the emotional read you felt in those quiet moments of touching another's soul.

> **Note:**
> The animation you do will outlast all of us. Make it something to remember.

Chapter 13

Important Points for Every Scene

What do you look for when you're evaluating a scene you've done? Almost every animator who's been around the block a few times will have something to say on the matter. And almost all that is to be said revolves around the points developed by the great masters of animation.

Use this list as a guideline to evaluate your work. (These points are signposts to aim you back to Chapters 10 and 11 if you need more detail on certain issues.) Scrutinize every detail to the best of your ability. When everything falls together and all the points are properly addressed, your work will begin to take on the same sheen of craftsmanship and skill as those in feature-quality animation.

13.1 Composition/Design

When you sit back and look at what you've done, really sit back and look at what you've done. Move your chair across your cubicle or office and watch your work play out at a different size than what you've grown accustomed to. Disassociate yourself from the "groove" you've been working in, and try to see it as if for the first time. Break it down into its basic compositional elements.

Watch your work play out through eyelids closed just enough so your eyelashes meet. This gets rid of a lot of the detail information and reduces what you're seeing to the basic compositional elements. This is how many painters break down the complexities of painting *alla prima* (all at once, usually on location) into design shapes they can more easily understand and make use of.

> **Note:**
>
> Another great thing you can do to help see what's "hiding in plain sight" is to mirror the image horizontally if you have access to post-processing software. This is what you do when you flip a drawing over and examine it on a light table. When you reverse the image like this, every minute error that you might have been content to live with leaps out at you. This stops the rationalization of inaccurate balance, weight, and proportion.

Watch your animation play out as a constantly transforming composition. Its final presentation will most likely be on the 2D plane of a screen of one kind of another. Evaluate your work with the same criteria any other 2D artwork would have to adhere to. (Your 2D piece just happens to evolve through time, that's all.)

> **Note:**
>
> Use the flow of silhouettes and design elements to lead the viewer's eye just as in a still image!

Watch the balance of positive (character) and negative (background) shapes. Watch how wedges and other design elements lead your eye around the piece as it plays out before you. Is your eye being led to where you want it to go? Is your focus in the right places to catch the important cues? Does your eye end up in a good place to link with the following scene? Does your eye start in a place that fits well with the preceding scene?

> **Note:**
>
> If *head and tail scenes* (the scenes that sandwich yours) are available to you as either *animatics* (timed storyboards with camera motion) or final renders, compile a movie of all three together. Watch the flow of your scene as it leaves the previous one and enters the next.

Before you even begin to delve into the finer points of an animation, its broad strokes must be strong, solid, and powerful enough to carry your attention, powerful enough to carry the audience's attention. The audience may never know your usage of design and composition to manipulate their perceptions; all they'll know is that your work feels powerful and they want to see more!

13.2 **Appealing Poses**

Your characters must first and foremost read clearly with the action that is taking place. Second, and second only by a hair's breadth, is the need for them to appeal to the audience. Remember, appeal does not mean cutesy! It means your audience must find some way to relate to and empathize with the character and what he's doing, how he's feeling, and what he's thinking.

Your characters must read clearly as two-dimensional representations of thoughts, ideas, and actions! Your primary tool in this area is, what else, silhouette.

Squinting your eyes, as mentioned in the previous section, will help you to lose the surface details of your character and see him more as a silhouette. You can also render your animation in Quickshade mode, saving out only the alpha channel and compiling the frames into an animation to see how your silhouettes are moving.

Examine your silhouettes for clarity of action, strength of design (the balance of broad and fine details, curved and straight lines, and clear shapes orchestrating the viewer's focus), and appeal. Your audience needs to understand your posing, find it interesting, and be able to empathize.

13.3 **Anticipation, Drag, Follow-Through**

Do your character's actions need to express the concepts of drawing through time?

Do your characters anticipate their actions (in accordance with who they are)? Do these anticipations help lead the viewer into the action? Do the anticipations help build, accent, and punctuate the rhythm of the scene?

Do your character's body parts exhibit their own mass as their individual momentums carry them along? Do they drag, unfurl, and follow-through, each in its own time? Do your overlapping actions add to the overall, believable fluidity of the piece?

13.4 **Weight/Timing**

Does your character, and everything you're animating in the scene, have the appearance of the weight and mass the audience would imagine it to have?

Do your timings imply the extra "oomph" needed to get those massive objects moving and then stopped again? Do your heavy objects (and body parts) accelerate much more quickly toward the ground than they do away from it?

Are your characters balanced, taking into account the perceived mass and motion of the character, his action, and anything he may be holding?

Have you used squash and stretch to give the audience that subliminal shorthand of sensation, implying the forces impacting your character?

13.5 **Entertainment Value**

Imagine looking at your scene through the eyes of someone who's never seen this production before. This someone may be considering an extra tub of popcorn or another soda. Does your scene have the riveting pull to keep him in his seat?

Are you presenting this scene in the most unique and entertaining way that is accurate for the character's personality?

> **Note:**
> Would anyone other than your mother want to see this scene twice?

13.6 **Characterization**

Do you feel the character's motivations, thoughts, dreams, and non-verbal comments through watching him move in the scene? Does he feel like the same guy you saw in the scene before?

Are his secondary actions serving to support his character? Are the secondary actions letting the primary idea of the scene shine through uncluttered?

> **Note:**
> Acting, not action, and always in character!

13.7 Character Evolution

Has your character progressed along his story arc from the time your scene began to the time your scene ends? Have the situations evolved him subtly, almost imperceptibly?

> **Note:**
> This can be a tricky one to nail. Subtlety is the key. As the saying goes, "It's easier to show the transition of five hours than five minutes." Still, your character has to be in a continual state of evolution in order to remain believable. Change is the only constant. Your character must continually grow emotionally, spiritually, and intellectually with everything he encounters in order to possess that elusive spark of life. Developing an inner dialogue that no one else need know about can help. But being attuned to the script and to the overall arc of his character as you work is key to getting these subtle changes to read, almost unnoticed, as your scenes play out.

13.8 Storytelling/The Distillation of One Main Idea

Scenes in filmmaking serve one of three purposes: to develop the mood, to develop the character(s), or to tell the story. Everything else is distraction and should be done away with (hopefully before it ever touches an animator's hands). Your scene has one main purpose in this film. Make sure you understand what that purpose is before starting work on the scene. And make sure that that one main idea reads clearly through your scene; everything else is support.

> **Note:**
> Is the reason for this scene being in the film clear?

13.9 **What's Best for the Production (Don't Grandstand)**

I hate to say it, but nobody likes a show-off. Nobody likes to be intentionally "upstaged." Yes, you may be capable of doing some wonderful, flashy bit of action, but ask yourself, "Is this in character? Is this developing and defining the story? Would anyone else in their 'right mind' do this scene this way?" (You know if the real motivation behind your work is to say, "Hey, look at me!" And others will know it too.)

Animation is heady business. And when you're first cuttin' your teeth, it is so hard to hold back! You want the whole world to know all the great things you can do! It's not about you, it's about the production; you can handle those juicy acting scenes better than those stuck-on-themselves "stars." Someone just has to notice, right?

Sit back and chill. Take some deep breaths. You will eventually get noticed. The work reveals the craftsman. It may be tough to sit tight when you get long shots or crowd scenes while others get the ones rich with pathos. Let your work speak for itself. People will notice, and they'll notice you for all the right reasons. They'll notice that you always do what's best for the scene; that your work, no matter how small on screen, always reads with integrity, subtlety, and character. They'll notice that your work gets done on time and with a minimum of corrections. Nothing goes unnoticed in a production — the good or the bad. Remember that.

Animation is teamwork. Together, everyone from the janitorial staff to the director makes the film. The director orchestrates your visions; your visions sculpt your character; your character creates your scenes; all the scenes together craft the movie; the movie will be there forever. Make it something you are proud to have helped bring into this world. Do so with strength, honor, and integrity.

Chapter 14

Additional Practice Scenes

Now you know everything it takes to make good animation. But knowing and doing are two entirely different things. Animation must flow naturally and inevitably, like good acting. Thinking about the different parts of it too much usually gets you into trouble. What you need to do is practice the concepts so that they become as much a part of you as your own breathing. You need to learn them so well that you can forget them. You need to free your conscious mind from thinking about which controls produce specific results. You need to allow your unconscious mind to "feel" what is right, what needs to be done.

This is something you will attain with focused practice. You will need to take at least one step toward that goal every day. You don't have to sit and practice for hours and hours every single day; just make sure that you do at least one small thing toward being a feature-quality animator every single day. By doing this, you *will* get there.

> **Note:**
> I like to think of it this way: You've got a certain number of so-so animations in you. The breathtaking animations are sprinkled in this pack of so-so scenes, but you've got to get all those mediocre animations out of the way to make room for the good ones. So you'd best get moving!

The steps you take have to be good steps. Practice makes permanent, not perfect! Make sure you're practicing something worth ingraining within you!

This is where I wanted this book to stand out above all others, even the rare, good ones that cover both the basic and the advanced material, the ones that make things understandable. But how can I help you learn to judge for yourself what is good animation and what needs work when I can't stand over your shoulder and encourage your best work? I can do this by giving you good quality animations you can explore as 3D scenes to compare with your work, scenes you can pose-copy move-for-move in your earliest stages of learning the craft. With pose-copying (as we did in Chapter 10), you'll know immediately when your work is exactly as it should be. It will be like having me right there with you, showing you all the mechanics it takes to make a scene flow with life and entertainment. By balancing between pose-copying and creating your own scenes you will quickly wean yourself from needing my help. This is the quickest and surest path to becoming the animator you've dreamed of becoming.

> **Note:**
>
> An important thing to remember is that good animation takes time. The feature studios worth their salt will often give an animator two weeks to work on a three-foot (2-second) scene. Don't rush yourself! If it takes a guy who's been doing feature-quality animation since 1976 two weeks to get a three-foot scene out, don't beat yourself up if you can't get a feature-quality scene out in a day!

14.1 The Technique

This is the technique I begin with when teaching students in person, whether they are potential animators working for me, students, or friends. Through the balance of pose-copying and creating original scenes, you learn what to do, fast. And you begin internalizing good habits right from the start. Using derivations of this technique, you will be able to find the next logical steps in nearly anything you wish to learn. (You can use a variation on this technique to learn how to draw or paint in a particular style.) If you're being dropped into a production where you have to match a predeveloped style, you can use this technique with movies of approved scenes. You can also assimilate much more quickly the sensibilities of the great masters by working from clips of their traditional animation in this fashion.

For your first scene, choose a scene from the Scenes to Copy section (Section 14.3). These scenes are all ready for you to load in and have you move the character to exactly match pre-existing animation on the life drawing model. Work with your first scene for a week (or more) if you need it; make sure everything is an exact match — timing, posing, everything. Don't let your character deviate one iota from the life drawing model. (Yes, this can be tedious.) Give yourself as much time as you need, there's no rush! Just kick your feet back and enjoy the ride!

Next, pull a scene from the Scenes to Create section (Section 14.4), where you're only given direction. Look through them and find something that sounds fun. Go through all the applicable steps outlined in Chapter 12 in preparation for settling in to work. (If you fail to plan, you plan to fail.) Give yourself half a day to a day to get your bearings on how you're going to handle the scene (I do). Then settle in to working on that scene for one to two weeks — however long you might need to make sure everything is as spot-on as you can make it.

> **Newbie Note:**
> It's fairly common for this second scene to give you fits. Don't worry about it too much. Just do your best. Enjoy the process of exploring! "Run and find out!" (*Rikki-Tikki-Tavi*)

When you feel you've spent as much time with this second scene as you can without losing your mind, take another scene (or another two, if you feel really wobbly about things) from the Scenes to Copy section. Give the scene(s) a week or so (each), enough time to get everything absolutely perfect. Then go back to doing another scene where you're taking it from scratch. You should notice things getting significantly better this time around.

Go back and forth between copied scenes and original scenes until you feel you've got your "chops" down. Then, instead of pose-copying something from the Scenes to Copy section, make a movie of it from a stationary viewpoint and work entirely from this movie. Compare your work either by feel or by loading items from the scene you're copying. Use Loading Items From Scene only to compare; revert to using the movie alone when making adjustments.

Again, alternate original scenes and scenes copied from a single-view movie. Keep at this until you feel really sharp, able to understand what visual cues translate into 3D coordinates. Then, take a foray into what's outlined in Section 14.5; I think you'll like it.

You can come back to this technique, or your own modification of it, whenever you feel like you need a little "boost" in your skills. It is the quickest, surest way to sharpen, to learn, and to train your internal senses of what works. You're building muscle memory, good habits that you don't have to think about to employ. You'll just get a feel for what's right and what a scene needs.

Continue to study the basic and advanced animation mechanics as you do this. Make sure your mind knows what your body is learning. "Gut feelings" can take you fairly far, and with your mind attuned to the conscious, logical understanding of the principles of animation, there will be nothing you can't handle.

> **Newbie Note:**
> After you begin to feel pretty good about what you're doing, you'll probably find yourself going through a short period where you feel like you're just starting out again. You may feel like you can't quite seem to remember how to get things into place or the controls suddenly feel awkward, when everything was feeling almost natural only a few days before. *This is normal!!!* This is considered to be the "mammalian learning curve," when what we hold in short-term memory gets transferred to long-term memory. The information is temporarily inaccessible while the synaptic structures are being constructed in long-term memory. Just keep at it! Once those long-term memory synapses get physically shifted around to hold that info, you'll be on top of the world again!

14.2 Life Drawing

You'll find a collection of images to practice life drawing from in Extras\Life_ Drawing\Images\ and scenes to pose-copy in Extras\Life_Drawing\Scenes\.

Life drawing is a great way to unwind. You don't have to worry about the same issues you do when your character is in motion; you just kick back and get that one pose you see in front of you. It's a great way to relax and get centered before starting your workday, and it's a good way to get loose and get past those "stiff" first poses.

Take your life drawing further than what you see in this book. If you have a laptop that can run LightWave, take it with you to a life drawing class. Take it with you at lunch and capture quick gesturals of the people you see around you. Life draw from the TV or a movie. Life draw from poses you find in paintings, sculptures, cels. Expose yourself to as much as you can. And have fun!

> **Note:**
> All that you truly examine adds to what you are capable of seeing!

> **Note:**
> Draw with verbs, not nouns!

14.3 Scenes to Copy

You will find scenes to copy in Extras\ScenesToCopy\. Use these in conjunction with "the technique," or to compare your take on a situation with mine. Each scene's title will let you know a little of what the scene is about, and the .txt file associated with it will give you direction as to the scenes to create. Work both with scene ideas that sound interesting and scenes that you have zero interest in.

> **Note:**
> Usually, being turned off by a subject is a good sign that there is something you need to learn there.

14.4 Scenes to Create

This section contains lists of directorial comments on scenes. With some, you may have to create your own simple props. Have fun with the process! These ideas are for you to springboard from. Take them, push them, make them entertaining; make them your own! The only directorial edict I'm going to issue is that you have to be able to imagine your finished scenes fitting in flawlessly amid a collection of the best animation you've ever seen. Take your time; do the best work you are capable of doing.

There are no deadlines here. There are no PAs rushing about, desperately trying to make quota. Dive into the scenes, and forget about (real-life) time for a while. Lose yourself in the process of simply doing. Play! Have fun! Let your fun shine right through the screen to your audience!

Actions

These are just bits of action you should get under your belt. Each of these actions incorporates many of the basic and advanced animation mechanics. I'd like you to go through each of these actions twice; one time, perform the action as straightlaced and realistically as you can, then do it as cornball and cartoony as you can. With the realistic pass, make it as true-to-life as you can, make it feel like it has been motion-captured. With the cartoony pass, really push it to the extremes; give Tex Avery and Chuck Jones a run for their money! Whichever you do first is up to you, but you may find your realistic scenes benefiting from the looseness you work into your cartoony scenes.

Make the action read well in silhouette. Give the characters a reason for (and an opinion on) doing whatever they're doing. Make your work entertaining, both in the doing and in the watching!

▶ Swing a baseball bat

▶ Do a golf swing using a driver (the golf club used to really belt that ball out of there)

▶ Do a golf swing using a pitching wedge to get the ball out of a sand trap and onto a nearby green

▶ Throw a javelin

▶ Do an Olympic-style hammer throw

▶ Throw a shot put

▶ Shoot a basket

▶ Throw a football

▶ Pitch a baseball

▶ Dive from a diving board

▶ Yo a yo-yo

▶ Swing on a swing

▶ Use your hands to "walk" across a set of monkey bars

▶ Skip rope

▶ Juggle (a real juggle and then a "cartoon, cascade" juggle)

Walk Cycles

Cycles need to loop seamlessly, so that someone watching them wouldn't know which keyframe marks the loop's start/end. (If Frame 0 is the same as Frame 28, I make a preview or movie from Frames 1 to 28.) Watch for "pops" and problems with acceleration as the cycle nears its head and tail. I generally don't use the motion graph's "pre" and "post" behavior to repeat the cycle. When I want to integrate the cycle into a scene, I copy the keys manually for as many times as I need the motion to repeat itself. This way I can have unique action happen before and after the cycle if need be.

> **Note:**
> A cycle will amplify any problems an animation may have. Your audience will catch the third time what they missed the first (and begin to rant and rave about it after the tenth). Make sure that everything is as polished to perfection as you can get it.

DIRECTION: Walk cycle: You're a businessman late for an important meeting but trying very much not to show it.

DIRECTION: Walk cycle: Do an exaggerated sneak-walk.

DIRECTION: Walk cycle: Do a "cool walk." (Think Fat Albert and the Gang kind of thing.)

DIRECTION: Walk cycle: Do the absolute weirdest walk you can think of (something that would fit in with the Monty Python "School of Silly Walks" skit).

DIRECTION: Walk cycle: Do a light jog.

DIRECTION: Walk cycle: Do an all-out run.

DIRECTION: Walk cycle: Do a walk showing your character as light-hearted and happy as a character can be.

DIRECTION: Walk cycle: Do a walk showing your character in the depths of misery.

DIRECTION: Take the "all-out run" you did, and copy your keys to extend it. End with your character stumbling and falling, coming to a rolling, skidding stop.

DIRECTION: Using your "light jog," animate your character blithely running along, not paying attention to where he's going. Life is good until he runs smack into a brick wall.

DIRECTION: Take your character from standing into any of the cycles you've done and then back to standing again.

DIRECTION: Using your "light jog," have your character running along when he spies someone gorgeous and comes to a screeching halt. As gallantly as possible, have him do an about-face and strut sexily past the object of his attention.

DIRECTION: Using one of your run cycles, blend this in a cartoony fashion with a stealthy sneak and then go back to the run. (Think of cartoons where the character is going full-tilt, then has to sneak by an open doorway, then goes back to his full-tilt run.)

Scenes

Use your creative license to handle these scenes in the most entertaining way you can think of. Create your own histories for the characters, devise reasons for them being there, opinions on what it is they're doing, and thoughts about where they are going next.

Play with multiple camera angles. First, establish the scene with a longer shot, letting the audience know what is going on and where the character fits into his surroundings. Use medium shots and close-ups to showcase the action and to create strong, storytelling, design-oriented silhouettes. Allow your timing to sculpt the feelings of the audience; lead them down the emotional paths you want them to follow and at the pace you decide!

Craft these scenes so that your audience will find something within them to connect with as they watch them. Let your scenes remind them of similar situations they've experienced. Choreograph them so those watching it will want to see it play through again, so that they want to see what happens next!

DIRECTION: You're walking down the street and stop because you find a coin lying there. You pick it up, and give it a quick flip into the air; heads you'll keep it, tails you'll leave it for someone else. The coin comes up tails. Get rid of the coin in an entertaining way.

DIRECTION: You're sitting in a chair, lost in thought and a little bit bored. The phone rings. You leap up to answer it and trip over another chair in your rush, tumbling haphazardly to the ground.

DIRECTION: Using the ChromeFox setup in conjunction with your character, animate him trying to coax a timid, wild animal to him.

DIRECTION: Opening a letter: The contents are beyond your wildest hopes. You leap for joy!

DIRECTION: Opening a letter: The contents are depressing beyond measure. You collapse into the chair behind you or down the wall and onto the floor. The key here is drama (perhaps even angst)!

DIRECTION: It is "high noon." Two chaps face off in a duel of "finger-pistols" (just pretending their fingers are guns). They draw! One "hits" his opponent who fakes a dramatic death. (Really play with camera angles with this one! Try to get that Old West kind of feel!)

DIRECTION: You take a sip of coffee and jump because it is too hot, fumbling the cup. You spastically juggle the cup, trying to save it, finally having to leap out of the way as it crashes to the floor.

DIRECTION: You're putting up a fence. You lay another board up, pull a nail from behind your ear, and absently hammer until … you bash your thumb with the hammer!

DIRECTION: You are breaking into an old "dial" safe. With your ear to the mechanism, you eloquently turn the combination. You hear the click of success, then rubbing your hands together in anticipation, you open the door.

DIRECTION: You sidle up to a locked door. First, making sure no one is looking, you kneel and begin to pick the lock. The tumblers fall into place and you stand, peering about to see if the coast is still clear. You quietly turn the knob and back inside, softly shutting the door after you.

DIRECTION: Like a musketeer of old, you draw your sword and gallantly salute!

DIRECTION: Animate your character pulling an arrow from a quiver on his back, knocking it, pullin' it back, and lettin' it fly!

DIRECTION: Do the ol' '50s sitcom bit with the character screeching on a chair because of a mouse.

DIRECTION: You are the coolest hepcat in town. You've got your back turned to the audience at a poetry reading. You're snapping your fingers and tapping your foot to the beat of the jazz band. You motion for the band to stop. You turn, pose, and bow.

DIRECTION: It is freezing and you're improperly dressed, waiting for the bus. Rub your arms, stomp your feet, blow into your hands to try to warm yourself up. Amid this action, look at your watch, and listen to it to see if it is still running.

DIRECTION: You are shoveling snow. You stop to rest for a moment, wiping your nose on your sleeve, then start back to work.

DIRECTION: You're swinging a pickax at a spot on the floor. Hearing a "thunk," you stop digging, kneel, and carefully brush away the dust to find a handle of sorts. Using all your might, you lift a heavy case from the ground.

DIRECTION: Like the hags in *Macbeth*, you eerily stir a cauldron.

DIRECTION: Like in the old TV shows, do a sliding leap over a car hood.

DIRECTION: Two characters: One character kneels before the other, slipping a ring on the standing character's finger in a proposal of marriage.

DIRECTION: Two characters: The two characters run into each other's arms, one swinging the other around in a loving embrace.

DIRECTION: Two characters: One character hikes the unconscious other character over his shoulder and carries him.

DIRECTION: Two characters: Animate a round of "rock, scissors, paper."

DIRECTION: Two characters: One character slaps the other in the face (as in a soap opera).

DIRECTION: Two characters: Animate a tug-of-war where someone lets go of the rope, sending the other flying.

These scenes aren't just for practice. These are the kinds of things that will get you a job. Set aside movies of your absolute best work. (Don't expect anyone to see "potential," period!) Blend these best-of-the-best together to make a demo reel no longer than three minutes. (You lose your audience after three minutes, no matter how good your work is.) Put a nice, strongly graphic plate at the beginning, letting the art director know who you are and how to contact you, repeating it at the end. Burn it to a CD, put it on the Web, and/or render it to VHS. (Just as a side note: Most "art folks" and management tend to be on Macintoshes. Saving your reel as a QuickTime means they're not going to have to work to see your work.)

Leave your audience wanting more! Don't show everything you've ever done! If you have brilliant work and really poor work on the same reel, the person reviewing it will probably wonder if you have the sense to know what is good and what isn't. Only put your best work on the reel! If this means your reel is thirty seconds, fine! It is far better to have thirty seconds of feature-quality work than it is to have three (or ten) minutes of forgettable work.

Easy power! Leave them wanting more! Have them so enticed about what your work shows you can do for them that they'll fly you across the country just to talk with you!

Do not put anything but your absolute best on your reel!

And don't worry if you didn't make the models or IK the setup yourself. (I included these high-level models and setups so you wouldn't be stuck with great ideas and no way to execute them if setup just isn't your thing. Use them!) In most larger studios, animators only animate. In the smaller ones, you generally do have to be a jack-of-all-trades. So use this information to target your job search. Do you want to do everything, or just focus on only one thing? Do you enjoy setup as much as you do animation? Don't settle for the first job opportunity that comes along, even though it will be tempting. (Don't rationalize yourself into a job you will come to hate.) Target what you do for a living to what you love to do!

Newbie Note:

Please don't feel like you've got to rush through this whole training thing. You've got your entire life ahead of you to perfect this art. Make every step the best, absolute best you can make it. Remember that you will only achieve feature-quality animation if, and only if, you give yourself the time you need to achieve it!

14.5 **Where to Go Next**

So, what's next? Learning from the masters what you wish to be taught. You've reached a plateau where you can see the path before you. You can understand what you need to learn. You know what kind of animator you wish to be. In the distance, you can see the next logical steps that will take you there. This is where you branch from the teachings in this book and take your own path to where you wish to be.

You know what kind of animation just sets your world spinning. For you, maybe it's the beautiful work of Hayao Miyazaki. Maybe it's the way-out shorts of Tex Avery or the brilliance of Chuck Jones. Perhaps early Disney makes your heart pound, or the later works of that studio line your shelves. I want you to dive into that work that you love. I want you to immerse yourself in it, live it, breathe it, and sleep it. I want you to use the pieces that make the blood rush in your ears to complete your training.

I want you to take your laserdisc, DVD, or VHS version of whatever is your favorite animated film of all time, and using what you've learned of character setup, craft a character of similar proportions to the one you either wish you were or wish you were with. Then, I want you to find your absolute favorite scene with him in it, and recreate his every motion with your own character. Your job is to make your character hit you with the same emotional wallop that this movie character does. You and you alone will know when you're there. And when you are, you'll know you are on the path on which you were meant to be!

Continue working like this for as long as feels right. Craft your own stories; build your own dreams into a reality you can share with others. Use everything you can to help you get to where your dreams are as tangible as the clothes you wear. And may your journey be one of wonder, excitement, and joy beyond measure!

Chapter 15

Digitigrade Characters

> **Note:**
> This is an advanced chapter. It assumes that you understand the
> details of character setup. (It does not hold your hand.) If there
> are parts where you are lost or confused, return to the earlier
> chapters on character setup for a refresher, and/or load in and
> examine one of the pre-built setups from the companion CD.

So what do you do when you have a character who walks on his toes?
How do you get your *plantigrade* (flat-footed) character to walk
heel-to-toe without having the animation be an exploration of
counterrotation? *Digitigrade* characters (those who walk on their
toes) need a bit of a change to the foot/leg IK in order to make things
work smoothly. These changes (and their derivations) can help any
character who needs special handling with their feet.

Figure 15.1. The structure of a fox.

It is important that you understand the underlying structures of whatever being you're working with, whether real or imagined. As mammals, we all have basically the same parts. Understanding how the parts are used in different "chassis" is key to building successful setups that allow for intuitive posing!

> **Note:**
>
> Even delving into the subtleties that few people will ever consciously notice can increase the power of your work. For example, the front paws of a canid (a member of the canine family) are larger than the back; this helps to absorb the impact of their leaping gait. Cheetahs have no clavicle; only muscle and ligament hold their upper arms in place. This evolution is an adaptation for speed; the shoulder "joint" will slide back three to six inches during the compression stroke of their run. Knowledge like this is essential if you are attempting to recreate reality. And your fanciful beings will become all the more real when they are grounded in an understanding of physiology that would actually work.

Note:

There is more to quadrupedal motion than can be covered in this book and still get to all the things I feel are important as a strong foundation for animation. I'm including the ChromeFox model for those who wish to "leap ahead." If you choose to work with this or another quadrupedal character, take the time to deeply explore how they, or similar creatures, really move. There is almost no wasted motion in a quadruped's motions. Every movement flows perfectly into the next, like a wave flowing through their bodies. Contra-posto plays a key role in everything they do. Watch for reversals of the pelvis and shoulders on heading, bank, and pitch. The lumbar section of their back gives power to their gallop; knowing where the rigid pelvis attaches and how much this section actually flexes during the compression phase is key. There is so much more than just knowing which "foot" comes first in a walk cycle.

Newbie Note:

If you have an anatomy class somewhere in your future, try renaming the bones to their scientific names: metatarsals, metacarpals, scapula, femur, radius, ulna, etc. When you're working with the "proper" names every day, they sink in faster than you might think possible!

15.1 Bones

These bones are the same bones as in your character's skeleton. However, they are angled differently and of different lengths, taking into account the different positions and pivot points of the various body parts. We still have a puller for the leg, and we still have a control to rotate the knee. It is the foot where the change comes into play.

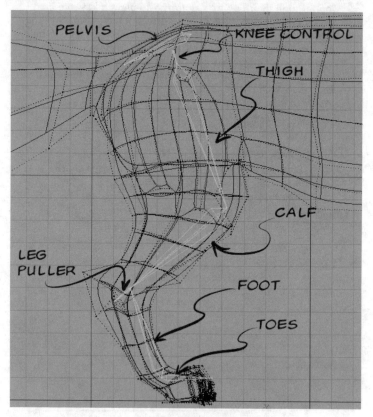

Figure 15.2. The bone layout for the fox's hind leg.

The one major difference is that the foot control is reversed. In this new setup, the toes will be used to position and angle the foot; the foot bone will only be rotated. Rotating the foot bone will move the goal that will be attached to its tip, compressing and stretching the thigh/calf section of the leg.

The hierarchy for the leg is as follows: Pelvis => KneeControl => Thigh => Calf => LegPuller. And the hierarchy for the foot is: Toes => Foot => Goal (where Goal is a null object that will be added in Layout).

Figure 15.3. The digitigrade leg setup with IK active in Layout. (Thigh is set to solve for IK on two axes, while the calf only solves on one. LegPuller is using a goal strength of 80.)

Figure 15.4. This setup allows you to keep the character's toes firmly rooted on the ground while the "heel" of the foot causes the leg to flex.

Note:

Think! Imagine! Be!

Note:

As you work with characters that walk on their toes, whether they be quads or bis, always remember joint flexibility and proper distribution of weight. Feel the extra spring in the step that always walking with your heels off the ground gives you. You aren't restricted by platforms like high-heel shoes, and you have complete mobility through your entire range of movement; you have the strength in your calves to carry out whatever action you dream! And remember that even though your legs may be at a collection of angles (not the straight, rigid, locked form of a standing human), all your angles still must add up to a constant, structured balance.

15.2 Plantigrade Modifications

You can use modifications of this digitigrade setup to create enhanced setups for your plantigrade characters as well. It is wise to have a "stable" of these special-case setups so you can pull just the right one for the job at hand — or foot. (The proper tools make all the difference in the world.)

Figure 15.5. This setup is made by adding one bone to the digitigrade setup. It makes it a lot easier to roll the character's weight from heel-to-toe as he walks. The new bone is the same length as the foot bone but heading in the opposite direction, with the toes set as a child of this new bone. The new bone doesn't control the character's points directly; it only controls the toes and foot which do.

> **Note:**
> "Enhanced" or special-purpose setups can save a lot of time in the long run, but they can also offer too much to think about for a novice. And while they may ease some tasks, they may complicate others. Only through playing and experimenting will you know what tools fit your style of working.

Explore! Experiment! The sky is the limit! And remember, if it works, it's got to be good!

Chapter 16

On the Path

> **Advanced Note:**
> This chapter is more for those just starting out, finding their bearings, getting a handle on how to get to where they'd like to be. Still, you may find some interesting suggestions in Sections 16.3 and 16.4. These sections may give you some new ideas or help to rejuvenate your career!

There is a wealth of knowledge out there from which you can learn. But you have to know where to look and how to see what you watch. And though you know the films that inspired you to pick up the pencil or stylus, what about other animated works out there, the other worlds of symbolism and inspiration; how do you find them? (How do you weed through the mountains of mediocrity that line the video store shelves?)

16.1 Support

There's a lot of good out there, and there's a lot of not-so-good, too. Having friends also interested in animation gives you a wealth of viewpoints outside your own. They can direct you to what they like best, and past the things they've sat through and afterward wondered why they did. This group of friends can also be the momentum it takes to keep going during the rough spots. (Everyone has times when they feel like they're going nowhere. A good strong base of friends can help you look objectively at your work, and see your progress and your achievements.) Look to the Internet for camaraderie if your local base of fellows isn't what you would desire. With the resources available with just a quick trip to your favorite search engine, it shouldn't be that hard finding a crowd you can connect with!

With a group of friends also interested in learning 3D animation, there's almost nothing you can't do! If there's one who is further along than the others, he can shine a light on the pitfalls. If you're all at the same level, all the better! With a group of close, dedicated friends, you'll be learning through a camaraderie that rarely exists in "The Industry" today.

Get together and draw out your own plans for making the short film you've always wanted to see. Find a particular style of animation you'd like to know how to do, something you'd like to have in your case-o'-riffs. Make your animation fit that style. Let the motions, characterizations, timings, character designs, and background designs all seem to be a 3D evolution of the films you've seen in that style!

> **Note:**
> A series of short films is a fantastic way to hone your skills. You
> see what you would like to be able to do, and you know what
> you are currently capable of. Use each short film as a step-
> ping-stone for the next. Build on what you learn. Let each work
> showcase what you feel confident doing, while still pushing
> your skills to the next level. Easy power! Heavily stylized films
> are often easier to create than ones that recreate reality. Your
> first short may be heavily shadowed, like film noir, so you only
> see the parts of the characters you feel confident animating. Or
> you might make use of conventions that bypass the more chal-
> lenging points of advanced animation mechanics. Work with
> your limitations; use them creatively! Build on them and let
> them lead you to where you want to be!

16.2 Editing

The problem with watching a film — any film, whether animated or
live action — is that everything is intricately woven together to
carry you deep into the story. It can be hard to figure out exactly
what was done to tell such a compelling story. Using a jog shuttle on
your DVD, VHS, or laserdisc player helps you to understand most
motions, but how do you understand how the pieces fit together so
well? How do these individual bits seamlessly recreate the
"dream-time" patterns of events that allow us to completely accept
the elements we are being shown as a contiguous, powerful story?
How do you learn to piece your scenes together so that they also
tell an accessible, lucid tale?

Learning to be a successful editor can take years upon years of
schooling and practice. (A great editor can make horrible camera
work and/or performances look stellar.) Even so, you can begin to
grasp some of the concepts by watching movies with the sound off.

Music and effects key to our emotional centers as few other
stimuli do. The score and *foley* (sound effects) of a movie are often
considered "invisible actors," and are every bit as important as the
other lead actors in sculpting the way we feel. When you watch a
movie with the sound turned off, you are able to distance yourself
from the events on the screen. You are able to see the positions of

the characters as one scene cuts or dissolves to another. You are able to see the directions in which the characters and backgrounds are moving, and how this complements or contrasts with the previous scene. You are able to see the positions of multiple cameras as they intercut to tell the story of the conversation going on. You are able to see how the director choreographs establishers, longs and mids, close-ups and extremes. You get a peek at the gears and cogs of the movie, all working in harmony.

> **Note:**
> Watch. Learn. Copy if you need to. Do everything you can to understand why things do what they do. Apply this understanding to your own work and make it yours.

16.3 Watching Movies

The breathtaking animated films of today are so polished that you may have anticipations going back 24 frames or more before the actual action itself! There is so much subtlety woven into modern feature animation that unless you have the experience to (almost) do this level of work yourself, you can't see what's being done to create it. Go back to the early days of animation, and study and learn by watching the masters hone their skills!

In the early days of animation, most folks were at the same level of skill where you are right now. They were still working with understanding advanced animation mechanics, and figuring out how best to work them into the scenes they had. When you watch these early shorts and features, you get a chance to see beyond the polish. You get a chance to see how the animators were thinking, problem-solving, how they reasoned through their scenes. You can understand their processes because their work is around the same level of ability as yours is right now! You can clearly see their thoughts on squash and stretch, anticipation, drag, follow-through, timing, weight, balance, and all the other things that make good animation great. The art of a master makes what he does look effortless; that's what mastery is! You'll be there someday. Luckily, you can, through their early works, watch them as they learned. You can study their solid logical steps toward their own mastery of the craft. Through an understanding of how they made their progress, you will be able to follow as well.

The old silent films are wonderful to watch too. There is the genius use of physical humor and pantomime storytelling in the works of Chaplin and Keaton. There are the incredible, graphic, painting-like visuals in films like *Metropolis* (1926, Director Fritz Lang). There is the groundbreaking editing and storytelling of *Bronenosets Potyomkin* (*Battleship Potemkin*) (1925, Director Grigori Aleksandrov).

> **Note:**
> Watch for the discoveries of lighting, camerawork, editing, and acting that have laid the foundations for the filmmaking of today!

Foreign films are replete with symbolism. It may take several viewings of a heavily symbolic film to begin to get the meanings that may be clear to a viewer from that culture. Symbolism deals in a kind of *archetypal imagery* (imagery that strikes a chord within the viewer regardless of experience or culture). You may not get the same messages or meanings as someone from that particular culture, but you will remember how the play of images made you feel. You can use similar metaphors in your own films, sculpting intricate patterns of emotion.

I've heard some "American" animators speak condescendingly about the works of Japanese animation, or anime. What these animators seem to miss is that often, the budget for an anime feature is less than what a single thirty-minute episode of a Saturday morning cartoon would cost to make. There is much to learn from these masters of a limited budget. They know when something has to move with the fluidity of "ones," and when a single, held frame will suffice. The master directors of anime know how to spend their budget wisely. And the delicate, finely crafted stills are so beautifully done, so full of symbolism, that often these are indeed the strongest ways to deliver the empathic vision of the scene.

> **Note:**
> Make an effort to learn as much as you can. "I do not like"
> often means "I do not understand."

As far as modern animation, I'm only going to name two that may have slipped by your radar. *The Iron Giant* (1999, Director Brad Bird) and *Cats Don't Dance* (1997, Director Mark Dindal) are two of the most brilliantly executed (on all levels of production) animated features of the "modern age of animation." Their story, storytelling, character designs, characterization, acting, animation, editing, scoring, and everything about them is absolutely heads and shoulders above most other modern animated features. (This is, of course, my opinion. And the reasons for their slipping through the theaters like greased lightning I'll leave to you to ferret out once you've entered the ranks of feature animation.)

16.4 Other Studies

An animator has to be the epitome of a Renaissance man (or woman). You have to be well-read, in both fiction and non. You have to have experience in many, many areas. (I like to think that this includes an understanding of all things rhythmic, from the earliest "early music" to the current beats pounding the dance floors on Sunset Boulevard.) You have to know how things work, and you have to understand how you would feel were you to be thrust into a myriad of different lifetimes. You are the ultimate method actor.

As an actor/animator, books that will help you immensely are *To the Actor* by Michael Chekhov and *Audition* by Michael Shurtleff. *To the Actor* will help you to get in touch with the energies that let you become different beings. There are exercises in that book that will astound you in terms of how much it will open up your perceptions of your worlds, both outer and inner. *Audition* will help you to quickly break down a scene into pieces you and the audience can relate with. It gets you to identify the motivating factor behind all interactions, as it exists within all scenes: love. Everything we do and everything we don't do is motivated ultimately through this single, unifying force. And through this single, unifying force, your audience will see themselves in what your characters do.

To help you plan your scenes, I recommend studying *Film Directing Shot By Shot: Visualizing from Concept to Screen* by Steven D. Katz. This book explains, better than any other, the rules and conventions used in filmmaking. It will help you to understand what you're seeing as you watch movies with the sound off. It shows you examples of how famous directors have storyboarded their scenes. It will help you more than any other resource I can think of on how to plan your production so that you get a finished product, and that this finished product is the one you had hoped for.

For another point of view on the principles of animation, my highest recommendation goes to *The Illusion of Life: Disney Animation* by Frank Thomas and Ollie Johnston. There is a lot of history in this book, and a lot of important information that is woven conversationally in the text. (Because of this, it is something that should be read cover to cover.) In it, you'll find many of the hows and whys of films and characters you've grown up with.

How do you find out what you "should" be doing? Read and do the exercises in *The Artist's Way: A Spiritual Path to Higher Creativity* by Julia Cameron. It is a great way to learn how to "enjoy the process of doing" and figure out where your dreams are leading.

How do you get an interview at the "big studios"? *What Color is Your Parachute?* by Richard Nelson Bolles is a fantastic resource for both people just starting out and those doing a 180 after already having had a successful career as something else.

Don't stop there. Explore your world; see where the hidden doorways lead! Take acting courses, take directing courses, find out how to do things in live action or on stage. Study physics, quantum mechanics, biology, mathematics, history, mythology, storytelling, and anything else you think might be exciting. Remember, your mind is a muscle, and if you keep exercising it, it'll just beg for you to give it more! Take a course on animal communication; how better to "become" your subject than "meeting them halfway" in understanding?

The key here is to light a fire under yourself to enjoy the process of learning! Animation is a life-long pursuit. You will never reach the point where there's nothing more. There is always something more! If you can train your mind/body/soul to enjoy the process, to regale in that which you do not know (… yet), you will have a life the likes of which most would never believe!

Chapter 17

Finding the Character

In the previous chapters, I've talked a lot about letting yourself live as your character. For some of you, this phrase instantly connects with experiences you've had where you have done this. You know what it means to imagine yourself so thoroughly as some other being that you know what it is to experience life through another set of eyes, for a while. Though similar to the "lands of make-believe" we visited as children, this kind of focused visualization is much more.

This is similar to how the shamans of different cultures call to them the wisdom and knowledge of the different archetypal beings. By allowing themselves to so fully let the essence of another being flow through their entire focus, they have access to information they would not otherwise have. We as animators must do very much the same thing. We also work with archetypes, letting their essences flow through us and into our work. The characters we animate are much more than "everyday Joes," even if our project is grounded firmly in the "realistic" vein. Our characters are something more than real. They are, in essence, symbols of ways of being. Just as to a medicine person the falcon may represent sharp, clear-seeing quickness and sureness in our work, Perdita (*101 Dalmations*) represents the essence of maternal love and strength, feminine caring, and gentleness of soul.

Ours is with the place of storytellers within the global fire circle. We work in ideals and in symbols that evoke change within our audience. And just as the shaman draws through him the essences of the totems (the archetypal symbols as represented through the exemplification of an animal) of his traditions, so we draw through us archetypal symbols in the forms of the characters with which we work.

The shaman allows his senses to reach out, to touch and be enveloped by the essence of the totem spirit; everything about him becomes influenced by this connection. To look at him with your feelings, his essence would be that of the totem, not the man. As actors, we let the essence of our characters envelop us as we work; in the final animation, all you feel is the being of the character, not the artist.

Animation has the capability to crystallize, to transform, to completely winnow out all but that which needs to be there. We as animators have the ability to perfect a performance. We don't have to create it all at once, on stage or in front of a camera; we can work at it slowly, delving into it, making sure that each and every movement sculpts the feelings we intend. The characters we work with can be perfect in their conceptualization, in their encapsulation of ideas, essences, thoughts, gestures, and purposes. These characters are so much larger than life, they are archetypes representing core motivations within us all!

But how do you get into character? How do you explain the techniques, how it feels to don another's essence, to "shapeshift" as it were? How do you teach the techniques that facilitate these transformations to someone who has never been able to do this? Well, the truth is, at some point or another in our lives, we were all able to do this. Perhaps this was a long time ago, before those "looking out for our best interests" told us to stop daydreaming, or get our noses back into our books and our feet back on the ground. At some point in our lives, we were like Calvin from *Calvin and Hobbes*, living alternate lives battling incredible odds or receiving beauty and adulation. At some point in our lives, all of us knew how to live as another, for just a little while.

At this point in our lives, a lot of us have to shed this "stuff" (for lack of a better word) that has been heaped upon us as we tried to conform to what we thought was asked of us. In this area of visualization, of acting, of shapeshifting, we have to unlearn how to be responsible, respectable adults. We have to relearn how to be kids again. The great thing about relearning this now at this point in our lives is that now most of us are indeed adults (or on the verge of being there), and we can look at the disapproving and say, "Go take a hike, I'm working!" This is our job now! It is our privilege and our duty to daydream, to wear another's essence as our own for a little while. This is what we get paid "the big bucks" (well, hopefully) to do! And we are completely, unequivocally, and altogether within our rights.

You have reached a point in your life and career that by dedicating yourself to the pursuit and study of animation, you have given yourself all the credentials you need to do all the wishing, daydreaming, pretending, play acting, role playing, and everything you wanted to dream as a youth but never had the time to do or the vocabulary to defend! This is one of the many reasons why this job, above all others, is the best job in the world! Let the producers, critics, and hangers-ons — those who wish they had the guts to actually do what you're doing — let them all have their fun thinking they're getting the good part of the deal. You know that the magic is all within you. And it is your magic that touches the audiences, making them wish they were what you have dreamed. And it is this wish that keeps the cycle turning anew.

17.1 Radiating Focus

What we are doing, living moments as "another being," is actually method acting. *Method acting* is the art of becoming the character you are portraying. You aren't just putting yourself, as you are in day-to-day life, into a set of strange circumstances. This is actually becoming the character you are portraying, through and through, mind, body, and soul.

I don't think anyone out there would dispute that the single best source for studying method acting is the book written by Michael Chekhov himself, *To the Actor*. There is no way I can come close to putting in text the kind of guidance, the kind of experience Mr. Chekhov has with teaching this kind of acting. I will, however, do my best to present for you the things I have learned over my career that have helped me the most. This chapter is in no way a replacement for *To the Actor*. I cannot recommend strongly enough that you read and study that text and its exercises. You will be surprised at how much it will help you as an actor and animator, and how much more enjoyment you may find in the simple, educated study of experiencing life.

An animated character radiates his essence to the audience with everything he does. We've explored how silhouette, gesture, and arc of motion are all used to create this experience on the two-dimensional plane of the screen. But how would you, personally, radiate? If you were to try to radiate your focus right now, how would you do it? Being louder? Being more forceful? No. There are many strong but gentle, shy characters who radiate their focus without ever raising their voice or "bossing" another around.

This "radiating focus" is a little like the focus in the martial arts. You project your mind, your being, and your essence into a point and let that projection guide your actions. With your mind leading, your body follows. And though your audience may not be able to "see" this focus, they will be able to read what it is doing; they will read it through every line of your body, with the very way you interact with the space around you.

The first step in being able to produce something is to be able to perceive it. These first exercises are designed to help you get comfortable with focusing your awareness and using your perceptions to experience, create, and control your radiating focus.

Exercise 1

Sit in a relaxed position, either in a comfortable chair or cross-legged on the ground. Rest your arms on your thighs so your palms hang loosely, facing downward.

Start by listening to your breathing. Remember how it sounds to hear someone breathing while they're deeply asleep. Remember how this sounds, the pattern of intake, pause, outflow, pause. Remember how the breath sounds as it flows through the sleeper's trachea. In remembering the sounds, allow your own breathing to fall into this rhythm.

> **Note:**
>
> This pattern of breathing is the "deep breathing" people talk about in association with meditation. We've all heard this kind of breathing, and we all seem to know instinctively what it means. There is something in this manner of breathing that kicks our mind into producing the brainwave patterns that come with being either deeply asleep or in a deep meditative state. And I find that having people reproduce the sound/feeling of hearing someone else making this pattern of breathing (no, not snoring — that doesn't count) is the quickest way for the light-bulb of understanding to go on, as it were.

It may surprise you, even if you're familiar with meditation, as to how quickly this breathing technique lets you drop into the "hum" of a meditative state. Your stress levels lower, your heart rate slows, and you have access to a great deal more of yourself than you do when you're in "daily do mode."

After about two or three minutes of listening to yourself breathe as if asleep (without actually falling asleep), bring the attention of your mind to your hands. Allow your imagination to explore your hands. Visualize the focus of your mind running along every fold of every finger. Allow your imagination to touch the surface of your palms, exploring the areas between your fingers, between your forefinger and thumb, along the backs of your hands, and over your fingernails. Imagine every detail, every crease and fold. Imagine the temperature difference as your body warms the layer of air nearest your skin.

Now, think about the surface of your palms, the inside surfaces of your fingers again. With your eyes closed, you can imagine the exact angles each of your fingers has in relationship to each other and to your hand itself. This close, mental scrutiny draws your focus to what you are exploring. You are focusing on your hands, how it feels to have them, how it feels to be inside and around them.

Now I want you to concentrate on letting a bit of a light, gentle tingling build within your hands. This may not happen right at first; if not, imagine it to be there. Through your imagination and pretending, you will allow yourself to make it real. Believe in it; trust that it is there. It doesn't have to exist for anyone but you, and you are the only one who needs to know of its existence. By falling into this imagination, exploring it without rush or hurry, you allow yourself to believe in it; by allowing yourself to believe in it, it becomes real. Perception defines reality. Focus on it; wrap the imagining of it around you like a cloak. Allow yourself to drift into the sensation of this tingling in your hands.

Now allow there to be warmth along with the light, soft tingling. Let this warmth build slowly, but steadily. Allow it to radiate from your hands as if they were glowing. This glow builds softly, slowly. You can feel the warmth, the pressure of the warmth against your legs where your hands are nearest them. Your hands warm the layers of air around them. The soft, gentle tingling increases as does the glow of light from them, as does the warmth, building to a comfortable presence radiating from your hands.

Let the sensations of this stay with you, gently letting them be. Explore this radiating warmth, the soft, gentle tingling. When you're ready to come back to "normal awareness," take a deeper breath, holding it for just a moment, then letting it out. As you exhale, let the warmth, the light, the soft, gentle tingling dissipate from your hands. Flex your fingers gently, reaching, stretching, and curling them slowly in a wave. When you feel comfortable, open your eyes.

You have explored a meditative state in which you focused your attention and your "energy" on your hands, and allowed this focus to radiate from them. You have felt the effects of this radiating focus as warmth, and perhaps even the light pressure of it against other parts of you. With a little practice, you will be able to achieve this point of radiating focus without having to go into a meditative state.

The radiating focus is the "clay" we will use to sculpt our dreams and visions into a (almost) tangible reality that will directly impact our work as actors/animators. This radiating focus shapes the way in which we perceive and interact with our world. It can also shape how others perceive us in person.

My first dramatic experience with someone using radiating focus in this manner (outside of theater) was in a life drawing class many years ago. We were drawing from a model who was absolutely gorgeous; she was absolutely-take-your-breath-away drop-dead gorgeous. The time came for her to take a break. Wrapped in a robe, she seemed somehow more plain. I thought perhaps I had imagined this incredible beauty. When she stepped onto the plinth again, I watched as she, over the course of two seconds, seemed to transform again into this goddess-like beauty. What had happened? When she began to strike her pose, she had allowed her focus to radiate with her visions of ideal form and beauty. Everyone in the class noticed these transformations. Now, there are those who might say that it was only how she used her body (her posture and carriage) that made us perceive her as beautiful. I say there was more going on than just the mechanics of how well she struck poses worthy of the great masters. I say it was her "energy," her radiating focus, her complete belief in herself becoming this ideal, and allowing this belief to so overflow the bounds of her physical vessel. In this outflowing of belief, we too believed.

Exercise 2

Now we are going to work with exploring the physical presence of this radiating focus. Remember that though this may seem a lot like mysticism, this is simply exploring the worlds of imagination that we all knew and embraced when we were children. No one is watching to see if you're "doing it right." Success is measured only in how much you can let go and play! (And if you just don't feel like you're getting the results you think you should, pretend!)

Sit and relax again. Allow yourself to reach that strong, gentle "hum" of the meditative state.

When you're comfortable, bring your palms together in front of you, almost touching, about 1/3" apart. Hold your elbows out from your body; let your fingers form a flat extension of your palms.

Let your focus explore your hands again. Mentally, run your imagination down the length of each finger, into the closed spaces between them, along your palms, over the backs of your hands. Let your mind hover in the space between your hands. Let this space begin to build with the soft, gentle tingling you felt in the previous exercise. Let this soft, gentle tingling build into a warmth that fills the narrow space between your hands and fingers. Let this warmth build, forming an almost tangible presence of its own.

As you explore this focus, feel it as an almost magnetic cushion between your hands. This magnetic cushion not only keeps your hands from touching, but also draws them back together when you pull them apart. Explore the sensations, the pull as you separate your hands minutely, the push as you bring them minutely closer together. Explore this "surface tension" that exists between your hands and the radiating focus you've created. You can feel where the warm, soft surface of this essence exists — this place that draws your hands into perfect equilibrium.

Then, let this radiating focus expand, slowly, putting pressure on your hands to move apart. Let the focus grow, the warmth, the soft, gentle tingling press your hands farther apart, coming to another, comfortable space of equilibrium when they are about six inches apart. Feel the surface tension again, and let your hands be drawn back together, pulled with a power that extends beyond their backs as you pull gently apart. Feel them pushed apart by this magnetic cushion that now radiates in the expanded space between your palms and fingertips.

Explore the sensations. Then let the space between your hands narrow again. Take back into you the energy/focus you've used to create the warmth, the soft, gentle tingling that exists between them. Allow the space to close once again to about 1/3". Feel the focus that once kept your hands in this cushioned equilibrium seeping back through the palms of your hands, up your arms and into your heart. Take the energy back into you, let its light fill you. And when you have let the space between your hands resolve to being about 1/3" again, explore the magnetic surface tension once more to know you're there. Gently push and pull your hands together and apart, feeling the radiating focus draw them again into balance.

Then, when you are ready to come back to "normal" awareness, open your fingers; let this field of softly tingling warmth envelop your hands like a cloud. Let your hands drift apart and your fingers bend slowly in a wave. Let the radiating focus dissolve softly back into you. Take a deeper breath, hold it for a moment, then let it out, and rest your hands at your sides. Feel your senses coming back to a more "normal" kind of awareness, and when you feel ready, open your eyes.

The focus we were exploring is something that need only exist for you, within the space of your own mind. Even so, you can see how it can have an almost physical effect on you. When you are working with an older character (Yar, for example, in Walt Disney's *Dinosaur*), you don't actually become old; you simply feel it, through and through, so that every action, every thought, and every belief you have is shaped by the radiating focus that exists within and around you as that character. Using this technique, you can turn around and jump onto a character who is as young as the other is old (Suri, also from *Dinosaur*), and with a few minutes of focused meditation, become the young girl as convincingly as you were the old man. You do this through the use of the radiating focus to permeate yourself with the character, inside and out.

Exercise 3

Let's do one more exercise with this radiating focus. With this one, we'll be exploring creating a focus, then letting it stand on its own without our "physical" proximity.

Relax, and attain the deep, meditative state again. Focus on listening to your breathing, hearing it sound exactly like someone else, deeply asleep. When you are ready, cup your hands together in front of you as if holding a delicate moth: hands close but not actually touching.

Let the soft, gentle tingling fill your hands; let it fill the space between them. Feel the almost physical presence of the tingling, noticing when the tingling begins to build into a warmth that caresses the insides of the curves of your palms and fingers. Let this warmth continue to build, the soft, gentle tingling continue to build. Let the sensations build. And as they do, through the imagery of your mind, see a golden ball of light forming in the open space between your hands.

This light is gold, bright, and comforting to "look" at. Allow these sensations to push gently at the surfaces of your hands and fingers, pressing them slowly apart. Let your hands spread as the sphere of golden light presses them slowly, gently farther apart. When the sphere reaches about 4" in diameter, allow it to build in strength, maintaining its current size. Feel the sureness of its light, the soft, golden warmth, the gentle, warm tingling of its surface build definition and confidence.

Raise your hands slowly, keeping the golden sphere within them. Raise the sphere up to your eye-level. Hold it there for a little bit, continuing to visualize its presence within your hands. Then, slowly, let your hands drop away, keeping your focus on the radiating, golden ball before your eyes. Allow your hands to drop to your sides, your breathing to continue as if one deeply asleep, and the sphere of golden light to hover in your mind before your eyes.

What to work for in this exercise is to maintain this radiating focus for as long as you choose. It takes practice. At first, it may dissipate or dissolve when you let your hands drop from its proximity. Your mind may wander, or you may lose its focus. This is natural. Practice this until you can keep the small sphere hovering before you until you choose to dissipate it, or to take the energy back into you.

You are exercising the parts of your mind that allow you to maintain a radiating focus while your thoughts are elsewhere. With practice, you will be able to maintain your focus while drawing, moving controls, or doing any of the other myriad tasks that present themselves to the digital animator (waiting through computer crashes, autosaves, network hiccups, or whatever).

Other explorations you can do with this particular exercise are to work with other colored spheres: blue, green, silver, etc. You can have multiple foci existing before you at once, each with a different color, moving them with your hands and with your mind. Explore! Play!

17.2 The Psychological Gesture

The *psychological gesture* is like a living gesture drawing. It is a gesture drawing you assume with your body. It is one of the points in Chekhov's *To the Actor* that has the closest correlation to animation. And like a thumbnail sketch or gesture drawing, it is more important that it *feels* like the essence of your character than it *looks* like him. The psychological gesture takes the idea, the essence, the one main concept of our character, and distills that thought into a physical pose you take on with your own body.

Like with a drawn silhouette, this gesture must be strong, simple, and interesting. It has to have all the qualities of good silhouette, even though you read it primarily with the feedback your body gives you as to the relationship of its parts. Working with this gesture before you animate, as you animate, holding the kinesthetic, empathic understanding of it in your mind as you move controls will have an amazing effect on the integrity of your work. You will create stronger, more powerful, more convincing animations that radiate with this essence of the character.

The psychological gesture is the distillation of all the attitudes, plans, thoughts, experiences, wants, and wishes of this character, drawn up into one physical pose. Why is it important for you to put yourself into this pose? Because the logical, rational mind will only take you so far. You are tapping into the kinesthetic, archetypal associations of the mammalian experience. Just as you were able to attain a meditative state by breathing as if one deeply asleep, there are certain keys that unlock states within our bodies that even though we might not understand them, their power is there nonetheless. They are like the fabled doors in the library at Alexandria: archetypal, symbolic, keying deeply to essences within the human experience.

Exercise 4

Imagine you'll be working on someone like Maleficent, the evil fairy from Disney's *Sleeping Beauty*. What is she? Who is she? How do you define her as an essence? You don't need to, at this point, delve into all the experiences that made her how she is; all you need to explore right now is how her primary impact on her world is, right now, this moment, as you see/feel/experience her during her performance.

Maleficent is a strong character, very strong. Her will is powerful and unbending. She is consumed with a desire to control and dominate. She is filled with hatred and disgust; the world is unworthy of what she has to give. Part of her appeal is in the power that radiates from her elegance, how each movement is carefully sculpted; nothing is left to chance.

Work with this essence. Use your own body as the loose initial strokes of a gestural drawing. In every angle of your arms, head, hands, legs, the shift of your weight capture the essence, the single, defining crystallization of this character. Feel the strength, the desire to dominate rising in your own carriage. You look down at those around you; they are not worthy of your most worthless thought. You command with your every gesture, yet you do not need to exert physical strength for this to happen. The presence and force of your will bends those around you, kings and paupers, to your control. Through this, your poise, grace, elegance are seen, felt, and tasted. Shape these feelings with your mind, feel them in your heart, allow them to sculpt your body.

Your gesture needs to be strong and well-crafted. Engrossing, encompassing the space around you, it chisels out of the very air the essence of your desires, thoughts, and needs. You are a living shorthand for the essence of this character. Repeat the gesture again. Allow yourself to settle into it from a nondescript "idle" pose. Allow the sculpting of your space to play a part of the gesture, the "getting there," a part of the idea itself. Repeat it again. Let the strength of your will increase, the desire to rule, dominate, control, the hatred, the disgust roiling within you, etching the breaths you take with acidic malice. Hold your poise as a weapon, capable through it of unleashing the fury of a thousand hells. The feelings seep, permeate your entire body, radiating outward from your mind/body union.

Figure 17.1. Perhaps your psychological gesture for Maleficent is something like this.

Exercise 5

Now, if we took a look at Peter Pan, we'd see some things that conflict with the "traditional" image we have of him with his feet spread wide, hands on his hips, and head thrown back.

Peter embraces much of the youthful joy of living, but he also consciously, willfully turns away from things that are "adult." These scare him. Were he to even contemplate that "grown-up" things would one day be a part of him, he would lose his powers. His abilities come not so much from himself, but from others' belief in him, from Tinkerbell, from the Lost Boys. In this manner, it is also Hook's belief in their conflict that gives him strength. So, Peter's confidence comes not from himself, but from the beliefs of those around him. He needs to portray enough of a mystique to keep these beliefs going; he is actually very dependent upon them. Yet, at the same time, he must keep everyone at arm's length. They can't get too close; otherwise they might see him for what he is, a scared little boy. To help effect this, he creates a personage that radiates a kind of unattainable perfection; he is the Pan, no one else can ever come close! He is dependent upon the energy of others, yet he can't look like he is; otherwise they would have power over him. This is a delicate balance.

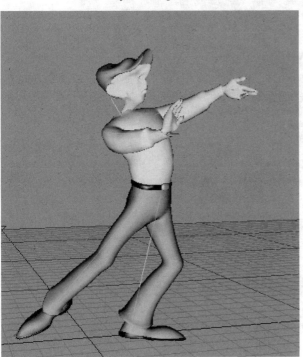

Figure 17.2. A psychological gesture for this idea of Peter Pan.

Exercise 6

There is a young girl in the film *Angel's Egg* by Yoshitaka Amano.
(This is one of those films so rich in hypnotic symbolism that it
takes many viewings to gain an understanding of it. It is brilliant in
the fact that there is barely one page of dialogue in the entire film!)
The entire film could seem to stem from psychological adaptation to
trauma; it could be entirely her vision of a schizophrenic fugue.

The young girl keeps all the bizarre occurrences, happenings,
and visions that take place in the film distant from her. Memory
seems unimportant, as does a vision of a future. She is withdrawn
with no desire to come in contact with the world in which she lives.
This isolationism isn't of weakness but of strength. She forces her
way through the film, protecting the treasure of this "angel's egg."

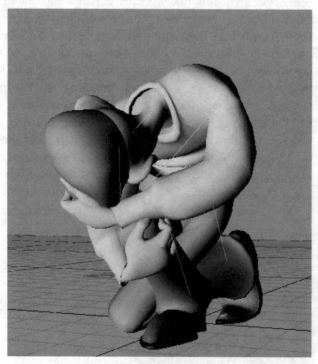

Figure 17.3. The young girl's psychological gesture may be
like this, shutting out everything but that which is within
her and her scope.

Exercise 7

Now, if we were to take someone gregarious, slightly hedonistic, with a kind and generous heart but whose mind is easily side-tracked, say, someone like Baloo from *The Jungle Book*, what kind of psychological gesture would capture the essence of him?

Baloo lives in the moment. He is open to receiving all the pleasures this world has to give with abandon. He means well, but sometimes his lack of foresight gets him into trouble. For him, the world holds very few things to be wary of. He embraces every new experience that holds the potential of enjoyment with the same kind of rapture as those he already knows to be groovy.

He is firmly rooted in this world, strong with base Chakra energy. You might spread your feet wide, grounding yourself and your energy, strengthening your connection to the earth and earthly things. He gives himself completely to the sensations of living, holding nothing back, knowing no fear. There is a beat, a rhythm to everything, and he can hear it. This beat moves everything he does in step with the rhythm of his world!

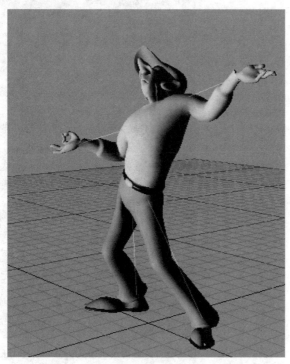

Figure 17.4. A psychological gesture representing Baloo might be something like this.

Exercise 8

Now we're going to look at a character with formidable power, but due to a lack of belief in herself, she allows herself to be swayed easily into fear. This character is Hitomi, from *Escaflowne*.

On Gaea, Hitomi finds that her "knack" for knowing the future is much more potent, so much so that she eventually finds herself shaping the reality around her with the force of her belief in what will happen. These are seldom conscious thoughts, and she often draws to herself "negative" experiences because she believes that this is what she is "supposed" to have.

She has physical strength and agility as a track and long-jump athlete, but she does not trust herself to be able to deal with what her worlds may throw at her. She doesn't exactly turn away from adverse experiences, but often wishes they weren't happening to her and doesn't confront them completely. She has a sense inside her of her own power, but she is afraid to trust it. She explores tentatively, touching but ready to draw her hand back at the slightest hint of being "burned."

Her one exception to her trepidation is where matters of her heart are concerned, but this again is born from a desire to find someone to protect her, so she doesn't have to protect herself.

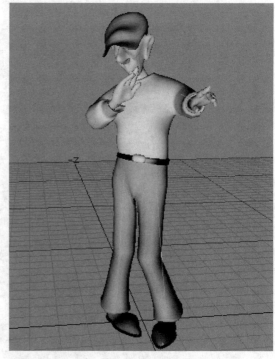

Figure 17.5. A psychological gesture for Hitomi might encompass something like this.

By studying the gestures, by allowing yourself to slide into them, you strengthen your connection with these archetypes as they exist within you.

> **Note:**
> I like to think of each one of us as being like the shards of a hologram. The image each one of us represents is the universe, the ultimate all of everything there is. Goddess, God, Allah, universe, etc. — this is the image, this is the hologram. If you were to take a hologram and break it in two, each half of that photographic plate would have the entire original image but from its own unique viewpoint. Break it into a thousand pieces, and you have a thousand complete representations of the original whole, but a thousand slightly different points of view. Within each of us is the understanding of everything there is, but from our singular viewpoint. The wonderful thing about our minds being as they are is that we can extrapolate from our own solitary point of view and understand many, many others. These archetypes exist within us all, balanced and blended, particularized to become the us of everyday life. How we balance the archetypes as they represent facets of ourselves and how we allow these facets to impact our world(s) defines us as beings. The archetypes, what the psychological gestures represent and help us make tangible to ourselves, exist within us. Understanding them (both the positives and the "negatives") is important, as actors, animators, and positive additions to this world and the worlds we touch.

The psychological gestures I've illustrated here are by no means "correct," or even necessarily "on target" for anyone other than me. They are right, for me, for my own point of view on existence. Try them on, allow yourself to don them from a "neutral" position; see how the gesture affects your own psychology as you draw nearer and nearer to the pose. How does the pose itself make you feel when you reach it? How does it feel to hold the pose? What are the differences you feel between successive repetitions of the poses?

Explore what you know of these characters to hone this psychological gesture to what you know to be true for how you see them. If you're unfamiliar with a particular character, go on the description I've included to craft something that you feel is a kinesthetic representation of that idea — simple, strong, interesting, powerful. Let the focus of the character swirl around you in an almost tangible mist. Your confidence in the "rightness" of the pose is your power.

> **Note:**
>
> There's a wonderful thing about high-energy physics. And that is the acknowledgment that the act of observing an event alters it. This is why Heisenberg laid out his "uncertainty principle," which says that you cannot simultaneously know both an object's position and momentum. You can see this if, instead of using photons to measure the position of a hot-dog cart, you were to use a '67 Camero to figure out where the hot-dog cart had been. Because of this, one can extrapolate this to mean that we each measure things slightly differently; even two people standing side by side experience the same event slightly differently. Both are correct, but both are unique. This holds true with our perceptions of beings as well. To me, Simba (to pick someone most of us are familiar with) is quite different from the Simba that you know. We're both right, and both very different. (Just as no two of your friends have the same impression of who you are.)

> **Note:**
>
> "Perspective" is the illusion created when you see things from only a single point of view.

Now, how do you apply this "psychological gesture" stuff to actual, practical use in a production you may be working on?

The wonderful thing about animation is that chances are you have more than just a collection of lexical symbols representing the idea of a character to work from (a script). You have character model sheets, pose sheets, storyboards, dialogue tracks, and probably video reference footage from the voice actor as he recorded the dialogue. This is a blessing that stage actors (and the folks whose job is to create these first passes at the characters' identities) don't have.

When you are analyzing anything creative — a script, a painting, a piece of animation — you have basically two separate directions you can take. Both directions start from the same point, the point of you interacting with this creative essence, and from there, they attempt to form an opinion on what it is that is being experienced. You have your logical, analytical, cerebral mind you can throw at the task, or you can use your empathic, intuitive, emotional side.

I'm not going to knock using your intellect to penetrate the layers of a creative experience. It can be a useful tool, but I am going to suggest saving "left brain" tasks for after your "right brain" has had its full shot at the matter. Someone's right brain, after all, had the directorial role in the manifestation of any creative experience. Using your empathic, intuitive, emotional right brain, you will be "speaking the same language" as the creator of the work, as he was deeply steeped in the process of creation. There are volumes of information that can be transferred in a moment through right brain centers. Allowing yourself to experience a piece as you would a psychological gesture, mentally wrapping the experience of the work around you, letting it penetrate through you, you are instantly and intuitively, kinesthetically, and empathically aware of everything from the pivotal to the trivial within the piece.

By using only your analytical mind (your left brain), you reduce emotion, sensation, and intuition to concepts. You blunt their edges so the impact is far less than it is with a more emotive experience. Using only the left brain to experience a creative work, you can far too easily drain it of warmth, feeling, and passion.

> **Note:**
> "The more your mind knows about a character, the less you are able to perform it."
> — Michael Chekhov

It is only through a blending, a balancing of both left and right brain functions, allowing each to do what it does best, taking turns at the proper time, that you can fully assimilate a creative work. After you are full of feelings, after the right brain has flooded you with the indescribable, your left brain must sift through the information, classifying it and aligning it with things you've already experienced, emotional states you already understand and can create with your own work. By letting the two halves of your mind work together, each doing what it does best and when it can do its best, you are beginning to unlock undreamed-of potential within the human mind.

> **Note:**
> The secret to life drawing isn't in drawing exactly what you see; it is in learning to draw your own imaginary model so well that you can instantly identify how the "real" model deviates from what you know.

This is why I have stressed throughout this book (when talking about the creative issues) to go by "feel." Does this or that have the "feel" it did when you imagined it, when you lived it, when you held the character's psychological gesture pose? Going by your "gut," you will be able to look at something and though you may not know why it doesn't quite "feel right," you know that you have to make another visitation at that part. You might not know exactly what it is you have to do to make it "right," but in trusting your intuition (right brain) and knowing how you achieved certain results before (left brain), you will almost always arrive at this point of "perfection" light-years ahead of trying to use only logic to solve the same problem.

Using every asset at your disposal, every technique you know, understand, and have internalized, approach your creative issues as first "gut feelings," then holding that feeling close, not letting it falter or disintegrate, turn your analytical mind loose on the task of using your tools to recreate that gut feeling within the medium at hand. Your right brain provides a road map, your left brain provides the means to get there. And this is why you need to internalize the tools and techniques so well that you can forget them. You need to trust your left brain implicitly to know how to take you there. You don't want to get in its way as it's doing its job — you'll just slow it down! Allow your left brain the luxury of using every trick, ability, and skill you can give it. You and your right brain will just be along for the ride, getting there with as much enjoyment and ease as you can.

So, with the materials given to you — the storyboards, the dialogue tracks, the script, the pose sheets, the test animations — allow yourself to craft a psychological gesture for the character. You don't need to be "right"; this is just a jumping-off point. (And besides, the only person who can say whether your psychological gesture is "right" is you — even the director can only make suggestions or improvements; he is also just another point of view on this tool you will use to create a final product.) Try the character on. Your right brain will know if the psychological gesture fits or not. Your intuition will tell you if one part of your gesture rings true, while the rest needs to be shifted.

Ask yourself what the main, focusing thread of the character is. Even if all you get is a vague inclination from this question, give it a go. You may only get a feeling for a part of the gesture, say for a hand or an arm, the cant of your pelvis, the shifting of your weight. Let this lead you onward, let it help sculpt the rest of your body. For a character who seeks interaction with his environment, you feel that at least one arm needs to be thrust outward. Adjust it until it rings true. Palms open, facing upward to receive inspiration from the Divine, perhaps facing outward as if to ward off a blow. Cup your hands together as if asking for alms. Gnarl them to fearful, evil claws, grasping at power you cravenly desire.

Just getting one part of your body to resonate with the character's psychological gesture will continue to lead you onward, each part falling into place almost without thought. You will know when your gesture is there. The pose itself will lead you. You can build on a psychological gesture for another character you already know to have power. You can build the power within you by reaching a pose you know you can settle into with comfort and ease, building your focus, letting it radiate from you. Then you can use this energy to sculpt what you intuit of the character into an archetype of form and gesture.

Drop the pose, shake it off, then assume it again. Each time, make small adjustments as the feelings come to you, honing it, sharpening its focus closer and closer to the ideal represented by the character. By honing the psychological gesture, exploring,

367

adjusting, perfecting, you are allowing the energies that focus within this character to move also through you. You are becoming the character yourself!

The psychological gesture, by the very nature of its archetypal symbolism, resonates with key parts of your own being, unlocking and opening pathways within you. You feel the character begin to stir and awaken within you as feelings and understandings that are not your "normal, day-to-day" self. You begin to know how this character would hold his hand, head, or torso, you begin to know what this character's timings and responses would be. You know this because you feel this essence moving within you. You can look at a keyframe you've done and know in an instant whether it fits with the essence that this psychological gesture holds.

There is such information within the psychological gesture, this single, intuited pose because your own body is moved, through and through, by the condensed energy of the character. His core, his most primal motivating goals and ideals, his experience is now yours. The information contained within a single, psychological gesture could take a thousand books to explain the hows and whys of a character. Yet, you know it, through and through. You know it because while you exist with the psychological character, you are one with the character's soul.

This is a key difference between the "left brain" and the "right brain." The left brain is the mind that likes to cubbyhole things into nice, orderly arrays. It is almost entirely responsible for us being able to encapsulate information and knowledge so that it doesn't need another living being there to propagate it; it is responsible for writing. Left brain information changes little from observer to observer. The left brain is the key to standing on the shoulders of giants when those giants are no longer there to help us.

Right brain is the mind of intuition, of "knowing," of "feeling," of "intuiting." Its realm is much more volatile. When right brain stimulus isn't there, right brain experience dissipates, like smoke in the wind, leaving (usually) only a left brain symbol of the memory of the experience. Music, with its ability to convey emotion and, at its best, information across language and cultural barriers, slips like a mist through the fingers of your mind after the last echoes have played themselves out (unless you have trained your mind to "replay" this kind of information — something anyone can do with practice). A painting, deep and visceral, moving you as no other work you've seen ever has; how does it look when you turn away from it? You may be able to remember bits and pieces of it, or remember symbols of it. (He was holding a bronze plate of smoldering herbs — I think there was a fan of raven-wing feathers in his other hand.) But the instant knowing, the emotional, empathic, perhaps even "telepathic" conduit of bidirectional informational flow is reduced to the memory of echoes when the experience of the right brain stimulus is gone.

A balance of both left and right brain is required as an animator. (And I think working to attain and maintain a balance of left and right brain functionality will serve you best as you move through life.) You can train yourself, you can hone the areas of your mind if you feel you are lacking in one or the other. Classes on symbolism and myth, the works of Joseph Campbell, and Eastern works of art can all help strengthen both your left and right brain, and the connection between them (the corpus colossum).

Your mind will give you what you ask of it. You can increase the aptitude of a lesser-used half of your brain. And you can increase the flow of information across the corpus colossum (and women, medically, seem to have a higher initial capacity for throughput). If you ask of your mind, it will be given. Our brains physically restructure themselves every single moment! Sound far-fetched? Consider that memory is stored physically, in the shape of synaptic connections!

If you feel you need help with right brain work, play short clips of a symphony or other musical work, and focus on replaying what you heard in your mind. Not just "remembering" but actually hearing it again in your mind, in its entirety. Practice hearing just the oboe or just the second violin, both as you replay it and as you listen with your ears. Practicing with the radiating focus is another way to increase your powers of experiential cognition. Imagine seeing the room in which you sit from another point of view, another vantage point, with or without your eyes open. Imagine what it would look like to be flying around your room, your house, or your yard. These are wonderful, quiet ways of honing your right mind and helping to strengthen its bridge to your left. And of course, studying painting (alla prima, "all at once," painting seems to have the strongest impact on training the right mind), acting, dance, music, any other "art" you can find enjoyable to study is only going to help you on your journey.

369

Can you have individual psychological gestures for certain scenes, bits of dialogue, or action? Certainly! They must all be refinements, dissertations, or explorations of the primary, core psychological gesture. Even for Cruella DeVille (*101 Dalmatians*), as close to bordering on "split personality disorder" as she is, each of the psychological gestures that represent her mood swings are still parts of her core psychological gesture. Her personality turns on a dime when she finds Perdita's puppies to be without spots, then again when she finds out that they will eventually become spotted. In each section of this sequence, she is completely within a different psychological gesture, but each one is an aspect of the core of who she is.

The shifts between scene- or sentence-based psychological gestures need not be as drastic as with Cruella. Subtle shifts show the character as he evolves and changes. And in order for a character to live, we need to see him evolve and grow. The things he experiences must have an impact on him that shifts him from where he was to where he will be. As with ourselves, a character's "present" is an ever-shifting conduit from his future to his past. I believe this is why Shan-Yu from *Mulan* was such a two-dimensional character. He looked the part of a villain, often he moved as one, and his dialogue was executed with believability, but very little was done to show any evolution within his character. He remains much the same at the end of the film as he began. This is boring to an audience, and unbelievable in storytelling.

The best kind of progression for a character to make through a story can be seen as a "spiral." This is the *mythic mode* of storytelling. The *masculine mode* of storytelling can be illustrated as a straight line, forever marching forward, never looking back, never revisiting the same position as was once held. The *feminine mode* of storytelling can be seen more as a circle. This is the kind of evolution that leaves the character right back where he was where he began, following the same path. ("Masculine" and "feminine" are only classifications of different modes of storytelling structure; this is not meant to be derogatory to masculine or feminine energy in any way.)

A mythic type of storytelling (or character evolution) is one that combines both masculine and feminine modes. The character "comes full circle" (perhaps two or three times within a story), yet at each revolution, he has progressed along a path and is not quite where he was when he began.

A key to the old mystery schools (even within the foundations of Judaism and Christianity) is to use storytelling to effect change within the audience. This is done by connecting with and then altering the mental focus of the audience. This is done through symbolism that leads the audience along paths that connect with patterns of archetypal levels within them. Archetypal levels are emotional states that are common to all, hard-wired into the fabric of our psyche.

Figure 17.6. A visual representation of the "masculine," "feminine," and "mythic" modes of storytelling.

> **Note:**
>
> Archetypal levels can be associated with the different Chakra points (energy centers) within certain aspects of Eastern philosophy (the Kundalini), from the "root" or Sacral Chakra representing grounded, earthly energies to the Crown Chakra representing the OverSoul, the connection with the Divine. A character's mythic evolution can be traced as his focus moves through each one of these archetypal foci: Crown, "Third Eye," Throat, Heart, Solar Plexus, Stomach, and Sacrum. Each of these represents an archetypal, psychological/emotional state of being.

Exposure to certain symbols actually causes chemical changes within the brain. (Though it may seem far-fetched, there are thoughts that are equivalent to a form; the reverse is also true.) The symbols that affect this kind of change upon us are *archetypical symbols*. This does not mean that these symbols are ancient, from times long ago and places long-forgotten. Archetypical symbols can be any symbol that has a strong and moving impact on the audience, an impact that is common regardless of the boundaries of language or culture.

In a mythic story, where the characters evolve along a spiral path, each "turn" finds them learning new things, not just remembering what they had once known but actually progressing forward, building new elements within their psyche. The symbology that incorporating Chakra centers represents is a wonderful overview to make sure that your characters are indeed evolving, and evolving archetypically (though any kind of association with archetypal traits will do, Eastern or Western). When you can see your characters moving from one focus to another, fitting more completely in a new archetypal state than the one they recently held, you know that the symbology the being of your character is exuding has evolved archetypically. Knowing this, you also know that you are making a deep and direct impact on your audience!

> **Note:**
> Symbols need not be a single, static image or shape. Symbols encompass ideas, essences, emotion, and experience; they are metaphor. Symbols can exist within any medium we can perceive!

The fact that symbols have actual chemical effects on the brain is why we spend so much time analyzing silhouettes (symbols) within our animation. It is why we work so hard to capture the essence of an idea or form in a series of drawings that combine to create motion. It is also why the best animators and actors are able to move us so deeply with the performances of their characters. They are not simply representing an occurrence, a happening; they are encompassing an archetype, carefully sculpted so the modern audience feels the subtle complexity of a living being, that is in essence himself, a subtly shifting, ever-flowing archetype.

This is the magic. This is why you and I have found such a pull toward animation that we have been drawn to becoming animators. This is why we must give this gift of experiencing a beautifully woven, powerfully moving story, with characters alive with archetypal ideals of mythic storytelling to others.

Acting, storytelling, animation — they are something more than "real life." Real-life gestures, actions, and thoughts don't have the power, the ability to stir us to our cores. They don't have the archetypal essences to move us into elemental states of being. "Real-life" gestures are too insubstantial, too weak, too splayed, or too specific. They do not fill our body and soul; our focus is elsewhere while we go through the motions of daily life. Archetypes and psychological gestures fill you entirely with their focus, body and soul.

The best acting is a subtle blending of archetype and everyday. Just as in every good drawing there is an element of caricature, within even the most "realistic" animation, there is archetype, there is mythic nature and structure, to move the audience, carry them along into "learning states," where they are receptive to the story you have to tell. Just as a mythic character would seem drastically out of place in the corner diner, a character who is only "real-life" gestures and motions would be hopelessly lost within good acting, within good animation, and within good storytelling.

Back to creating and working with psychological gestures. Though the feeling from the psychological gesture should be strong, full of power, stirring the soul, and honing the will, it should not encompass unnecessary tension. The crooked hands of a hag are clawlike from flexers and extensers battling with each other; a mother's embrace of her newborn is no less powerful, but done with the delicacy of a summer breeze. Power and strength come from focus, letting your focus radiate from within you, not from exertion of your muscles.

Just as in Exercise 6, the *Angel's Egg* girl's gesture and silhouette are not weak; they radiate with power and emotion. Concepts of softness, gentleness, laziness, or tiredness do nothing to reduce the strength of the psychological gesture; it is an aspect of it, but its power is still without question.

And just as the silhouettes we evaluate in animation are critiqued, so are the psychological gestures! They must be simple, as understandable as possible, able to be grasped in a split second, and without the need of the analytical mind kicking in for even a

373

moment. There should be nothing vague whatsoever about the pose. Psychological gestures also have to be interesting; they have to hold your attention. (If you are bored, your audience will be bored as well!) Use large, broad strokes, with fine detail in which to delve, leading the eye, leading the heart of the holder. Layer upon layer, the information within is almost fractal in its simplicity. There must always be something more.

As you work with psychological gestures, experiment with timing and tempo. The tempos of animated characters are as varied as Droopy and Woody Woodpecker; the tempos of your psychological gestures should be just as varied.

The tempos of the gestures in Figures 17.2 and 17.3 vary greatly. Tempo can be achieved in many ways, from the speed with which you assume the pose to the carriage of the pose itself (as in Figures 17.2 and 17.3).

A character's evolution can sometimes be shown just through simple changes in tempo, preserving the same essence of the psychological gesture. A change in tempo can also completely redefine a psychological gesture. If you assume the pose of Figure 17.1, slowly, deliberately, with great care in the arcs that resolve themselves into the gesture, the pose feels very much like Maleficent: elegant, plotting, patient, brilliant, and self-controlled. If you were to assume that pose quickly, in a flash, the pose might feel more like the first encounters with Beast in Disney's *Beauty and the Beast*.

Changes in tempo can show the progression of thought, the interaction of external stimuli, and the evolution of the character. Understanding tempo through experimentation and feeling its effects on your own psyche as you take on and work with psychological gestures allows you to use this powerful acting tool with subtlety and strength.

Using a different tempo for the character's inner thoughts and his outward actions can be a powerful tool for creating depth within a character. The character's actions may be slow, well-thought out, planned, and carefully executed, leaving not a nuance to chance. But his thoughts may move at lightning speed, formulating, testing, calculating, reassessing. Mandible from *Antz* is one such character. Gene Hackman's voice work suggested many instances where a myriad of possible things to say flashed through Mandible's mind as he searched for the words that would best further his desires. The animators brilliantly took this dialogue and worked in subtle pauses showing this train of thought, the differences between his inward and outward tempos. All the while, they preserved Mandible's connection to his psychological gesture (which might be similar to Maleficent's in Figure 17.1).

A quick outer tempo and a slow inner tempo can do much more than imply a "fast talker" covering for his lack of inner "oomph." This contrast can imply the practiced skill of an outright master. And this mastery doesn't have to be over something like swordsmanship; it can be something as mundane as shipping parcels. Practice allows the body to go on "autopilot," running quickly through familiar tasks as the mind relaxes.

How can you show these combinations, these contrasts? Our physical bodies can reach limits of what they are technically capable of showing. How do you let these subtleties read through? You do this by bringing into play techniques of the radiating focus.

When you've "entered" a psychological gesture, and your body has given you all it can give in terms of rotations and translations, don't just let it drop. Hold it for another ten to fifteen seconds. And as you hold it, plus it with your mind! You've reached a point where moving a hand or an arm isn't going to increase the strength of the gesture, so let the force of your presence that fills you seep beyond the physical bounds of your body, enveloping and sculpting the

> **Note:**
> When you finish with an experience such as combining radiating focus and psychological gesture, remember to take a moment to let the focus dissipate, to "take the energy back into you," or to reconnect with the centers of your own essence. This is as important as the gesture itself. It helps to outline a path to return to the gesture, and to yourself. C.S. Lewis remarked that the writing of *The Screwtape Letters* was one of the most unnerving things he had ever done; he had to *become* this creature jockeying to tip one man's soul toward evil. You have to give yourself a path back to yourself, as it were. (Archetypal symbols will create changes within you, just as they do within your audience. Some of these you may be thankful for; others you may wish to shed.) Method acting is a potent tool for creating the most powerful of performances; used properly, it can also help you to know yourself, and it can help with your own personal, emotional, and spiritual evolution. We can experience "challenging" lives as if they were our own, and then come back to the "safety" of our own, quiet existences. And by learning to appreciate who you are, with respect to another spirit you've known as well as your own, you not only know the character more deeply, but yourself as well.

space around you. Use the techniques we worked on in practicing the radiating focus to fill yourself with the essence, the energy, the archetypal focus of this gesture. *Feel* the essence of this pose within you, filling every corner of your mind's impression of your body; instead of a "sphere" of focus, your entire body is your focus, what your body represents is your focus, and it cannot be bounded by simple things like flesh. Allow it to radiate out from you, to fill the space around you with the very pressure of the gesture itself!

Exercise 9

Subtle changes within the form of a psychological gesture can completely alter its emotional keys within you, even inverting them entirely.

Take on the pose in Figure 17.7. As you go from your "rest" position to the gesture, say, "I wish to be left alone." Allow the sen-sations of calmness, of a certainty that you know what you want and that it is within your rights to ask for it to permeate your essence. Allow this to radiate through both your voice and your ges-ture. Repeat this until you feel a union with the essence you are working toward, your voice and your body. Everything should be an extension of the primary core of calm-ness, a gentle but firm strength of will to close one's self off from one's current environment.

Figure 17.7. A simple gesture suggesting calmness and closing one's self off.

Now, repeat the gesture, but this time, resolve it with your head tilted downward. What effect does this small change have on your feelings? Did it make you feel more stubborn, more insisting? These feelings should be added to the base you've already achieved. Repeat the gesture a few more times until these new colorings fill your psyche, your voice, and your body.

Now to alter the feeling entirely. Resolve the gesture with your palms turned to face outward and your head thrown back, tilting it to one side, your eyes closed. Now the pose radiates pleading, vulnerability; the trauma of an attack. Tears may well up, your voice may falter as you beg your perpetrator to leave you alone.

Explore different, small changes to this gesture (any we have gone through already or one of your own creation). What we are doing is building a sensitivity to the subtlety minute change can evoke. The more subtle the changes you explore, the greater depth of sensitivity you will find within yourself.

Subtlety and sensitivity are tools that will help you attain mastery. What you are working toward is to have a unity between your psyche, body, and speech. As you work with these and similar techniques, the definition between these elements will begin to blur. You will eventually be able to say with confidence that your body and speech, the poses that come through you are tangible representations of your soul.

The psychological gesture is a tool for yourself and your director only. It is not something to be shared with the "uninitiated" public. Like unfinished animation or rough thumbnail drawings, the psychological gesture requires a complete understanding in order to comprehend and appreciate it.

The psychological gesture is something that you "hold" with you as you draw, as you manipulate controls, as you examine your work for purity and truth to what you know to be the character. Your character will (most likely) never assume the psychological gesture on screen. The psychological gesture is an archetypal symbol, kinesthetically, empathically, and visually; and it is for you and you alone. It retains holographically all the information you know about the character. You can go to it mentally, emotionally, physically, verbally, any time you need to create, review, or revise. It is your tool through which you will do great works; keep it safe, and use it well.

17.3 **Characterization**

Character and characterizations are not the same thing. A *characterization* is a little thing you develop to personalize the character and help define him. This may be fumbling with his clothing, folding or hiding his hands, scratching an ear. These are little symbols that the audience comes to identify with your character.

Characterizations are "finishing touches," and can endear an audience to the character. The viewers can begin to expect, anticipate, and look for these personal features whenever your character is on-screen. They are symbols in and of themselves that serve to reinforce the character as a whole.

Someone being officious and trying to exert his presence within his surroundings could habitually rearrange the items around him, aligning them to right angles to the desks and shelves on which they sit. You could even build in a gag with this as the person with whom he must interact purposefully sets something askew again to assert his own dominance (especially if it is his space). If the pedantic character is subordinate, you can run a gag showing his resolve weakening as he fights with the desire to set the newly askew knickknack straight.

Someone who doesn't like to be around others could push items within their reach away from them. A dominant, intimidating person may have developed an unconscious habit of shaking his head "No" as if to interrupt the speaker. Someone who is shy may continuously glance away from someone interacting with him, at the ceiling or floor or at objects just beyond the other character.

Imagine and play! Rewatch old favorite films and try to catch the characterizations the great actors and animators bestowed upon their characters. But as you watch, build within yourself the intuition of what you yourself would do as that character.

> **Note:**
> "The ability to observe becomes more acute when you know exactly what you are looking for."
> — Michael Chekhov

17.4 **Character**

One of the most enjoyable and creative techniques for developing your character is something I was taught long ago in a college course on directing. It is a technique that blends everything in this chapter into a single powerful tool.

What is this tool? It is a technique Chekhov calls "the Imaginary Body."

The wonderful thing about learning this tool in a collegiate setting was that it lent validity to "flights of fancy" I had enjoyed since I was very young! No longer was I guilty of "daydreaming," "wasting time," "lollygagging," or being generally irresponsible. No, this was work! This was dedication to my craft, to my Art (with a capital "A"). This was my responsibility, what I needed to do in order to become the best animator/actor/director/writer I could be!

What using the technique of the Imaginary Body does for an actor is that it alters what you perceive through your body, and what others perceive of your body. Your physical body radiates with the essence of another, and its senses are filtered through this Imaginary Body. It can alter the way a thin actor carries himself to convince the audience beyond all doubt that he is indeed corpulent, and without the addition of prosthetic make-up! It is how a young actor can convincingly play someone aged, a male can convincingly play someone female, and how someone wise can play an imbecile, or vice versa!

What this means for an animator is that we begin to know and understand the character to a degree not possible any other way. We have lived as the character. We understand the intricacies of his being, his littlest habits and his grandest dreams, because we have become them, walked miles not just in their shoes but with their entire body! With this technique, there is no grasping as to what a character will do when you're handed a sequence to work on; you know, because you have been them, and when the need arises, you are them again.

Allow your mind and body to relax. Then, letting the creative powers of your mind radiate outward from your body, using the techniques of the radiating focus, and helped by an understanding of the psychological gesture, "clothe" yourself in an Imaginary Body that is the character. (You know what this character looks like; you have model sheets, pose sheets, CG models, and pre-production art.)

Within the same space as your own "physical" body occupies, you use your radiating focus to create the body you know to be your character. This body exists between your real body and your spirit. It touches your soul, as it moves your body. You begin to think as he does, to experience the world as he does, to move, to speak, and to evolve as he does. It changes your whole being, both psychically and psychologically. It transforms you entirely into this other being.

As you build this Imaginary Body, don't rush into moving around in it too quickly. Sit or stand quietly, becoming comfortable with the sensations of feeling with another's hands, of seeing through another's eyes, of breathing through another's nose. Let it become comfortable and natural to you. When you do begin to get up and move around, trust this Invisible Body to guide your movements. Trust it implicitly; don't try to sculpt it into the performance you might be expecting. Allow it to reveal bits and pieces of the character you may be as yet unaware of.

Let the character be your guide. Don't force things or try to overexaggerate things. Just let the experiences flow naturally around and through you. Only when you feel completely comfortable in this Imaginary Body should you rehearse the lines of your sequence.

To rehearse in this manner, as an animator, you can imagine the lines your character says, or you can let your dialogue track loop as you act out the scene. (Be sure to have the loop padded with silence at the head and tail so you can reposition yourself and analyze what you just did as the character!)

> **Note:**
> Some people have suggested venturing into public with this Imaginary Body as a means of exploring the character. I would caution against this. You have to look out for your own physical safety (say, if you're riding a public bus as a loud and boisterous character, and you are not naturally loud or boisterous), and the safety of the character himself. Any "emotional wounds" he may receive that aren't congruent with the story he must live may leave "emotional scar tissue" that could make it difficult for you to effectively play certain scenes.

In addition to the Imaginary Body, you can use the tools of radiating focus to help hone the character.

You can place (and maintain) your glowing, radiating focus in any of the archetypal centers (Chakras) to heighten the aspect of your character that they represent.

As your character evolves from one archetypal level to another, visualizing the radiating focus moving from one archetypal center to another will help lead you to experiencing that change yourself! And in experiencing it, you are more capable of portraying it through your art!

Moving your radiating focus from your heart to your head moves you from emotional to cognitive centers. Moving it to your crown enhances the connection with the Divine.

You can also play with foci outside the body as well. If you were to be animating a meddlesome, prying character, you could envision a tiny, hard focus just beyond the tip of your nose. Moving a focus to a few feet out in front of your eyes can enhance a sense of a keen, penetrating character.

If you have to play an absent-minded character, moving the focus quickly, just beyond his "mental reach," can effect a feeling of dishevelment. If you are asked to animate someone who is drunk, letting the focus wander aimlessly through his body will give you a convincing performance.

As the focus works through your own bodies (physical and imaginary), so it should work through your character's model as you animate. No one else need ever know where his focus is or of what kind, but you should know. You should know and feel this, beyond any doubt, as you watch your poses take shape before you, and as you watch the final scene play before you. You should feel your own memories of how the focus felt within you resonating in sympathetic vibration with what you see in your character's performance.

17.5 **The Animator's Trust**

These are only a few of the tools open and available to you. Perhaps I may be placing too much weight on what we do, but I feel that there is a huge trust placed within animators and other dreamers of this world. We have been given the responsibility to shape the visions and dreams of those out there, young and old. It is a place of honor. It is a position of responsibility.

I've always felt that we as animators should do everything within our power to create the best, most moving, thought-provoking, memorable, evolutionary, and powerful experiences for those who seek to be enveloped by the worlds we create, again and again. Not only does every new step to becoming a better animator make what you do more enjoyable and fulfilling, it makes your work more alive, more real (to both you and the audience). Study as much as you can, study everything you think might be interesting; it can only add to your well of experience. Do everything you can to fall head-over-heels in love with this beautiful, wonderful honor and gift we are given, this gift which we in turn give back to the world!

Advanced Animation Tools

Back when I was in art school, one assignment had us doing an 18" x 24" rendering entirely by stippling (making tiny dots) with a fine-point technical pen. It took most people about two weeks, and the only reason most of us actually completed this assignment was that our final grade depended on our having done so.

What a pedantic pain in the posterior!

But I tell you what, after that exercise, when we could again reach for that blessedly wide piece of charcoal or conté crayon to quickly lay in our shading, we had a newfound respect for the clarity and precision we were seeking in our renderings.

Let me be blunt. These new animation tools are fantastic time-savers, *and* they reduce the precision of mental focus required to produce quality results.

Basically, they allow/encourage you to be *sloppy*.

So, there you go. You've been forewarned.

Using these tools, you'll be able to double, triple, even quadruple your output for the same amount of effort you expend in creating your animations. And, I strongly suggest, that like all the top animators in the field, you make a commitment to yourself and your skills to continually revisit the basics of animation every year or so.

Revisit the basics without any of these timesaving tools to hone your focus of mind.

The quality of your mental focus will allow you to know your target, and then hit your target without the "hunt-and-peck" method that these powerful, effective advanced animation tools can allow.

> **Note:**
> Going in-depth on all the ins and outs of these advanced animation tools could be a book itself! I'm going to give you a taste of how these tools can be used here (how I've used these tools in a production environment). If you like what you see, use the problem-solving skills you've developed. Dive into LightWave's searchable, HTML help documentation to find all the gory details of these "super-mega-ultra-" powerful tools!

18.1 Dope Sheet

For years, the exposure sheet (X-sheet) has been the trusted companion to the animator. By using a stopwatch, making quick, easily adjusted notations on this "animator's spreadsheet," and previsualizing the scene before any labor-intense work is done, it allowed the animator to know his target, and then bring his skills to bear in hitting that target.

Thanks to animators all over the world calling repeatedly for a digital equivalent to this invaluable tool, the programmers of our 3D tools have now given us something far more powerful than any traditional animator ever knew. In LightWave, it's called the Dope Sheet.

Figure 18.1. Laid out horizontally (as opposed to the vertical layout of a traditional animator's X-sheet) we'll only be exploring the combination of the Items and Dope Sheet tabs. There's an incredible amount of power within this seemingly simple interface. (Check out the LW documentation to find out how you can modify nearly every aspect of your scenes, objects, lights, cameras, and even surfaces through this powerful tool.)

Note:

The beauty of working with the Dope Sheet is that you can quickly and easily lay in poses, and then slide those poses around until you get the timing you want. (Animation consists of posing and timing; this means that one aspect of animation can practically take care of itself.)

The danger of working with the Dope Sheet is that it doesn't require you to have as clear a pre-vision before actually starting your animation. While it is the end results that really matter, I strongly feel that developing and maintaining the skills to know your mark and then hit your mark is vital to being a good animator.

Figure 18.2. Let's say that I wanted to make a quick adjustment to the FlyBall.lws "Life-Drawing in Motion" scene you worked with earlier, that I wanted to make the point where the bat connects with the ball more "snappy."

Figure 18.3. The first thing I'd do (after loading the scene, of course) would be to open the new version of the Scene Editor (new as of 8.0) using **Scene Editor | Open... ^F1**, then right-click on the model with the animation I wanted to modify and choose **Expand child items (recursive)** to make all its bits and pieces visible in the Dope Sheet and accessible for manipulation.

Figure 18.4. Keyframes are represented for the items you can see on the left-hand side of the Scene Editor as little blocks, color-coded to whatever color you have set for that particular item. You can zoom your view by clicking and dragging on either end of the pan-handle at the bottom of the screen (just above the VCR-like play-control buttons) the width of the keys, and timeline rule marks (top) will smoothly update to reflect your zoom/pan settings.

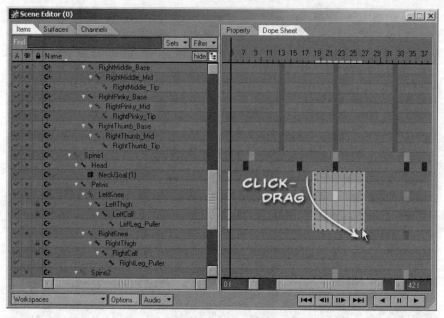

Figure 18.5. By (left) clicking and dragging in the Dope Sheet, you define a selection box. Frames that have been selected (including keyframes) lighten in comparison to the unselected frames. You can add to this selection by Shift-clicking elsewhere in the Dope Sheet...

Figure 18.6. ...And you can add *discontinuous* frames to your selection by Ctrl-clicking (and dragging) anywhere outside the dotted-line rectangle that represents the extents of the current selection(s).

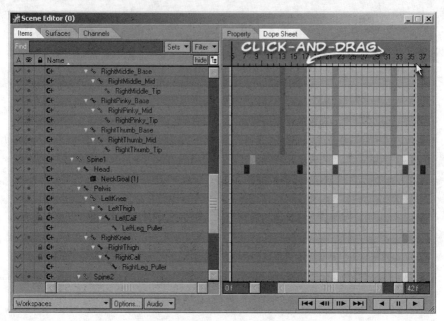

Figure 18.7. You can select keyframes for all the items visible on the left-hand side of the Scene Editor for a specific time range by clicking (and dragging) on the little rule marks on the timeline.

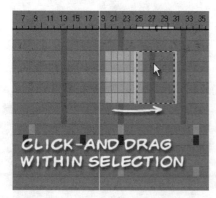

Figure 18.8. Once you have a selection defined, you can right-click and drag within the selected area and slide the selected keys left or right along the timeline.

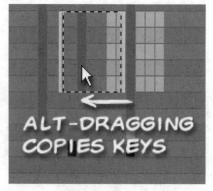

Figure 18.9. Alt-dragging drags a copy of your selected keyframes.

Figure 18.10. Dragging the ends of the selection stretches/squishes the selected keys in time.

Warning:

Stretching/squishing keyframes in time (as mentioned in Figure 18.10) will often result in those keys being on a fractional frame (i.e., frame 3.1415769...).

If a keyframe falls on a fractional frame, the only way to get at that frame is to activate General Options | Fractional Frames, and Shift-Left Arrow to Snap to Previous Keyframe (or Shift-Right Arrow to Snap to Next Keyframe).

If you're just putting the final adjustments on an animation, this doesn't matter since LightWave's renderer deals just fine with fractional frames.

However, if you're still planning on tweaking your work, this can be a pain in the posterior.

A fix to this fractional frame issue is to select the fractional frames in a Scene Editor (or leave them selected if you've just performed a stretch/squish action) and, from the right-click menu, choose Quantize. (More on Quantize below!)

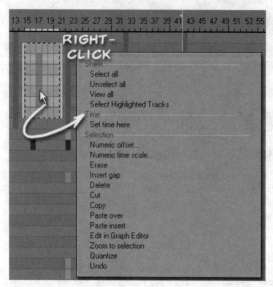

Figure 18.11. Right-clicking on a selection opens up a menu that gives you even more options.

▶ **Erase** clears the selected keyframes, leaving the surrounding keys in place.

▶ **Insert gap** "pushes" the keys that follow the selection forward in time by the number of keys selected.

▶ **Delete** removes the selected keyframes, "pulling" the keys that follow backward in time by the number of keys selected.

▶ **Cut** erases the selected frames, holding their values in memory.

▶ **Copy** brings the selected frames' values into memory.

▶ **Paste over** replaces the current selection with the values in memory. (The pasted selection doesn't have to be copied/cut from the same item.)

▶ **Paste insert** puts the values from memory into the selected track(s), "pushing" the keys that follow forward in time by the number of frames in the current selection.

▶ **Edit in Graph Editor** opens a Graph Editor window containing the function curves for the items to which the selected tracks belong.

▶ **Zoom to selection** causes the zoom settings to bound the current selection.

▶ **Quantize** removes any keyframes that fall on fractional frames, establishing the requisite keys on the nearest whole frames needed to retain the motion you'd see when stepping whole frame by whole frame through your animation.

▶ **Undo** will revert your selection to the way it was before you started noodling with it.

Figure 18.12. Here's an extreme case in which I created an oscillation along the X-axis, then squished the motion in the Scene Editor so that several keyframes were "condensed" to fall between the whole frames. After applying Quantize to the selection, you can see how the only keys that remain fall on frames 0, 1, 2, and 3, holding the animation I would have seen by step-framing through the animation, whole frame by whole frame.

So, to make the action of FlyBall.lws more "snappy" when the bat would hit the ball, first, I'd isolate the items that most clearly contribute to that motion: LeftHand*, Spine2, and Spine3.

Figure 18.13. I'd Ctrl-click and drag to create a discontinuous selection for the keys of LeftHand*, Spine2, and Spine3 that encompass that part of the motion. I'd drag the "far" end of the selection to squish the keys forward in time, accelerating their motion.

Figure 18.14. Then, I'd select and drag the keys of Spine2 and Spine3 that cause the upper torso to swing, leading the action of the arms closer toward each other. This increases the perception of the whip-like motion that "snaps" the action of the bat through the frame of contact with the imaginary ball.

In less than a minute, I've adjusted the timings of this animation, bringing even more life and snap into it!

> **Note:**
>
> It's so easy to get lost in "Tweaksville." Always use your head, and be honest with yourself as to whether you're making things *better* or just making things *different*.

18.2 Dope Track

LightWave's Dope Track offers yet another way for you to quickly and easily modify your animations.

Figure 18.15. You access the Dope Track by clicking on the little grip-textured doohickey right above the Time Slider. (You close the Dope Track by clicking on it again.)

Figure 18.16. The Dope Track is very much like the Time Slider, yet it shows "ticks" representing keyframes from *all* selected items (whereas the Time Slider only shows keys from the currently selected item).

Figure 18.17. Click and drag in the Dope Track to select key(s) that you can then slide about by dragging them left or right.

Figure 18.18. Right-clicking on the Dope Track opens a menu with similar editing functions as the Dope Sheet that act upon the currently selected items.

Figure 8.19. Dope Track's marker tools are very handy when you want to leave notes for yourself about when things should happen in your animation. You can even label markers (when the Time Slider is over the marked frame) to explain themselves when the Time Slider is over the marked frame.

The Dope Track supports a Channel-edit mode (see Figure 18.18) that you can activate to manipulate the individual channels of the selected items — acting upon only the currently selected manipulation mode (Move, Rotate, or Scale/Stretch).

Figure 18.20. The Dope Track also sports a Baking function to create keys on every frame of the selected range (established by right-clicking and dragging within the Dope Track) for all selected items. (This comes in handy when you have an item controlled by some function or tool you must remove before sending your scene to a render farm.)

18.3 Motion Mixer

Motion Mixer has been in LightWave for a while now, and as the kind of animator who enjoys creating animations "from scratch," it is something I never really explored until I had to do some minor crowd scenes for *Kaze, Ghost Warrior*.

In my career, I've been asked to use a lot of animation systems designed to blend different pieces and parts of animations together (like the "limited animation" seen frequently on Saturday morning cartoons like *The Flintstones*). The thing that sets Motion Mixer apart from all the other ones I've had to use is Motion Mixer actually *works*.

Figure 18.21. Motion Mixer is a multi-track, nonlinear editing/blending system. Here, you see the actor NinjaFox (from *Kaze, Ghost Warrior*) starting with the "StepBack" motion (the playback rate is controlled with a spline to get the perfect ease-in/out). He then moves into the "TurnToRun_Backwards" motion (sped up by 55% from its original animation), which flows into the motion "Run-Naginata" that will offset repeat for just over thirty frames, making NinjaFox run off into the distance.

This is the perfect solution for turning out television animation or video game cut scenes, especially if you have access to the motions used in the game itself!

Figure 18.22. The first thing you've got to have when you're wanting to work with Motion Mixer is a rigged character in motion. (The run cycle for the ninja in Sq04 of *Kaze, Ghost Warrior* is 24 fps, on *twos*.)

Super-Mega-Ultra Important Note:

Cycles...

The first thing most newbie animators ask to be taught is how to do a walk or run cycle. I suppose, from an outsider's point of view, it might make sense; after all, there's usually little "acting" in a walk or run, it's mostly just getting the character from Point A to Point B, right?

The truth be known, cycles are one of the most pedantically challenging things there are in the art of animation...for the reasons just mentioned. It is far easier to put yourself into the scene when you've got an emotional reason for being there, i.e., "acting."

There's one other reason why cycles are such a PITA repetition. The audience may not catch a bump, pop, or hang the first time through an animation, but every time that animation repeats itself, any inadequacies in the skill of the animation become multiplied exponentially.

Producing a good quality cycle requires the highest level of skill within an animator.

Luckily, we have options.

1) *Move the camera in for a close-up.* Bring the camera in close, if you can, when you've got a scene where you must show a character moving from one place to another. If you have the camera relatively "tight" on the head and shoulders, all you have to do is animate the spine, shoulders, and head to *intimate* a walk. Take a look at live-action films for a reference of just how rare it is to see the whole character walking or running.

2) *Dick Williams* and *Preston Blair.* (An artist is only as good as the material he or she references.) When you absolutely, positively have to show a full character running or walking, reference the best. The books by these two master animators are filled with frame-by-frame side-on and front-on frames from many different walk and run cycles. Do what the pros do — grab these books, reference, and modify!

> **Note:**
> Cycles to be used with Motion Mixer need to start and end on the same pose. (Motion Mixer will deal with making sure there is no "catch" as the cycle repeats itself.)

Once you've created a motion for your character, you open the Motion Mixer window: **Window|Motion Mixer F2.**

Figure 18.23. With the control bones of your character selected (all the bones that drive your character's motion — in the case of my riggings, these are Star through LeftThumb_Tip), click **Create Actor** and a window opens, requesting a name to identify your new Motion Mixer actor that will control all the items you have selected.

> **Note:**
> The Motion Mixer window doesn't have Pan/Zoom bars. To pan the view, you need to Alt-click in the view, and drag left or right. To zoom the view, Ctrl-Alt-click in the view, dragging left to zoom out and right to zoom in (just like getting around in any other viewport in Layout or Modeler).

Figure 18.24. When you have an actor assigned, Motion Mixer gives you some timelines to work with. Just as in a nonlinear video editing system, you can layer and join motion clips.

> **Note:**
> You can add and remove tracks by right-clicking on the timeline.

Under the Actor menu, you'll find that you can add any items you may find yourself needing to control in the future, remove items you realize you're not using, and scan XChannels of the actor items or external items for additional animation data (like Morph Mixer animation data). You can also completely free an actor from memory, and you can fine-tune your control over which specific channels of your character are driven with Motion Mixer by editing the actor map.

Figure 18.25. Within the Edit Actor Map window, you are presented with a list of all the items and respective channels that Motion Mixer will be taking care of. A check next to an item or channel name means that Motion Mixer will override that item/channel's data with its own, and will look to those channels for storing data for its motions. An [L] next to an item or channel means that the item/channel will not be driven by Motion Mixer.

Figure 18.26. With the run cycle ready that I want Motion Mixer to use as a motion, I click on **Create Motion** to open the Motion Mixer | Create Motion window. I choose to create this motion from all the actor items (by selecting specific items, I could create motions for just the hands, head, or feet by choosing Selected Items) and enter the frame range of **0-24** for my cycle. I also tell Motion Mixer to clear channels, which will leave me with a blank slate in Layout from which to create my next motion.

> **Note:**
> Motion Mixer enters your scene's start and end frames by default. Motion Mixer stores all the keys you have created for your animation, using only the entered frames for its motion so you can easily make adjustments later.

Figure 18.27. Selecting the appropriate motion from the Motion List (if necessary), click **Add Motion**, then click on one of the tracks to add the motion to the scene. You'll see that scrubbing the Time Slider in Layout moves your character through the motion *and* resets the character to his "blank slate" pose at the end of the motion.

Figure 18.28. You can drag the motion clip around on the timeline. You can also stretch/squish it by dragging on the end handles, making the motion play faster or slower than the original animation.

Figure 18.29. Right-clicking on the motion clip brings up a menu where you can add weight curves (for letting the underlying animation in Layout show through the Motion Mixer animation), TimeWarp curves (for controlling the change over time of the motion's playback speed), and Pre- and Post-Behaviours, which tell Motion Mixer what to do before the beginning and after the end of your motion clip.

▶ **Reset** causes your character to reset to his "blank slate" pose.

▶ **Constant** causes your character to hold his beginning or final pose.

▶ **Repeat** causes your actor to replay his animation from the beginning, again and again, at the same rate of speed as the motion clip.

▶ **Oscillate** makes your character ping-pong back and forth through his animation.

▶ **Offset Repeat** causes your actor to continue on with his motion. In the case of my run cycle, he runs into frame before the motion itself starts on frame 16, and keeps right on running out of frame after the motion ends after frame 40.

> **Note:**
>
> A motion clip or Pre-/Post-Behaviour is removed from the timeline by clicking Remove from their respective right-click menus.

Note:
Pre- and Post-Behaviours can be stretched as long as you need them to be.

Note:
TimeWarp curves are fantastic — they let you control the playing of a clip as it moves from 0% to 100% of its animation with a curve you edit in the Graph Editor just like any other curve! It's the perfect way to add variety to motions within crowds to keep the crowd characters from looking like carbon copies of one another. A TimeWarp curve is also the perfect way to easily, precisely control the ease-in and ease-out of a motion.

Figure 18.30. You can add a transition between two motion clips by selecting one, clicking on **Add Transition**, and then selecting the other. A bar appears between the two clips that automatically stretches to reach each clip's closest end.

Figure 18.31. By right-clicking on the transition, you can remove it, or edit the transition (function curve) in the Graph Editor, controlling how quickly and/or how smoothly the transition takes place.

Figure 18.32. You can also abut animations that are linked by a common pose (shown overlaid onto the Motion Mixer window). Here you've got the actor stepping forward, moving into a "ready animation," and stepping backward.

Now, with the animations I have strung together in Figure 18.32, I animated them all with the character starting at 0, 0, 0, which is fine for the "ready animation" that starts and ends at exactly the same place. But with StepForward, the character ends up one step forward, just as StepBack lands him one step backward.

Just putting these animations "nose-to-tail" as they are in Figure 18.32 causes the character to step forward, reset to 0, 0, 0, go through his ready animation, and then step backward (again jumping back to 0, 0, 0 because there is no post-behaviour telling him to stay where he lands).

Figure 18.33. Selecting the ready animation, I can click on the **Offset Editor** and specify from which motion currently in the timeline it should be offset and how. The Offset Type of Relative makes it so wherever the previous motion clip ends up, the current one begins.

Figure 18.34. What happens when you use Relative Offset on two animations that, while the first may end on the same pose that begins the second, are *facing in different directions*? You get some *serious* funk.

Figure 18.35. Motion Mixer offers a kind of offset it calls Character Offset that understands how to link up animations that were made facing different directions — so long as the end pose for one is the starting pose for the other. (You can even manually adjust the alignment of the character offset, just in case you find the need.)

You access Character Offset through the Custom Offset Type, where you set your desired offset on an actor item by actor item basis by clicking on the Type entry to scroll through the choices of Absolute, Relative, Relative XZ, and Character.

Figure 18.36. Using the different tracks/timelines in Motion Mixer, you can quickly layer/blend bits and pieces of animations into actions that look completely original. Here, separate animations of the head and hands are overlaid onto my standard Run_With_Naginata cycle.

What happens when you want to make a slight (or great) change to an animation you stored as a motion clip?

Figure 18.37. Selecting the motion clip you wish to edit, clicking on **Edit Motion** "drops" that motion back into Layout where you can edit and make changes to your heart's content. When you're done tweaking, just click **Edit Motion** again and you are presented with options to accept or discard the changes to the motion you just made, to restore the animation in Layout to the state it was in before you began to edit your motion, to keep what you've done in Layout, or to completely clear Layout's animation, restoring your actor to his "blank slate" pose.

Figure 18.38. If you need to change the in-point and out-point of a motion in your timeline, you can do this through the Motion Properties window, opened through the Properties option of the right-click menu for that specific motion.

Motions in Motion Mixer are stored with the scene file itself. (Which means that if you have a lot of complex motions, that scene file can get pretty large.)

You may find yourself wanting to "offload" some motions you don't use that often, choosing to bring them into a scene only when you need them.

Figure 18.39. Through the Motion Menu, you can save, load, copy, rename, and free (remove from memory) motions.

You can save and load motions between different actors, *even if the actors have different names for their controls*! (Though the actors should have similar proportions.)

Figure 18.40. When Motion Mixer encounters an item in a motion it is loading that it doesn't have in its current actor, it gives you the option of ignoring that item or assigning that item's motion to something else in your current actor.

So, as you can see, there's a lot of power in these advanced animation tools. And I've just barely scratched their surfaces.

There is so much to dive into and explore with these tools. Their creators have really covered nearly every possible need and want a user might have.

The things I've shown you here in this chapter have been beyond value in the creation of my own film, *Kaze, Ghost Warrior.* The Dope Sheet allowed me to quickly lay in the poses of complex fight sequences and quickly adjust the timings for individual characters and their controls in a matter of hours rather than days. Motion Mixer let me animate an action once, stretching, blending, and applying it to other characters when there simply wasn't enough time to animate the entire scene from scratch.

I encourage you to explore these tools. Find out what they can do that is exactly what *you* need for your own projects. And share what you find — you'll be amazed at how far you can go when your focus is to simply enjoy the process of discovery!

"For if a human...is able to play, he can be taught. And if he is teachable, he is capable of unlimited development and accomplishment."
— J. Allen Boone, *Letters to Strongheart*

Chapter 19

Facial Animation

The principles of facial animation are the same as the principles of animation we've gone over for the rest of the character. All the rules still apply, all the skills still stand.

And this is why I'm going over facial animation now, here, at the end of the book….

You must be good at animation if you wish to be good at *facial animation*.

At Disney, the characters' bodies were animated *first*, approved by the director *before* any facial animation was even begun. Why?

The character must be able to *sell* his performance with pantomime alone if it is to be truly believable. Facial performance is just "icing on the cake."

I can't stress this enough.

Watching your character perform, evaluating silhouette, timing, the illusion of weight, following the arcs of motion, understanding squash and stretch, your character must deliver on his ability to convince the audience of the emotions he feels, the thoughts he thinks, his "past," his "future," and his opinions on both. *And all this must be done successfully first, before any facial animation is even thought about.*

> **Note:**
> By knowing and understanding the principles of animation, you already know how to do facial animation; you just need to have someone show you how to use the tools designed for creating facial animation.

19.1 **Two Paths**

There are two main ways people have been doing facial animation: facial riggings and morph targets.

Facial Riggings

A facial rigging is, for most intents and purposes, the same as a character rigging. It is a system of bones and weight maps, IK, and FK that pull the points of the face, just as the character rigging pulls the points of the body.

I've never used a facial rigging in production.

From what I've seen of them, they appear to be powerful within the parameters they were designed to fulfill. But to my way of working, I've never been able to fully wrap my mind around them.

I much prefer the precision definition achieved by using predesigned shapes, sculpted in Modeler and then blended in Layout, to give me what I'm looking for.

Morph Targets

Modifying your character's face in Modeler, sculpting the precise definition you wish to see in an expression or phoneme, and then telling Layout to move the vertices of your character's face into that shape is by far the most common way of doing facial animation, regardless of software package. (Which is not to say it is the *best* way...it's just more common.)

Using Morph Mixer, you can layer morphs onto each other, controlling their mixture with sliders that affect a percentage (negative or positive) of that morph's influence. The cumulative effect of this is that (as with layering motions in Motion Mixer) you can quickly and easily sculpt shapes that appear to be completely unique, yet still retain the precision of "pre-sculpted" definition.

There are two main approaches to working with morph targets: "tiny bits" and "big bites."

The "tiny bits" method is common at large studios with lots of people and lots of time to do the work. With this method, each section of the face has its own morph target. The outer, middle, and inner part of each eyebrow would have its own targets for up, down, in, and out.

Using the "tiny bits" method, animators get a lot more controls to more precisely craft their facial expressions in Layout. It makes for a lot of flexibility and a lot more work (a.k.a. time).

The "big bites" method sculpts specific shapes for common applications (like the phonemes that make up dialogue) and also "modifiers" to be layered/blended onto/with those common shapes to create diversity.

> **Note:**
> To tell the truth, I always favored the "tiny bits" method of morph target facial animation as being able to produce beautiful, lifelike, asymmetrical facial performances…until *Kaze, Ghost Warrior*.
>
> I didn't have the time to go all out and do the tiny bits method, and so I had a new software package made to my specifications that would push the big bites method into a whole new valence shell.
>
> Mac Reiter, the programmer for Timothy Albee's Facial Animation, succeeded well beyond my hopes and expectations. When you look at the scenes of *KGW* done using TAFA, it's hard to imagine those as simply modified phonetic poses.

19.2 Endomorphs

LightWave has the ability to store modifications to a model's geometry for application in Layout (morph targets) within the model's file itself: endomorphs.

Endomorphs are vertex maps (just like the eight maps we use to assign points to move along with their respective bones) that store data based on how much a vertex has changed from its base position.

> **Note:**
>
> Since it takes a little practice to know how to model facial geometry to retain the "landmarks" we've come to identify as the human face, I've included a new model on the CD for this book — Mr. Cool. (Mr. Cool has two base versions, both *with* and *without* facial modeling, so you can animate the body without being distracted with thinking about facial animation, and then when you're done, you can swap out the standard model with the facial model.)
>
> Objects\BaseChar\MrCool\MrCool_Facial_Blank.lwo is the "raw" Mr. Cool model that has all the geometry modeled and weighted but none of the facial morph targets modeled.
>
> Objects\Final\MrCool_Facial_F.lwo is Mr. Cool weighted and with all the facial morph targets I'll be talking about in this chapter already created for you.
>
> (Objects\Final\MrCool_Facial_F_FA.lwo is the Timothy Albee's Facial Animation version of Mr. Cool. We'll explore this model in the next chapter.)

Figure 19.1. Mr. Cool has the same proportion, scale, and weight maps as ThinGuy. He can be swapped onto the riggings we've been using with ThinGuy in Layout, following the steps in Section 7.3.

Figure 19.2. In the lower right-hand corner of Modeler, among the series of lettered vertex map buttons is one with an "M" on it. This "M" button lets LightWave know you want to be working with the morph style of vertex maps. Selecting **(new)** from the list box to the right of the buttons opens a requester to name your new morph map.

> **Note:**
>
> For the purposes of facial animation, we'll be using relative morph maps — storing morph data as the amount of change with respect to the base object.

> **Note:**
>
> Just as with weight maps, a morph map without any data held within it is "forgotten" by Modeler when you select another map. If you were to change back to (base) right now, the new morph map you've just created would disappear.

Figure 19.3. My favorite tool for creating morphs is Magnet (**Modify|Magnet**). Magnet lets you drag (selected) points and polys around based on a two- or three-dimensional "sphere of influence." Right-click dragging in a viewport sets the position and extents of this influence. Left-click dragging then moves that geometry based on the falloff from the centerpoint as set in the Numeric n options window. (Working with the Magnet tool reminds me of sculpting in clay.)

Important Note:

When working with facial morph targets, it's important to preserve your model's symmetry. Unless you have a darn good reason not to, always make sure you've got Symmetry mode active while you're "pulling points."

Figure 19.4. On the left is our unaffected base model. Test_Morph, on the right, retains changed positions of the points we've moved in Mr. Cool's nose.

Figure 19.5. If we then changed the shape of the nose in our base model, we'll find that the points we moved in Test_Morph still move the same amount relative to their new starting positions.

So, in creating the different facial shapes we'll be using for our morph targets, it's really just a matter of carefully selecting the geometry we're wanting to affect, and then using the Rotate, Move, and Magnet tools. Using these three tools, you can create the entire range of facial expressions you'll need.

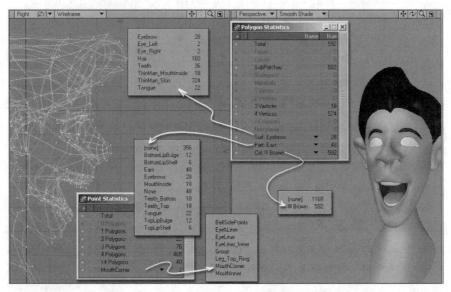

Figure 19.6. LightWave lets you group and select both polys and points in a variety of ways.

Because the ability to precisely select and isolate different areas of our model is so vital in creating the facial targets we'll be using, you'll want to use all the different ways LightWave lets you group and select geometry, both polys and points.

▶ Surfaces

▶ Parts (View | Selection Sets | Create Part)

▶ Sketch Color (Detail | Polygons | Sketch Color)

▶ Point Selection Sets (View | Selection Sets | Selection Sets)

In Figure 19.6, you can see that I've got nearly every area of Mr. Cool's head and face accounted for with some sort of selection set. The different surfaces themselves serve as a great place to start in isolating different areas of the model. When I need more refinement, I can add or remove the geometry I've assigned as parts — Ears, BottomLipBulge, Tongue, etc. I've got one sketch color, brown, assigned to the whole head so I can quickly select it and hide the rest of the body.

Between the fact that LightWave's toolsets restrict themselves to only working on selected geometry (when you have geometry selected) and that you can show/hide parts of your model at a moment's notice, you can quickly get at even the most challenging bits of your model, if you've planned ahead in his/her modeling.

19.3 Expression Morphs

The easiest "sculpting" you'll do is in the creation of the expressions for your model, the scowls, the grins, the puffing of the cheeks, etc. These are the best ones to get your feet wet with when you're starting out.

> **Newbie Note:**
> Just as with animation, it's probably best to count on starting over after you've done your first pass — you'll be much better in your second pass at this for having done so.

Note:

Morph Mixer *parses* the names you assign to your morphs, meaning that it will go through your names and try to make sense of them, and sort them accordingly. Morph Mixer uses a period (".") within the endomorph names to sort them into different groups. The part of the name *before* the period is handled as the group name, and the part that comes *after* is handled as the morph name. So, Cheeks.Puffed in Morph Mixer would simply be called Puffed, but would be grouped within the Cheeks group.

Any endomorph without a period to define its group membership is collected in Morph Mixer under a group named General.

BASE... PUFFED

Figure 19.7. Cheeks.Puffed. With symmetry active and the Thinguy_Skin surface selected, I just used the Magnet tool, setting its influence to encompass the cheek area but not the corner of the mouth, and dragged the points out and slightly forward in a Top viewport.

Important Note:

Making facial morph targets *isn't* like doing life drawing in 3D. *There is no right or wrong!* Don't fixate on trying to get things "exactly right" because there is no such thing. Just play and have fun! Find out what works for *you!*

The great thing about the way LightWave works with its endomorphs is that you can completely finish facial animation on an *entire sequence of scenes*, realize you don't really like a particular endomorph, then go into Modeler and make the needed changes to that morph. When LightWave reloads the scenes you've already done, loading the new version of the model, Morph Mixer references the new morph shape(s) based on endomorph name(s)! So just by "fixing" the model, you've also "fixed" all the animations that use that model!

So don't tie yourself in knots trying to figure out exactly what I did to get Mr. Cool's face into a specific morph shape.

Go play! Explore! Experiment! Have fun!

The important thing in everything you do is that if you are able to have fun doing what you're doing, you're learning without even trying!

CHEEKS SUCKED

Figure 19.8. Cheeks.Sucked. The opposite of Cheeks.Puffed. I simply created a new endomorph and, leaving the Magnet's regions where they were, dragged the points of the cheeks inward and back.

Note:

LightWave [8]'s update to Morph Mixer now lets you easily do morphs with a negative percentage. So, morphs like Cheeks.Sucked aren't really necessary anymore — all you need to do is Cheeks.Puffed and run that morph into the negative percentages and you'll get pretty much the same result. Though sometimes, like with Brows Scowl and Surprise, you'll want specific shapes for each, in which case you'll want to model both morph targets.

Figure 19.9. Eye.Brow_Scowl and Eye.Brow_Surprise.

Figure 19.10. Mouth.Frown and Mouth.Smile_Closed. Notice how even the cheeks, lower lids, and "wings" of the nose are affected by the smile and frown (just like in real life).

Figure 19.11. Mouth.Smile_LipsOpen and Mouth.Smile_MouthOpen. Being able to isolate the upper and lower lips made Smile_LipsOpen a snap! Selecting the geometry of the lower jaw and rotating it about where the jaw attaches to the head in real life (up near the front of the ear) made Smile_MouthOpen look natural.

You get the idea. You can browse the different endomorphs in the Facial_F version of Mr. Cool to see how I chose to do things with him.

The list of expression morphs I've included with Mr. Cool are:

Cheeks.Puffed

Cheeks.Sucked

Eye.Brow_Scowl

Eye.Brow_Surprise

Eye.Closed

Eye.Lid_Lower_Dn

Eye.Lid_Lower_Up

Eye.Lid_Upper_Dn

Eye.Lid_Upper_Up

Mouth.Corner_Back

Mouth.Corner_Front

Mouth.Frown

Mouth.Lip_BOTTOM_Dn

Mouth.Lip_BOTTOM_In

Mouth.Lip_BOTTOM_Out

Mouth.Lip_BOTTOM_Up

Mouth.Lip_TOP_Dn

Mouth.Lip_TOP_In

Mouth.Lip_TOP_Out

Mouth.Lip_TOP_Snarl

Mouth.Lip_TOP_Up

Mouth.OpenWide

Mouth.Smile_Closed

Mouth.Smile_LipsOpen

Mouth.Smile_MouthOpen

19.4 **Asymmetry**

Organic systems are rarely perfectly symmetrical. The facial expressions we go through on a moment-to-moment basis are a perfect example of this. From lopsided smiles to "speaking out of the corner of one's mouth" to doing a "Spock" eyebrow thing, we've come to associate asymmetry with life.

> **Note:**
> Just as with the body's animation, you want to avoid twinning in facial animation at all costs.

So, if we want asymmetry in our morphs (we just spent so much care in building so they would be perfectly symmetrical), we've got to split each symmetrical morph into left and right halves, which we can control separately in Morph Mixer.

First, to make this task as easy as possible, we've got to find a way to quickly separate the left, right, and centerline points of our model.

> **Note:**
> I've done the creation of these point selection sets for you with the Mr. Cool models in the Final directory, but not with the model in the BaseChar directory in case you want to follow along.

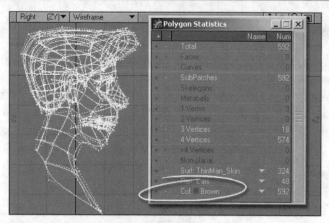

Figure 19.12. Selecting all the polygons with the Sketch Color: Brown (which I've already assigned to the geometry of the head and neck) I press = to hide unselected geometry.

Figure 19.13. Pressing / to drop my selected polygons, I select one or two polygons I know belong to the hair, and press] to select connected. With the hair selected, I press - to hide selected (leaving me with a bald Mr. Cool).

Figure 19.14. Focusing my attention on a Top view, *with nothing selected* in Point Selection mode, I press **"** (quotation mark), which inverts my selection (inverting a selection of "nothing" is a quick way to select all geometry of your current selection mode), and press = to show only the points of Mr. Cool's head.

Figure 19.15. Very carefully, I select all the points along X=0. (It's easiest to do this in a maximized view, and still I like to zoom in really close to make sure I'm getting the right points.) Then, I click **View|Selection Sets|Selection Sets** to assign these points to a point selection set I name **Head_Center-line**.

Figure 19.16. Having assigned the points along X=0 to a point selection set so I can get at them easily later, I hide them so I can clearly see the points of the left and right halves of Mr. Cool's head.

Figure 19.17. I select the points of the right side of Mr. Cool's head and assign them to a point selection set named **Head_Right**.

Figure 19.18. I hide the points of the right side of the head and assign the points remaining on the left to a point selection set named **Head_Left**.

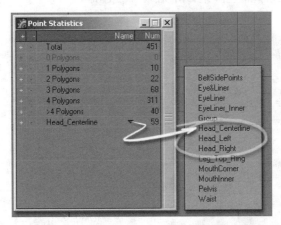

Figure 19.19. Now, through a Point Statistics window, I can instantly select the points I'll be using in the next steps.

427

Figure 19.20. Using the Point Statistics window, I select the points associated with the Head_Left point selection set. And in a Windows|Vertex Maps Panel window, I scroll down through the list of my morph maps until I come to Mouth.Smile_Lips-Open. Right-clicking on the morph's name, I choose **Copy Vertex Map**. In the window that opens, I name the copy **Mouth.Smile_LipsOpen_L**.

Figure 19.21. Working its magic only on the points I have selected, LightWave copies the morph data assigned to those points to a new morph map named Mouth.Smile_LipsOpen_L.

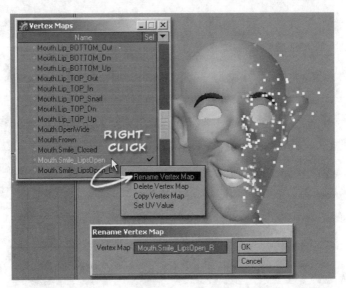

Figure 19.22. Returning to the Mouth.Smile_LipsOpen morph map, still with the points of the left half of the head selected, I press _ (underscore) to remove the morph data from those points. Then, right-clicking on the morph's name, I choose **Rename Vertex Map** and add an "_R" to the end of its name.

So, now that we've got the left and right sides of Mouth.Smile_ LipsOpen assigned, you may be wondering about the points along the center of the model. You may have noticed that for the left side of the head, those points remain as they are in the base pose, yet for the right side of the head, those points still reflect 100% of the position data we "sculpted" for that morph.

We can't simply copy the centerline point data along with the rest of the points of the left side of the head; Morph Mixer's effect is additive. If the centerline points for left and right morphs both held 100% of their "sculpted" data, the points along the centerline would move twice the amount we originally sculpted when both left and right morphs were active at one time in Morph Mixer.

What we need to do is to apply 50% of the position data we sculpted for this morph map to the centerline points of both the left and right morph maps.

Figure 19.23. Using the point selection set Head_Centerline to select the points along X=0 of the head and setting Mouth.Smile_LipsOpen_L as the active morph map, I click on **Map|Morph|Apply Morph**. From the selection list, I choose **Mouth.Smile_LipsOpen_R** (which has the centerline points at their full "intensity") and set the Strength to **50%**. After clicking **OK**, 50% of the positioning data from Mouth.Smile_LipsOpen_R is applied to our selected points. (See Figure 19.25 to compare the results.)

Figure 19.24. Now, we need to copy the vertex map data for those points back onto the points of Mouth.Smile_ LipsOpen_R, so that both morphs contain position data that is 50% of the originally sculpted position data.

Figure 19.25. The left and right versions of the Month.Smile_LipsOpen morph are perfect mirrors of each other, and with their centerline points being 50% strength versions of the original, when these two morphs are combined in Morph Mixer, we'll get a perfect rendition of what we symmetrically sculpted for this facial expression.

This process of splitting the morphs into left and right versions needs to be repeated for every facial expression, except those in which the lower jaw moves. (In the case of Mr. Cool, these exceptions are Mouth.Smile_MouthOpen and Mouth.OpenWide.)

> **Note:**
>
> If you're thinking that this morph "splitting" business is pedantic, manual labor, I completely agree with you. But it's one of the things that's just the way things have been done. The good thing is, you don't have to like it, and if you use Timothy Albee's Facial Animation, you don't need to do it — TAFA does this for you!

19.5 *Re-Symmetry*

Okay, so now you've got all your expression morphs all asymmetrical. What happens when you want to make adjustments to that matched pair of morphs and you want exactly the same adjustment to be applied to both halves?

Figure 19.26. With Mouth.Smile_LipsOpen_R as the active morph map, we simply apply the morph data from Mouth.Smile_LipsOpen_L with a Strength of **100%**...

Figure 19.27. ...And both halves become
whole again!

Delete the Mouth.Smile_LipsOpen_L morph map so you don't
forget it will soon contain out-of-date data.

Activate Symmetry, make your changes, re-split your morph
into left and right halves, and you're back in business!

19.6 **Dialogue Morphs**

Having had all the practice you've just accumulated with creating the expression morphs, creating the dialogue morphs is going to be a lot easier.

Dialogue morphs are the facial shapes that create the different phonemes we use to form words.

Figure 19.28. "Sculpting" dialogue morphs isn't diffi-cult; it just requires observation, knowledge of the tools, and a sense of *subtlety* (as appropriate to that particular character).

The best way to see how a dialogue morph should be con-structed is to study your own face as you make the different phonetic shapes in a mirror.

As with expression morphs, there's no need to worry about get-ting things perfect, because there is no such thing as "perfection." Just play and explore, knowing that by making a change for the better to your model, you are also bettering all the scenes that use that model.

> **Note:**
> I prefix my dialogue morphs with Dial. so they all fall under a
> Dial. group within Morph Mixer (and so the default settings
> within TAFA recognizes them as dialogue morphs).

I was able to do all the dialogue for *Kaze, Ghost Warrior* with a
grand total of fifteen dialogue morphs. These are shown in Figures
19.29 through 19.43.

> **Note:**
> Bear in mind that these are American English pronunciations.

Figure 19.29. A (**A**ce).

Figure 19.30. *ah* (**a**bsolve).

Figure 19.31. *E* (**E**at).

436

Figure 19.32. *eh* (b**e**d).

Figure 19.33. *F* (**F**ace, **V**ase).

437

Figure 19.34. *K* (**K**usac, **G**arras).

Figure 19.35. *L* (**L**unch).

Figure 19.36. M (**M**an).

Figure 19.37. O (**O**h).

Figure 19.38. oo (b**oo**t).

Figure 19.39. *P* (**P**eas, **B**eans).

Figure 19.40. r (**R**ight).

Figure 19.41. S (**S**un, **Z**oo).

Figure 19.42. *T* (**T**ip, **D**id, **N**ice).

Figure 19.43. *th* (**th**is).

442

As you can see, we're not concerned with the sound of each phoneme, but rather the shape of our mouths as we make the sounds. You'll notice there is no shape in the above list for the "H" sound in the word "Hat." This is because we can use percentages of the shapes *A*, *ah*, *E*, or *eh* to provide any number of visual interpretations of that sound.

> **Important Note:**
> Remember that animation isn't about recreating how it looks to do something, it is giving a *visual impression of how it feels to do something*. This holds equally true for character and facial animation alike.

19.7 "Plussing" Morphs

What happens when you're watching your facial performance and you say to yourself, "Gee, things look good, but everything is just a bit too subdued"?

Are you stuck with having to re-model a morph target in LightWave if you want to boost or reduce its intensity? Heck no!

You can use Apply Morph to apply a morph *to itself*, fiddling with the Strength percentages (positive or negative) until you get the "volume level" you're looking for.

Figure 19.44. In the center is the base morph for the *th* phoneme. On the left is the result of applying the morph to itself with a strength of –30%, effectively reducing its intensity by 30%. On the right is the result of applying the morph to itself with a strength of 100%, effectively doubling its influence on the model.

19.8 Morph Mixer

So, how do you put all this facial sculpting and splitting to work and get a character to speak? Through the magical manipulations made manifest through Morph Mixer.

Figure 19.45. Scenes\CharacterSetups\MrCool_Facial_Setup has (the Morph Mixer version of) Mr. Cool all set up and ready to go on the ThinGuy rigging we've been using.

Figure 19.46. With Mr. Cool selected, I open an Object Properties window and, from the **Deform** tab, **Add Displacement|Morph Mixer**.

Figure 19.47. Double-clicking on the plug-in's name in the displacement list opens the Morph Mixer window. (You can also open a plug-in's window by selecting it and then choosing Edit|Properties.)

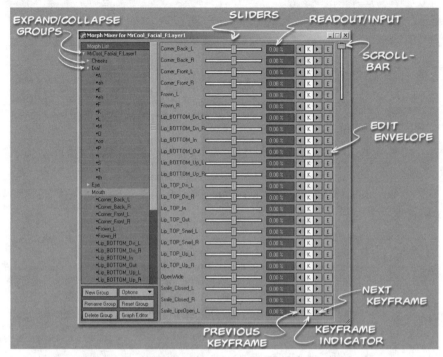

Figure 19.48. The Morph Mixer window itself. You expand and collapse your groups of morphs by clicking on the little triangles to the left of each group name. The currently selected group has its morphs displayed in the "action area," where you see sliders you can quickly move between −100% and +100%. In the Readout/Input box you can see the value of the slider and enter values by hand. When you have more morphs than the window can display, a scroll bar appears in the upper-right corner of the window. You can edit the envelope for any morph by clicking on the "E" button to its right. And using the left and right triangles, you can quickly jump to the next and previous keyframes for that morph. The Keyframe indicator shows when your current frame holds a key for a morph.

Note:

Morph Mixer has some helpful keyboard/mouse combinations for working with keyframes within a *group* of morphs that I use frequently:

▶ Clicking on a keyframe indicator that shows that there is no key on the current frame for that morph will create a key on the current frame with the current value for that morph.

▶ Clicking on a keyframe indicator that shows that there is a key on the current frame for that morph will remove the key on the current frame for that morph.

▶ Shift-clicking on a keyframe indicator that shows that there is no key on the current frame for that morph will create keys for all morphs at their current value on that frame.

▶ Shift-clicking on a keyframe indicator that shows that there is a key on the current frame for that morph will remove keys on the current frame for all morphs.

▶ Ctrl-clicking on a keyframe indicator will set a key on the current frame for that morph with the value of 0%, regardless of whether or not there already is a key on that frame.

▶ Shift-Ctrl-clicking on a keyframe indicator will set keyframes at 0% on the current frame *for all morphs*.

Figure 19.49. After you get the hang of understanding how each morph affects the face and how they interact with each other, it's just a matter of applying the same knowledge of silhouette, anticipation, timing, and all the other principles of animation you've already learned to this new set of controls.

Advanced Note:

In the Mr. Cool facial setup scene, you'll notice a black null named Eye_Mover. This is used by the surfaces of the eyes as a reference object to control the position of the painted texture map of the eyes' coloring.

Figure 19.50. Under the Texture Editor for the Eye_Left surface, you see where I have set Eye_Mover as the reference object. Since this is surfacing information, it is saved *with the object* (not the scene). And in order for it to work properly, the scene must already have an object named Eye_Mover loaded

This isn't the greatest way to do eyes that are neither spherical nor ovoid, but it works passably, and it's free.

Newbie Note:

Surfacing is something beyond the scope of this book on animation, but if you'd like to add that skill to your growing list, *Essential LightWave 3D 8* (1-55622-082-0) covers surfacing in great detail. (The book is designed to give you the same level of LightWave aptitude that I had after working on *Babylon 5*.)

19.9 **Sample Workflow**

The first thing you need to do when you want to work a scene with dialogue is to figure out how long that scene will need to be.

If you've "timed-out" your storyboards into an *animatic* (moving storyboard — see *CGI Filmmaking, The Creation of Ghost Warrior* (1-55622-227-0)), you already know your scene length.

If you're uncertain of how long you need/want your scene to be, it's usually okay to have your scene be as long as your dialogue track (assuming you don't need a head or tail on the scene to give you some room to play with in editing — again, see *CGI Filmmaking*).

> **Note:**
>
> Even when I'm rendering to NTSC (the U.S./Japan television standard), which runs at 30 frames per second, I always do my work at 24 fps. This is in part because I started off working as a traditional animator working at the frame rate for theatrical films. There are two other reasons why I like working at 24 fps: Though most laypeople couldn't tell you why, 24 fps looks like "movies" and 30 fps looks like "video." And when you're working at 24 fps, you're saving your render farm from having to render six more frames per second — and that time saved adds up quickly.

Figure 19.51. Here, I've loaded the file Audio\ManyYearsAgo.wav into a work-scene created from Scenes\CharacterSetups\MrCool_Facial_Setup.lws. Looking very closely at the representation of the audio wave that appears in the timeline, I see that it ends right around frame 36. (So I'll be setting my scene length to **36**.)

Project LW3D CHAR. ANi'a 2	Character(s) MR. Cool	~~LIFE CHAPTER~~ CHAPTER 19	~~SCENE~~ Section 8			
Action	Dialogue	Layer 4	Layer 3	Layer 2	Layer 1	Camera Instructions
1						
2						
3						C(1), So Not Much
"MANY YEARS AGO..." 4	M					Body Animation is needed.
5						
6	A					
7						
8	N					
9						
10	E					
11						
12	A					
13						
14						
15	S					
16						
17						
18						
19						
20						
21	A					
22						
23						
24	G					
25						
26						
27						
28	O					
29						
30						
31						
32						
33						
34						
35						
36						

Figure 19.52. Printing out the X-sheet (located in the Extras folder in the Content Directory), I use the arrow keys to step-frame through the scene in LightWave, making note of the mouth shapes that I feel are creating the sounds I hear.

Figure 19.53. Moving to **frame 4** (where I've indicated on the X-sheet that the "M" sound should be), I move the slider for the "M" morph to 100% (a key is automatically created for that morph). To create keys on all the other channels (so they stay at 0% until I tell them to move), I Shift-click on one of the other morphs that doesn't have a key on frame 4.

Figure 19.54. Moving to **frame 6**, I Shift-Ctrl-click on a keyframe indicator to set 0% keys for all my dialogue morphs at this frame, then move the "A" morph's slider to 100%.

I repeat this process for the rest of the line of dialogue, using my X-sheet as my guide.

Setting my scene length to 36 and centering the head nicely in the upper-left viewport set to Perspective Textured Solid, I create a preview.

> **Note:**
> Sometimes LightWave needs to play through your preview a few times before audio and video sync up properly.

If you've been following along with Mr. Cool on your own, using my X-sheet notations to guide your own placement of dialogue morphs, you'll notice that things look a little funky at the beginning of the scene: There's too much action going on for me to believe that Mr. Cool is actually saying those words.

I jump to **frame 8** and, by Shift-clicking on one of my dialogue keys in the Morph Mixer window, remove all the keys I'd put in for the "N" sound ("T"=100%, all the rest 0%).

A new preview shows that the dialogue now reads just fine!

After the dialogue morphs are doing what they need to be doing, it's just a matter of scrubbing through the timeline and using the other morph groups to "sculpt" the different facial expressions that complete the performance.

Super-Mega-Ultra Important Note:

Less is more!!!

It seems to go against logic, but the more keyframes you have in your dialogue morphs, the worse your dialogue will read!

You want to have the absolute barest minimum number of keys to convincingly convey the *impression* of the spoken line.

When you watch the great Disney classics and step-frame through their dialogue performances, you'll see that what you *thought* was a "spot-on" lip-readable performance actually falls much more in the realm of *suggestion* than it does the land of *simulation*.

This is why I strongly recommend against using any kind of "automated" lip-synch package. Work from these packages may be correct simulations, but they are *grossly incorrect* when it comes to good animation.

My rule of thumb is that you should never have dialogue keyframes closer than every other frame. I try to have as much space between the dialogue keyframes as possible, wherever possible, always keeping in mind the *rhythm* we talked about earlier in the book.

Note:

The best way to do facial expressions is to follow the time-honored way that's been used in animation for a hundred years — use a mirror. Hang an inexpensive mirror (safely) in your work area so you can see both you in the mirror *and* your character on the screen without moving your head. Watch what your own face does as you deliver the lines convincingly and recreate that performance for the character.

After you get used to the controls, you'll see that doing facial animation in this manner isn't difficult, it's just moderately time-consuming. I find that if it takes me x amount of time to do the animation of the character's body, I can expect that it will take me the same amount of time to do the facial as well.

19.10 **Recycling**

One of the greatest things about the way LightWave stores its endo-morphs "inside" the model itself as deviations from a base pose is that if you use a finished head as a base from which to sculpt another head, the new head will retain all the morph targets of the first!

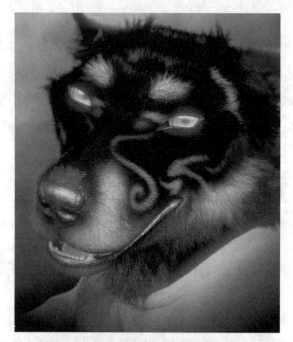

Figure 19.55. In doing *Kaze, Ghost Warrior,* the first character I did was Itsua, the bartender. I spent a good week and a half getting all his point weights, surfaces, and morph targets to be as good as I could make them.

After Itsua was moving well on his rigging and speaking and acting well with his facial morphs, I took him into Modeler and (saving him as a new model first) started dragging his points around until I had a new character. And because this new character's morph data was based on the distance each vertex was from its "base" position, nearly all of the morphs created for Itsua were fine for this new character as well!

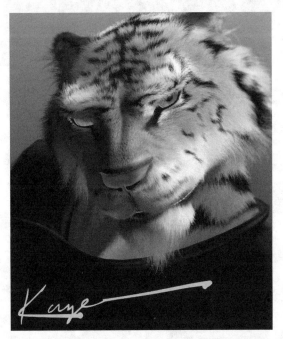

Figure 19.56. Kaze was created from pulling points on Itsua's head model. And even though feline and lupine muzzles have many differences, Kaze's morph targets only need minor adjustments after I had finished resculpting Itsua's head into Kaze's.

This ability to recycle both the body's weight maps and the dialogue morphs is just one more reason to like LightWave!

Timothy Albee's Facial Animation

> **Note:**
> This section was written while Timothy Albee's Facial Animation was still in pre-alpha. Many workflow improvements have already been implemented, not the least of which is a streamlining of the internal code to allow for frame rates of over 110 frames per second while working on the film resolution version of Kaze's head at a level of Sub-D smoothing equal to LightWave's level-2 SubPatch setting. Check out http://Kaze-GhostWarrior.com for current information.

So, what you saw in the previous chapter is the way facial animation has been done in 3D for quite a while now. It's a good technique — it's precise, but it's slow. (And because it is slow, there's less of an impetus to explore, play, and try new things with a performance.)

With the production of *Kaze, Ghost Warrior*, I needed something that would give me the rich, lifelike, asymmetrical performances I want out of my characters, and give me access to all the best tools from both traditional animation and CGI animation. (After all, traditional tools have been honed over the course of over a hundred years. It'd be foolish to ignore their advances!)

With the disappearance of my old favorite tool for facial animation, I took that as a sign that it was time to stop wishing and start doing. Teaming up with programmer Mac Reiter, together we created a facial animation package that does everything that I, as an animator, ever wanted a facial animation package to do (and what Mac has planned for v2.0 makes even my head spin).

Using the core of this tool on *Kaze, Ghost Warrior* (even though the tool was in pre-pre-alpha), I was able to do in twenty minutes what would have taken me about a day and a half the old-fashioned way.

20.1 Remember Yoda?

Isn't it amazing that in the original *Star Wars* series of films, in which Yoda was a foam and cloth puppet, he lived, thought, and felt. His performances (by Frank Oz) were works of powerful acting, regardless of the fact that Yoda, without Frank, was painted plastic.

I've yet to really see that kind of touching performance in a CG character.

I've got theories as to why this is so, and they stem from my training as an actor, an animator, and a director.

As an actor, you are taught (in the "method" school of acting) to forget yourself and actually become the person you are portraying. Performances are spontaneous, flowing from the heart, and millions upon millions of subconscious decisions affect the subtle pauses and movements, which the audience interprets as cues to hidden thoughts and feelings.

As an animator, you spend hours and hours on a few frames that go by in the blink of an eye. Preparation and planning are integral, and changes are painful. It's easy to lose sight of the performance amid the myriad of keyframes, slider-controls, and sheer volume of time it takes to create a performance in animation.

Facial Animation uses interfaces familiar to both CGI animators and traditional animators. The X-sheet and dialogue "scrubbing" tools allow for the fastest timing-out of dialogue I've ever used, allowing for quick and easy modifications of the keyframes without the hassle of remembering sets of arcane numbers (unless you really want to). And the Function Curve Editor lets those born and bred on CGI animation have the familiar spline curves they've come to know and love so well.

But the real power of Facial Animation is in its ability to record a puppeteered performance using facial palettes.

A puppeteered performance holds all the subconscious nuances that are the cornerstone of powerful acting. It also holds far more keyframes than could be easily added and/or manipulated simply by moving sliders.

And a puppeteered performance can be created and recreated in as much time as it takes to play the animation in real time.

This is a huge plus for directors who can now, in walk-throughs, help hone a facial animation performance to perfection, rather than having to go away and come back the next day to see the changes the animator interpreted from the director's words!

20.2 A Separate Program?

What? Not animate facial animation directly in LightWave? What's the big idea?

Remember a while back when I said that you must first sell your performance with your character's physical animation? That wasn't just lip service. That's the way we did things on *Dinosaur*, and the way all the top studios get the best overall performances to tell their stories.

If you can convince an audience of the character's emotional state and motivations without facial animation, then what you do with a facial performance will crank up the intensity and believability of that performance tenfold.

So, two separate programs help to make it absolutely positively clear: When your character's physical performance sells the shot, then you move on to adding facial animation.

20.3 **FA's Interface**

Figure 20.1. Timothy Albee's Facial Animation consists of several floating windows you can position and resize to suit your needs and your desktop space.

Figure 20.2. Main window. The Main window of FA shows your model in real time, subpatched (Sub-D surfacing), textured, and lit with up to eight lights you can position and change in color/intensity. You have complete rotational control over the main head and "icon heads" (that show your current facial palette) at all times, even during playback.

Note:

The geometric white lines over the image in the above illustration are visual guides that may be turned on and off to help you in knowing the extents of the capture plane, and give you a visual representation of the currently selected blending mode. (FA supports several different kinds of blending modes for recording its puppeteering data — certain kinds of facial morphs work best with specific blending modes.)

Figure 20.3. Playback controls. The Playback control window lets you control the playback and recording of your scene data. In addition to providing you with standard VCR controls, you can set the speed independently for playback and record. (The Record button is only active when you are working with a puppeteering track in the X-sheet.) When you have a selection highlighted in the X-sheet, you have the option of having your recorded performance punch-in and punch-out, recording over only your selected frames (with the default three-second pre-roll to get into the feel of your animation beforehand).

Figure 20.4. Control window. The tiny, little control window gives you quick access to other Facial Animation functions. Clockwise from upper left, the FA button opens the Expression Palette window, the shaded sphere opens the Geometry Visibility window, the wavy lines open up the Function Curve/Graph Editor window, and the spreadsheet-like button opens the X-sheet window.

Surfaces ▼
Eye
Fur
Gums
Lenses
Nose
Teeth

Figure 20.5. Geometry Visibility window. The Geometry Visibility window lets you choose which parts of your model are visible as textured solids, shaded solids, or wireframes, or hidden completely. Clicking on the triangle beside Surfaces will let you choose to set your visibility from LightWave's surface names, parts, or sketch color.

Note:

You should plan on having your model on the first layer for Facial Animation, but if you absolutely, positively must have your model on some other layer, you can specify which layer(s) FA should use for saving animation and which it should show under the Options menu.

Figure 20.6. Morph File. The Morph File shows GL pictures of your character's visible geometry that can be rotated separately (by Shift-dragging on the icons) or as a unit to show the most informative side, or as a whole (Ctrl-drag to make all icons follow your current icon's rotation, Alt-drag to add your rotation to all other icons). Labels for the icons are generated from the morph name that follows the prefix (Dial.Oh would be labeled "Oh").

Note:

In FA, endomorph prefixes are stripped (the morph name before the first period) and are grouped on scollable pages similar to Morph Mixer's groups. Morphs with the prefix "Dial." are grouped on page 1, the "Dialogue" page. Other morphs are grouped alphabetically on their respective pages labeled with their group prefix. (Endomorphs without a prefix are grouped last, under the heading "General.")

Figure 20.7. Facial Palette. Like an artist mixing colors, the Facial Palette lets you mix your endomorphs in real time. Each icon represents a quadrant of the Main window. When in test mode (holding the "T" key), you can see the influence of the current morph palette on your model by moving the mouse around the Main window's active capture area. Moving your mouse closer to the corners of the Main window will blend that morph target more and more onto the model, all in real time!

Note:

By default, Facial Animation parses your endomorph list, grouping *pairs* and *quads* together based on the naming convention described in a moment in Section 20.4, "Morph Targets and FA."

Through the drop-down list box, you can select a facial palette from among those FA has created via parsing your endomorph names and from among those you've created and modified. You can also use the arrow keys on either side of the list box to scroll visually through your facial palettes.

New palettes can be created by clicking on the "new" icon in the upper-left corner of the window, and a palette can be deleted by clicking on the "x" box in the upper right. Palettes can be renamed by click-dragging over the current palette's name.

As with the icons in the Morph File, these can be rotated in real-time by Shift-left-click-dragging on them. (Alt and Ctrl dragging work similarly to the way described for icons in the Dialogue tab; however, rotations in the Facial Palette are mirrored across your current centerline axis.)

36 Frames						
AUDIO	V	Dial 1	X	Dial 2	X	Smi
	1	LS.43 mm				•
	2			_BLANK		
	3					
	4	LS.43 mm		LS.43 mm		
	5					
	6					
	7	LS.34 A				
	8			_BLANK		•
	9					
	10	LS.37 ee				
	11					•
	12					•
	13					
	14	LS.33 ah				•
	15			LS.42 rr		
	16					•
	17					
	18					
	19	LS.40 ss		_BLANK		
	20					•
	21					
	22					
	23					
	24	LS.41 kk				
	25					
	26					•
	27					
	28	LS.36 oh				
	29					
	30					
	31					•
	32					•
	33					
	34					
	35					
	36	LS.43 mm				•

Figure 20.8. TAFA's X-sheet. X-sheets (exposure sheets) have been a staple of traditional animation for over 75 years. It's a mystery why only in-house tools at the major studios, programs designed to be used in traditional animation, and old Amiga animation programs make use of this time-proven, intelligent way of laying out animation information.

On the leftmost track, you see a waveform representation of your loaded audio track (which you choose from under the File menu). Facial Animation defaults the length of your animation to the length of your audio clip, with respect to your frames per second setting (which can be set from the Options menu).

> **Note:**
> You can also load and clear dialogue and set scene length by right-clicking on the X-sheet's Audio track.

Click-dragging over the Audio track will "scrub" the dialogue, letting you play each frame of your recorded dialogue at a fixed frequency as quickly or as slowly as you move your mouse. Your model's animation in the Main window will follow in real time as you "scrub." Clicking on a single cell within the Dialogue track will play just that one frame of audio.

Facial Animation automatically provides you with one Dialogue track, onto which you can drag and drop dialogue morph icons from the dialogue morph file, or Alt-click on a cell to insert the most recently selected dialogue morph.

Once a morph target is in a cell, click on the cell and press the Delete key to remove it.

Right-clicking on a cell brings up a menu from which you can choose to have that cell be the model's neutral (base) pose, represented with a large red "X" within that cell. You can also cut, copy, paste, delete, and add keys from a list with this right-click menu.

Ctrl-left-drag on a cell with a dialogue morph to interactively set the percentage of that target's influence on the left side of the centerline.

Ctrl-right-drag on a cell with a dialogue morph to interactively set the percentage of that target's influence on the right side of the centerline.

> **Note:**
> You adjust *both* "halves" of a dialogue morph by simultaneously holding both the left and right mouse buttons while Ctrl-dragging on a dialogue morph on your X-sheet.

The cut, copy, and paste functions of the X-sheet work much the same way as in a spreadsheet program. Drag to select a group of cells, then Ctrl-x, c, and v to cut, copy, and paste, respectively. You can quickly move a selected group of cells by dragging up or down on the selected cells.

> **Note:**
> Double-clicking on the track's name selects the entire track, letting you easily copy all your work to another track for trying out new ideas.

Right-clicking on the track's name lets you rename, activate/deactivate the track, or choose to delete it altogether.

Right-clicking on an empty part of the X-sheet's top row lets you add more dialogue and/or facial tracks. (You can have as many tracks as you'd like — FA will play three tracks as quickly as it plays three hundred!)

Figure 20.9. Puppeteer tracks are created by choosing Puppeteer when right-clicking to add another track to your X-sheet. They function in much the same way as Dialogue tracks, except that you only see "dots" to represent the presence of a quad-keyframe within the Puppeteered performance.

Note:

By default, Puppeteer tracks are assigned the name of the active facial palette they have recorded. However, this can be changed by right-clicking on the name of the Facial track.

Selecting, copying, and pasting of these quad-keys works the same as it does with dialogue morphs in a Dialogue track. Using the right-click menu on a cell on a Puppeteer track to add a quad-key will add a quad-key with the current, interpolated values for that frame.

Ctrl-left-dragging on a quad-key opens up a small, square window with a "dot" representing the quad-key's position within the four quadrants to which the Facial morphs are assigned. Drag the "dot" to adjust the quad-key's position information, watching the result in real time on the model in the Main window.

> **Important Note:**
>
> All this manipulation of the X-sheet can be done *while the animation is playing*! You can instantly see the results of your adjustments as you make them.

> **Note:**
>
> Selecting a group of cells of a Puppeteer track sets a "Punch-In/Punch-Out" range for re-recording that section of puppeteering. (By default, you get a three-second Pre-/Post-Roll, heralded by audio beeps to get you set to record, and to let you know when recording has started and ended.) Once the "Punch-In/Punch-Out" range has been set, you still need to click on the Punch In/Out button in the Control window to activate the "Punch-In/Punch-Out" recording mode.

> **Note:**
>
> Clicking on a cell in a Dialogue or Puppeteer track sets that track as the active track for recording or manipulation.

Figure 20.10. Function Curve Editor: Dialogue view. The Function Curve/Graph Editor reflects the data of the currently active track in a way that may be more familiar to 3D animators who didn't start out as traditional animators.

When a Dialogue track is active, the Function Curve/Graph Editor shows the keyframes for the currently selected Dialogue track. Keys representing the percentages for the morph on the left side of the centerline are represented in green, and keys for the model's right side are represented in red.

Select and drag keys up and down to change their values. Select and drag keys or the dialogue labels left and right to change the frames on which they exist. (Dialogue keys consist of both a left and right value, and will always remain as pairs.)

The Function Curve/Graph Editor's "highlight" moves in conjunction with the timeline's. You can cut, copy, and paste keyframes in much the same way as by using the X-sheet for that Dialogue track.

Right-clicking on a keyframe opens up an edit menu for that frame, from which you can also set values numerically for the left and right halves of the dialogue key.

Figure 20.11. Function Curve/Graph Editor: Puppeteer view. The quad-keys that comprise the stored performances for the Puppeteer tracks are "split" to represent percentages along the Y axis of the capture plane for the left and right halves of the model. Keys and curves in green represent data for the left half of the model, and keys and curves in red represent data for the right half. And as with dialogue, keys are paired and remain together when being moved, deleted, copied, cut, or pasted.

The horizontal centerline represents the 0% influence of the respective curves. The top of the chart represents 100% for the top facial morphs, and the bottom of the chart represents 100% for the bottom facial morphs.

Cut, delete, copy, and paste key functions in the Facial Function Curve Editor work the same as they do for dialogue.

Right-clicking opens up an edit menu for the frame directly under the mouse from which you can also set values numerically for the left and right halves of the facial quad-key.

20.4 Morph Targets and FA

Facial Animation can use the same morph targets you created in the last chapter for Morph Mixer. However, FA is a lot smarter when it comes to understanding how morphs are created.

Facial Animation will split your morph across the X=0 (center-line) axis for you, so you don't need to have separate morph targets for left and right sides of your character. (Your centerline axis can be changed under the Settings menu.)

Facial Animation will parse your endomorph names to automatically sort Dialogue morphs from Puppeteer morphs. (The default prefix for Dialogue morphs is "Dial." This can be changed under the Options menu.)

Facial Animation will also parse your Puppeteer morph names to automatically create facial palettes with morph pairs (by ending your endomorph name in ".U" for "up," and ".D" for down) or quads (by ending your endomorph name in ".UL" for "up left," etc.). (These letter codes can also be changed under the Settings menu.)

Figure 20.12. Here you see the complete listing of Mr. Cool's morph targets for Facial Animation. (There are nineteen fewer morphs than what are required to give the same range in Morph Mixer.)

All targets beginning with "Dial." will be sorted (alphabetically) in Facial Animation's Dialogue group within the morph file.

Facial palettes will automatically be created for all morph targets ending in ".U" and ".D", where the ".U" morph will be assigned to the top two squares and the ".D" morph will be assigned to the bottom two squares (both morphs will be split along the centerline axis by default).

Facial morph targets (not beginning with "Dial.") not ending in ".U" or ".D" can be set to appear in a facial palette of their own or to remain unassigned until you do so manually. (Yep, you guessed it — you choose how Facial Animation handles these morphs under the Options menu.)

20.5 **Integration with LightWave**

After you've laid in your dialogue shapes, honed them with perhaps a second or third dialogue track, and recorded your puppeteering tracks, Facial Animation gives you two ways of interfacing its data with LightWave.

If you don't ask FA to "split" your morphs for you (if you're using a model that has separate shapes for left and right morphs like we created in the previous chapter), you can choose to export a file that can be read directly by Morph Mixer (Options|File I/O|Load Endomorph Mix within the Morph Mixer window).

You can also have your animation data "mixed-down" to a Motion Designer .mdd file that can be applied as a displacement to your model. (See the Facial Animation or LightWave documentation for details on how to apply a Motion Designer .mdd to an object.)

> **Note:**
> The rules of applying a Motion Designer .mdd file to a model is that the model must be set to Subdivide After Motion or Last. And after adding the MD_Plug Displacement handler, within the MD_Plug interface you'll need to make sure you have Key-Move set to ON so your keyframed movement in Layout still affects the mesh.

I've never found anything to yield faster, better facial animation than this blending of traditional animation, CGI animation, and puppeteering. In short, Facial Animation is what I always wished existed — and now it does. And rather than it being a proprietary tool of a huge mega-studio, it is something you have access to bringing into your own productions!

Chapter 21

In Conclusion

So how do you feel?

You've learned how to set up a character and how you can modify that setup to create anything you desire. You've learned the controls, and probably surprised yourself with how easily you took to life drawing in 3D. You've followed me in animation, and you've begun to create your own. And now you realize that this dream of yours, this dream that you might never have told anyone about, this dream of becoming an animator may indeed be possible!

I'll let you in on a little secret... You *are* an animator! You've followed me through the exercises, you've made your own artistic decisions, you've learned all the tools you will need to become a feature-quality animator. The rest is up to you. If you don't believe me, go take a look at one of your old scenes. I imagine it looks like it was done by a completely different person. You've got confidence in your abilities now. Even though the road to mastery stretches out over the farthest horizon, you know you can get there under your own power! You've seen the logical steps that have brought you this far, and you can look down the path and see where the next ones are. And you know that whatever the path brings, the sights you'll see will make the journey worthwhile!

Congratulations! I'm really proud of you! You've proved to yourself that you *can* do this; you can fulfill this dream that you've had perhaps for as long as you can remember! It is a wonderful path that lay open before you; where you go now is entirely up to you.

> **Note:**
> Realize though that with power comes responsibility. "We are such stuff as dreams are made on." (Prospero, *The Tempest*) And although you may see all the ways in which you can (and must) improve, others will begin to hang their dreams from the high points of your craft. Make your dreams that others see be the best and brightest they can be! And when those who have shaped their lives to your work ask for your help, be kind. Lend them a hand, for they are the ones who allow you to be who you are.

Remember as you journey this path that we are storytellers. No matter how interesting the technology we may use to create our visions, our magic exists only in how we connect with the audience. It is in characters you want to be or to be with. It is in situations you wish you had lived. It is in scenery you wished you had touched. We are creating dreams for others to hold. Tell the stories you wish you had been told, and in them, let us dream with you.

I wish you well on this wondrous journey. I look forward to seeing your work, whether it be television, feature film, video game, Internet, or some completely new medium as yet undreamed of in the minds of common men. May the beauty of your vision shine far into the future!

Be well, my fellow animator!

Timothy Albee

Index

About the CD

The companion CD-ROM is organized into the following directories:

▶ Audio—Example .wav file

▶ Book Images—Full-color versions of all the images in the book

▶ Extras—Animation timer/time-base converter, artwork by Timothy Albee (including animation drawings, paintings, and 3D renderings), life drawing models, and 3D scenes to study and learn from

▶ Images—Images needed for exercises in the book

▶ Objects—Objects needed for exercises in the book

▶ Scenes—Scenes needed for exercises in the book

Warning:

By opening the CD package, you accept the terms and conditions of the CD/Source Code Usage License Agreement on the following page.

Additionally, opening the CD package makes this book non-returnable.

CD/Source Code Usage License Agreement

Please read the following CD/Source Code usage license agreement before opening the CD and using the contents therein:

1. By opening the accompanying software package, you are indicating that you have read and agree to be bound by all terms and conditions of this CD/Source Code usage license agreement.

2. The compilation of code and utilities contained on the CD and in the book are copyrighted and protected by both U.S. copyright law and international copyright treaties, and is owned by Wordware Publishing, Inc. Individual source code, example programs, help files, freeware, shareware, utilities, and evaluation packages, including their copyrights, are owned by the respective authors.

3. No part of the enclosed CD or this book, including all source code, help files, shareware, freeware, utilities, example programs, or evaluation programs, may be made available on a public forum (such as a World Wide Web page, FTP site, bulletin board, or Internet news group) without the express written permission of Wordware Publishing, Inc. or the author of the respective source code, help files, shareware, freeware, utilities, example programs, or evaluation programs.

4. You may not decompile, reverse engineer, disassemble, create a derivative work, or otherwise use the enclosed programs, help files, freeware, shareware, utilities, or evaluation programs except as stated in this agreement.

5. The software, contained on the CD and/or as source code in this book, is sold without warranty of any kind. Wordware Publishing, Inc. and the authors specifically disclaim all other warranties, express or implied, including but not limited to implied warranties of merchantability and fitness for a particular purpose with respect to defects in the disk, the program, source code, sample files, help files, freeware, shareware, utilities, and evaluation programs contained therein, and/or the techniques described in the book and implemented in the example programs. In no event shall Wordware Publishing, Inc., its dealers, its distributors, or the authors be liable or held responsible for any loss of profit or any other alleged or actual private or commercial damage, including but not limited to special, incidental, consequential, or other damages.

6. One (1) copy of the CD or any source code therein may be created for backup purposes. The CD and all accompanying source code, sample files, help files, freeware, shareware, utilities, and evaluation programs may be copied to your hard drive. With the exception of freeware and shareware programs, at no time can any part of the contents of this CD reside on more than one computer at one time. The contents of the CD can be copied to another computer, as long as the contents of the CD contained on the original computer are deleted.

7. You may not include any part of the CD contents, including all source code, example programs, shareware, freeware, help files, utilities, or evaluation programs in any compilation of source code, utilities, help files, example programs, freeware, shareware, or evaluation programs on any media, including but not limited to CD, disk, or Internet distribution, without the express written permission of Wordware Publishing, Inc. or the owner of the individual source code, utilities, help files, example programs, freeware, shareware, or evaluation programs.

8. You may use the source code, techniques, and example programs in your own commercial or private applications unless otherwise noted by additional usage agreements as found on the CD.

Warning:

By opening the CD package, you accept the terms and conditions of the CD/Source Code Usage License Agreement.

Additionally, opening the CD package makes this book non-returnable.